Nil.

THE BIG V

A History of the
Vitagraph Company

by

ANTHONY SLIDE

The Scarecrow Press, Inc.
Metuchen, N.J.   1976

By the same author:

Early American Cinema
The Griffith Actresses
The Films of D. W. Griffith (with Edward Wagenknecht)
The Idols of Silence
Early Women Directors

COPY
PN
1999
.V5
S55
c.1

Library of Congress Cataloging in Publication Data

Slide, Anthony.
    The big V : a history of the Vitagraph Company.

    "The films of the Vitagraph Company, 1910-1915": p.
Bibliography: p.
Includes index.
    1. Vitagraph Company of America. I. Title.
PN1999.V5S55   791.43'0973   76-21247
ISBN 0-8108-0967-2

For
Marian Blackton Trimble and Lucille Smith,
the co-founders of this book

CONTENTS

ACKNOWLEDGMENTS

I am tremendously grateful to the Academy of Motion Picture Arts and Sciences, and its staff, which has encouraged me in the research for this volume since I began work on it in 1971. In particular, I must thank June Banker, Sam Gill, Alice Mitchell, and, above all, Mildred Simpson. Other institutions which gave me access to whatever research materials I needed include: The Los Angeles County Museum of Natural History (John Dewar), The National Film Archive (Elaine Burrows and Pat Coward), The Library of Congress (Rita Horwitz, David Parker, Pat Sheehan and Paul Spehr), The American Society of Cinematographers (Charles G. Clarke), and the Library of The University of California, Los Angeles.

Kevin Brownlow, John Cunningham and Bert Langdon screened films from their collections for me. Norma Oldfield kindly loaned me stills and other materials relating to The Battle Cry of Peace. Robert Giroux gave me access to an unpublished interview with Lillian Walker.

I must thank the following members of the Vitagraph family for sparing the time to talk or correspond with me: the late William P. S. Earle, Frank Hulette, Zena Keefe, the late James Morrison, Jane Novak and Arline Pretty.

Jean Paige (Mrs. Albert E. Smith) very graciously gave me access to her late husband's papers, and allowed me to read the unedited version of Two Reels and a Crank. Mrs. Marian Trimble offered me much valuable information concerning her father, J. Stuart Blackton, allowed me to quote from unpublished articles by her father, and more importantly, gave me her friendship. In London, Jan Zilliacus, Larry Trimble's daughter, talked to me at length about her father and his work.

Finally, I wish to thank Robert Gitt for his help and

encouragement on this project for the last three years, and Edward Wagenknecht, who read through the manuscript, and made many valuable additions and changes.

Anthony Slide
Washington-Los Angeles

Chapter 1

THE BEGINNINGS

Why a whole volume devoted to the Vitagraph Company of America? The answer is simple; because Vitagraph was the most important of the early production companies. It was the only one to survive through to the Twenties; and not only to survive, but to prosper. The Biograph Company, with D. W. Griffith as its director-in-chief, might be considered Vitagraph's artistic superior, but to the film-going public, Vitagraph's releases were the more popular. Vitagraph co-founder, Albert E. Smith, summed it up when he wrote, "Griffith was like an artist who paints one picture--Vitagraph was like a magazine or a newspaper, who has a clientele that it must furnish a supply to regularly."93*

The Vitagraph Company might well be considered the M-G-M of the 'teens. It established the star system, and built up a roster of players that included, at one time or another, Betty Blythe, John Bunny, Norma Talmadge, Clara Kimball Young, Corinne Griffith, Larry Semon, Antonio Moreno and Alice Joyce. The company also gathered together the finest technical staff available, and placed them under contract. By 1912, according to Smith, Vitagraph "had 400 people in our stock company and quite a small army of photographers, printers, developers and other workers in different branches of the business."93

Vitagraph was the brainchild of two young Englishmen, J. Stuart Blackton and Albert E. Smith, who built up a tiny New York-based company to a multi-million dollar concern. This book is the story of their life's work. It might also be considered the story of the development of the art of the motion picture, for Vitagraph contributed as much to film art as did Griffith. But Vitagraph did more than create an art form; it established the business of film-making, a business that

---

*Superior numbers in the text refer to the bibliography.

1

was to remain relatively unchanged until the decline of the studio system in the Fifties.

Not only did Vitagraph perfect the studio system of film production, it also devised an almost perfect distribution set-up. Indeed, one of the chief reasons for Warner Brothers wishing to purchase Vitagraph in 1925 was Warners' need for film exchanges and an established sales system to handle its product. In Europe, also, Vitagraph had well-run branches; its European headquarters in Paris did as much business as the parent company.

Both Blackton and Smith had given some thought to the reasons for Vitagraph's successful evolution. In 1913, J. Stuart Blackton explained, "Picture making can hardly be said to have developed. The art itself is an evolution--its branches developed. Everything was so absolutely new that the first producers had to evolve their own standards. For instance, there were no experienced picture players. The pioneers had to find out the best and proper course to pursue. Out of the early successes and failures had been created the present day motion pictures."94

Albert E. Smith, in 1919, took a hard-headed businessman's look at the film industry in relation to Vitagraph's rise. "It was the struggle in the early days of the industry that taught me the value of studying the public wants and co-operating with the exhibitor. This co-operation must be of the practical kind. It should start at the boxoffice and take the basic form of giving the exhibitor only such pictures as the public will patronize. No other consideration should be allowed to interfere with this rule."

****

J. Stuart Blackton and Albert E. Smith met in 1894, through a mutual friend, another Englishman named Ronald A. Reader. Reader, who was employed by the Royal Insurance Company, spent his spare time entertaining anyone who could be cajoled into watching his magic tricks. He was particularly impressed by would-be prestidigitator Smith and would-be cartoonist Blackton, both of whom had been appearing, somewhat infrequently, on what was known as the Lyceum circuit, consisting of smoking parties, church affairs, etc.

One fateful evening, Reader introduced the two men to each other at his Harlem boarding house. He thought the one could inspire the other, and was determined to be the catalyst in the friendship of the two men. As William Basil Courtney wrote in 1925, "if either Smith or Blackton had been a lady he undoubtedly would have married them to one another."[26] The three men decided to combine their acts, and initially called themselves The Royal Entertainers, in honor of Reader's employer. The Royal Entertainers lasted only a few months, and then became The International Novelty Company.

According to Albert E. Smith, The International Novelty Company made its debut in Haverstraw, New Jersey, before an audience of two.[92] Others have recorded that the trio toured with their act as far West as Iowa. How true this is, there is no way of knowing. One thing is certain: on Friday, December 7, 1894, Reader, Smith and Blackton appeared at Parshall's Hall on New York's 167 Street, for the benefit of the Church of the Holy Faith, under the auspices of the Helping Circle of King's Daughters. The men were not billed as The International Novelty Company, but as "The Celebrated Reader, Smith and Blackton Combination."

The program began with a piano overture, played by Miss Florence Hayden. Then followed Ronald Reader "with a succession of surprises concluding with Cassedega Propaganda, a new spiritualistic enigma in which the ghost of a departed enchanter plays a prominent part." Blackton came next with "a comic travesty introducing one of his funny faces, cartoons in black and white, artistic landscape and marine painting." Albert E. Smith, billed as "the Komical Konjurer," introduced "some original novelties, including his celebrated cabinet mystery." To conclude the entertainment, Smith assisted Blackton in presenting kinetoscopic paintings, which would appear to have been a series of magic lantern slides, painted by Blackton.

What happened next to Reader, Smith and Blackton is clouded in mystery. The act appears to have been practically discarded, with Reader returning to the insurance business, Smith taking a job as a bookbinder, and Blackton joining The New York Evening World as a cub reporter. In July of 1895, Smith claims to have seen an Edison kinetoscope, a peep-show type machine, enabling one person at a time to view a short strip of film, and suggested to Blackton that if a method could be devised to project the film before an audi-

ence, it might be just the boost The International Novelty
Company needed.

In the meantime, on April 22, 1896, Blackton was
asked by his newspaper to interview Thomas Edison about his
projecting machine, which had given its initial presentation
at Koster and Bial's Music Hall in New York a day or two
earlier. In a lecture at U.S.C. on February 20, 1929,
Blackton recalled that historic meeting:

"I went into this room, and Mr. Edison was back
there in a corner busily engaged. His back was to me. I
said, 'Good morning Mr. Edison,' but he paid no attention
to me. I said a little louder, 'Good morning, Mr. Edison!'
Still he took no notice. I said it several times and then I
almost yelled, 'Good morning Mr. Edison!' I had been walk-

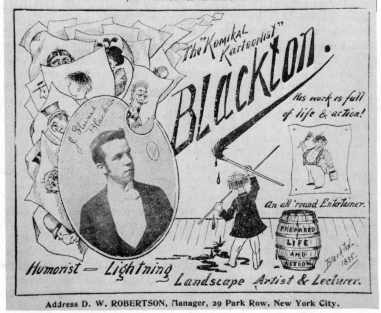

A page from the only extant program for the Reader-Smith-
Blackton Combination, dated December 7, 1894. Opposite:
the cover of the same program.

ing to and fro and then I walked right up to him and evident-
ly he saw my feet there, and he looked up and said, 'Hello
young man, what are you doing here?' I told him that I had
been sent out there by The New York Evening World to interview him. He said, 'You will have to speak louder, I am
stone deaf.' He beckoned me around to his right ear and by
means of a sort of bellowing I made him understand. He
said, 'All right, you have a good strong voice and I can hear
you, young man. Sit down.' And then he began to interview
me.

"Mr. Edison is probably the best informed man on the
greatest number of subjects of anyone in the world, and he
interviewed me about everything in the world connected with
the newspaper business, the police courts business, art,
sketching, writing, everything. And then, finally, I got a
few words in edgewise. Then he asked me, 'What is that
you have got under your arm?' I told him it was my sketch
book. He asked me if I could draw, and said that was the
one thing he wished he could do.... He asked me if I could
make a sketch of him. I said I would, and he sat for me
while I made a sketch of him. He was very pleased with it,
and said it was very good, and he said he would give anything to be able to draw like that. Here was a boy of nine-
teen, seeing Edison, making sketches for him and of him,
wasting hours that must have been valuable. He is the kind-
liest of men and the most colorful mind and man I have ever
met, and yet to think of him, Edison, shut away from the
world because of his deafness. In fact, he really seems to
have accomplished more because of that fact.

"Then he asked me if I could draw that picture of him
on a big paper on a board. I told him that I could and he
said, 'You come on out to the Black Maria,' and we did and
he had them get boards and wide white paper and some char-
coal, and right then and there he had the camera recording
your humble servant drawing a picture of Thomas A. Edison.
He said, 'Put your name on that board,' and 'this will be a
good ad for you. It will go all over the country in the show
houses.' I did, and that was my entrance into the motion
picture industry. I finished that picture with two others with
the name of Blackton, Cartoonist of The New York Evening
World, written over the top of that board. Then I came out
through the Edison workshop and shook hands with him. As
I was leaving, I asked if it was possible to buy one of those
machines that make these pictures. He said he didn't know
much about the business end of it, but he was sure they didn't

sell them. Then, he said, 'I am getting a little machine together now, and in about three, four or five months I am
going to put it on the market. It will be called the Edison
Projecting Kinetoscope, and will do everything the big machines would do.' I told him that I would very much like to
put in an order for one. He rang the bell for a boy, and I
gave the order for a machine."

According to Blackton, the projecting machine arrived
a few months later, along with ten films, for which he and
Smith paid $800. Smith, however, in his autobiography,
claims to have invented his own projecting machine, which
was used for the first time on January 6, 1896. However,
also in his autobiography, Smith publishes one of the patent
drawings for his machine, which is quite clearly marked,
"Application filed March 15, 1900." To add to the confusion,
there is no record of the Edison Company's ever making
available a film of Blackton sketching the inventor.

If this were not confusing enough, there is the problem of Smith's claim in his autobiography that Vitagraph
made a triumphant debut at Tony Pastor's Fourteenth Street
Theatre in New York on March 23, 1896. There is no way
this can be true, and many historians would be inclined to
believe that Smith is exactly a year off with his date; but in
Smith's still-extant diary for 1896, there is an entry, dated
March 23, "Tony Pastor's. Vitagraph. 2 weeks, $500."
The only explanation I can offer is that Smith was so im-
poverished in 1897 that he was forced to utilize an old diary
that he had kept from the previous year.

Only one thing is certain. Sometime in 1896, Smith
and Blackton formed the American Vitagraph Company.
William Basil Courtney wrote, "They thought well of the
first syllable of Edison's name for his projector, the Vitascope, and decided to adopt it with a more significant em-
bellishment ... Vitagraph, meaning life picture, life portrayals. A patriotic flare would help to touch popular interest; therefore the enthusiastic young partners, being English,
decided that the complete appellation should be the American
Vitagraph."[26] Courtney also indicated that the company's
business existence began in February of 1897.

The newly-formed American Vitagraph Company continued for a while to present much the same type of entertainment as was offered by The Reader, Smith and Blackton
Combination, with one major difference. Motion pictures

became an integral part of the entertainment. The most
popular film Smith and Blackton screened was of the Black
Diamond Express train, hurtling towards the audience, with
offscreen railroad noises provided by Blackton, aided by
assorted dish pans and metal sheeting. Vitagraph's moving
picture entertainment became a permanent part of the bill
of fare at Tony Pastor's Fourteenth Street Theatre, and
Ronald Reader rejoined Smith and Blackton to act as projectionist there.

The partners began to expand their activities. An
office was rented in the Morse Building on New York's
Nassau Street, for the princely sum of $150 a year. Addi-
tional Edison projectors were acquired, as the American
Vitagraph Company began presenting film programs as part
of the evening's entertainment at more of New York's vaudeville theatres, beginning with Proctor's 58 Street and 23
Street Theatres. The partners hired their first employee in
1898, a magician's assistant named John B. French. He
began as a projectionist, and remained with the company until
it was sold to Warner Brothers. Soon afterwards, a second
employee, Morris Brenner, was hired as an office boy and
clerk-typist.

The next step was an obvious one; film exhibition
naturally led to film production. On May 16, 1897, on the
roof of the Morse Building, Vitagraph filmed a sixty-second
subject, The Burglar on the Roof, featuring Blackton as the
burglar. Mrs. Olson, wife of the janitor of the Morse
Building, failing to realize that it was only a film, attacked
burglar Blackton with her broom. The camera was operated
by Albert E. Smith. Smith and Blackton also organized The
Commercial Advertising Company, to produce magic lantern
slides to advertise various businesses and products. It remained a successful subsidiary activity until other matters
forced the partners to shut it down in 1900.

Vitagraph produced other film subjects on the roof of
the Morse Building, some of which were sold outright to the
Edison Company, but the initial novelty of moving pictures
was wearing off, and theatre audiences were beginning to
make it plain that film was no longer welcome on the vaudeville program.

Then, on February 15, 1898, the U.S. battleship
Maine mysteriously exploded and sank in Havana harbor.
The Hearst newspapers wasted no time in putting the blame

for the explosion on Spain, and anti-Spanish feeling was soon rife throughout America. Smith and Blackton decided to display their patriotism through the medium of the motion picture. As Blackton recalled at his U.S.C. lecture, "The first war picture made was <u>Tearing down the Spanish Flag</u>.... Our background was the building next door. We had a flagpole and two eighteen-inch flags, one of them an American one and the other a Spanish flag. Smith operated the machine, and I, with this very hand, grabbed the Spanish flag and tore it down from the pole, and pulled the Stars and Stripes to the top of the flagpole.... The people went wild. Of course, it was wartime, and their emotions ran high, and then while the flags were but eighteen inches in size, the picture showed a thirty-six-inch flag. That was the beginning of making the miniature look like the real thing."

The Spanish-American War and the events leading up to it proved a Godsend to the American Vitagraph Company. When the bodies of the dead from the Maine explosion were brought for burial at Arlington National Cemetery, Albert E. Smith was on hand to film the occasion. The footage was an emotional success when screened in New York.

William Randolph Hearst chartered a boat to take newspaper correspondents to Cuba to cover the war activities, and, through the intercession of William A. Brady, Smith and Blackton were able to secure passage on the ship. Accompanying the two pioneering film-makers was a camera-cum-projector, built by Smith, and affectionately known as the Dunderberger. Smith and Blackton were apparently able to shoot film of Theodore Roosevelt and his Rough Riders at San Juan Hill, the first war newsfilm ever taken. I say apparently, because despite the amount of space Albert E. Smith devotes to this adventure in his autobiography, and its recounting in William Basil Courtney's "History of Vitagraph," published in 1925, J. Stuart Blackton's daughter tells me that neither her father nor Smith ever set foot in Cuba.

On May 2, 1899 came news of Admiral Dewey's defeat of the Spanish fleet at Manila Bay. Having no film of the event, Smith and Blackton decided to recreate the battle, using a water tank, cardboard cut-out model ships, and plenty of smoke provided by Blackton's cigar. <u>The Battle of Manila Bay</u> thrilled audiences at vaudeville theatres in New York, as did Vitagraph's newsreel film of Dewey's triumphant return to America. Possibly for the first time, motion picture film had been used not only to incite patriotic fervor, but

also, and more importantly, to bring the general public first-
hand accounts of international events.

Of the Spanish-American War and its impact on the
American Vitagraph Company, William Basil Courtney wrote,
"An elaborate argument could be based on the premise that
the only important contribution of the Spanish-American War
to the history of the United States lay not in the acquisition
of territories and pension lists, but in the impetus it gave
to the work of Smith and Blackton in placing the foundation
blocks for the motion picture industry. It is at least an
interesting commentary on social history that the pictures
and the work that Smith and Blackton did then have done
more to promote the general happiness of, and are recalled
most familiarly by, the average citizen who cannot recall
whether Dewey's first name was Abraham or Grover."[26]

The year 1898 had been an exciting and important one
for Vitagraph; 1899 proved equally special. The magazine
Mahatma reported that "at the review of the Astor battery on
January 23rd, 1899, Mr. Smith broke all records in photography and caused considerable newspaper talk by taking an
animated picture of the parade on Union Square at 4.00 p.m.,
and developing, printing and exhibiting it by 9.00 p.m., the
same evening at several New York theatres."[70] Blackton
scored a comic success in the "Happy Hooligan" series,
filmed at New York's Rye Beach.

The year 1899 also brought a third partner to the
American Vitagraph Company in the large and portly shape
of William T. Rock. "Pop" Rock, as he was affectionately
known, was also English, having been born in Birmingham,
England, on December 31, 1853. He entered the film industry in 1896, after being offered rights for the state of
Louisiana to the Edison Vitascope by Raff and Gammon,
which handled the projectors. Rock recalled:

"I took my machine and started for New Orleans. We
had the May Irwin Kiss, and a lot of scenic stuff. Bill Reid
was my operator. I made a contract with the West End Park
for four weeks and we packed them in, renewing my contract
and continuing to play the West End for several seasons.

"July 18, 1896, Wainwright and Rock (Walter Wainwright was my partner) took a storeroom in New Orleans at
623 Canal Street. We fitted it up as a showroom with chairs
and a projection booth. We ran this show from July to

J. Stuart Blackton in his characterization of "The Happy
Hooligan."

October. We also showed pictures in Jack Greenwald's
Theater. Our profits on the summer's business were about
$2,000 for each of us. We were the only state rights
owners out of about forty who made good with the Vitascope;
all the others went broke on the deal. I attributed our success to the fact that I knew something about electricity and
Bill Reid knew how to handle film."[84]

Rock returned to New York in 1897, and opened a
small office at 125 Street and 3rd Avenue. Here he bought
and sold films, and here, one day, J. Stuart Blackton came
to trade some Vitagraph productions. Why Rock was invited
to join Vitagraph is unclear, but join he did, and in 1900 the
Vitagraph Company of America was incorporated. Rock was
named president, Smith was the treasurer, and Blackton was
the secretary.

Possibly, "Pop" Rock had the maturity that his youthful partners lacked. Age was certainly not the only difference between him and Smith and Blackton, for Rock was
loud-mouthed, blustering and always ready with a choice
swearword, all of which his partners were not. He would
always wear diamond cuff-links, studs and rings--"He was
made for diamonds," recalled Blackton's daughter--and had
curious penny-pinching habits. When Vitagraph opened its
own theatre, Rock would go around, turning off the exit
lights, which he considered unnecessary.

Between 1900 and 1905, Vitagraph expanded at a fair
pace. The Company moved into new offices in the Morton
Building at 110-116 Nassau Street, paying a rental of $500 a
year. More employees were hired: August Wenz as a
machinist, Max Held as a projectionist, and "Doc" Willat as
an assistant projectionist. The partners also hired G. M.
Anderson, later to gain fame as cowboy star Broncho Billy
Anderson and co-founder of the Essanay Company. Anderson
joined Vitagraph around 1902, and stayed with the Company a
year or so. Smith and Blackton were also, of course, out
in the field, filming such events as the Galveston flood of
1900 and the 1904 inauguration of President Theodore Roosevelt. In May of 1906, Vitagraph advertised "genuine and
authentic" films of the San Francisco earthquake, five subjects ranging in length from 100 to 200 feet.

The next step in Vitagraph's history was a major one,
the separation of the production of motion pictures from the
business of selling them. Rock could handle the latter from

the Nassau Street offices, but a new studio was needed, with
room for expansion.   Land was purchased at East 15 Street
and Locust Avenue, in the Flatbush area of Brooklyn, close
to the Brighton Beach elevated railroad.   Ground was broken
in August of 1905, and shortly thereafter, even before any of

The first building at Vitagraph's Flatbush Studios.

the buildings were completed, the first film was in production.   It was titled The Adventures of Raffles, the Amateur
Cracksman, and featured J. Barney Sherry, who must be
honored as the first actor employed by Vitagraph.

     The film was produced by arrangement with Kyrle
Bellew and Liebler and Company, who claimed the dramatic
rights in the work.   In return for authorizing the production,
actor Bellew asked Vitagraph to film him in the sword fight
from his current Broadway success, A Gentleman of France.
This the Company did, and the result was a five-minute film

titled The Great Sword Combat on the Stairs, which Vitagraph
listed in its catalog as a comedy.

As the following news item from Views and Film Index
for August 25, 1906 indicates, the Vitagraph Studio did not
become fully operative until late 1906. "The new factory
which is being built by the Vitagraph Company of America at
Locust Avenue and Brighton Beach Railroad, Brooklyn, is
nearing completion and will be ready for occupancy about
September 15th. The cost of the building is $25,000. The
building which is made of concrete blocks is supplied with a
100 horse-power engine which will operate a dynamo, to
furnish electric light, heat and power for the machine shop
and dark room. There will be a complete outfit of Cooper
Hewitt lights in the studio. Special apparatus and stages
have been made for taking novel pictures with special scenic
effects. The entire roof and upper part of the building is
covered with a specially designed prismatic glass. This
construction of glass diffuses and intensifies the rays of light
so that shadows are not perceptible."

Smith and Blackton next decided to build up a regular
stock company of players and directors, the first members
of which were William Shea, William V. Ranous, Hector
Dion and Paul Panzer. The last starred in another of the
early films to be produced at the new studio, Monsieur
Beaucaire, based on the Booth Tarkington play. One-reel
in length, Monsieur Beaucaire marked the last appearance
of J. Stuart Blackton before the camera.

In 1908, Vitagraph further expanded with the opening
of a Paris office, to distribute their productions throughout
Europe. Ronald Reader was appointed to head the Company's
European operation. Reader kept the Company aware of anything which did not go over well on the continent. On February 2, 1909, he wrote to Smith, "Avoid as much as possible all religion in pictures.... I say this as customers
object to priests, crosses, etc., unless they are really
necessary." The importance of the Paris office should not
be under-estimated. Before the First World War, Vitagraph
undoubtedly released more of their productions in Europe
than they did in the States. Actor James Morrison recalled
that a film was not considered completely finished until the
Paris office had indicated its approval of the subject.

Smith and Blackton each headed their own company of
players and directors at the studio. As Smith wrote, "There

was a friendly rivalry between the two groups. If Blackton's side produced an especially good picture, my aggregation would not rest satisfied until they had bettered it. So this friendly rivalry worked for the good of the business." It was a busy time for the two men. Blackton wrote to Smith, away on a European trip, on February 15, 1908, "Took five pictures this week--that's the record.... Am doubling in brass these days--upstairs set, focus and grind the crank-- then downstairs and join negative."

In January of 1909, Vitagraph released a film on Making Moving Pictures, an indication of the rise of public interest in the motion picture. For by now, no longer were films part of a vaudeville bill. Nickelodeons had sprung up in their thousands throughout America. Film had come of age, thanks, to a large extent, to the Vitagraph Company. When President Taft was inaugurated on March 4, 1909, Blackton and three assistants were given special places to film the ceremony, and less than two days after the event, Vitagraph had the film in release.

Annette Kellerman came to the Vitagraph studios in August of 1909 to perform "her daring feats as well as her physical culture exercises and diabolo playing." In October of the same year, the Company began to supply suitable music scores to accompany its film releases. The Moving Picture World on December 18, 1909 announced that Vitagraph was to send a company of players to Jamaica to film instructive and entertaining stories. "Such enterprise helps to maintain the motion picture as the most educational development of the century."

On February 14, 1910, the Vitagraph Company began to release three reels of film a week. Aside from its business and technical staff, thirty actors and actresses and seven directors were under contract. Its profit in 1910 was over $600,000. The International Novelty Company must have seemed a long way away to Smith and Blackton then.

Chapter 2

J. STUART BLACKTON

Albert E. Smith modestly wrote in his autobiography, "I think I should say in all fairness that credit for most of the artistic success of Vitagraph for the first twenty years is due to Mr. Blackton."[93] Without a doubt, J. Stuart Blackton was the creative genius of the Vitagraph Company; he was a colorful personality in silent film history, whose contribution to the cinema has never been fully analyzed.

James Stuart Blackton was born in Sheffield, England on January 4, 1875; the exact year is in doubt as Blackton constantly changed his date of birth to make himself appear younger than he was. "He was as cagey about his actual age as are most women," recalls his daughter. Blackton claimed in many Who's Who entries to have been educated at Eton. Not only is this untrue, it is also impossible, as Blackton left England at the age of ten, too young to have obtained an education at England's most prestigious public school.

According to Blackton, his father had been a cele- brated Victorian portrait painter, which may be correct, as Blackton demonstrated a natural ability to paint, and in the 'teens even published a book of marine studies. The foreword to this rare volume reads, "This little book and its contents-- verses, sketches and photographs, products of the author's pen, pencil, brush and camera--is affectionately dedicated to the many friends who love the sea--who love art, and poetry and all things beautiful."

Blackton Senior died while his son was still an infant, leaving his family in straitened circumstances. Mrs. Black- ton "demonstrated the indomitable spirit that is always Eng- land," as one writer put it, and emigrated to America with her entire family. After some basic schooling in this coun- try, J. Stuart Blackton set about providing for himself and

16

his family. As his daughter recalls, "The Blacktons lived
in dire poverty until my father pulled himself onward and
upward, by dint of his tremendous imagination and his enormous capacity for work, plus supreme self-confidence. It
was really a Horatio Alger story."

J. Stuart Blackton began his working life, at the age
of eleven or twelve, apprenticed to a carpenter. In his
spare time, he dreamed about and schemed for a life in
show business, a dream which came to fruition when Albert
E. Smith appeared on the scene. Chapter 1 of this book
tells of the fateful meeting of the two men in Ronald Reader's
boarding house, but it is perhaps worth recording here that
Blackton's daughter claims her father and Smith first met at
a carpenter's workshop, where the two young men were both
apprenticed.

In the early 1890s, Blackton married his first wife,
Isabelle Mabel MacArthur. The couple had two children, a
son, James Stuart Blackton Jr., born November 6, 1897;
died on December 16, 1968, and a daughter, Mariane Constance, born in 1901. Blackton divorced Isabelle in the
'teens, and married Paula Hilburn, who, as Paula Dean, had
appeared in a number of Vitagraph's first productions, including Raffles, the Amateur Cracksman and Monsieur Beaucaire. Paula died of cancer in 1930, and a year later
Blackton married Helen Stahle, who was also to die of cancer. In 1939, Blackton married for a fourth and final time.
The bride was Evangeline Russell, who had been living with
Blackton and his daughter in their North Hollywood home for
a couple of years prior to the marriage.

Some of Vitagraph's earliest film successes were
short subjects featuring animated drawings by J. Stuart
Blackton. One of the earliest extant examples of these films
runs for approximately sixty seconds, dates from around
1900, and is titled Cohen and Coon. Blackton writes Cohen
and Coon on a board, and then proceeds to change Cohen
into a stereotype Jew and Coon into a stereotype Negro.
The best known of Blackton's animated films was Humorous
Phases of Funny Faces, copyrighted in 1906, but which Albert E. Smith believed may have been started in 1904.

Aside from his animated films, Blackton had successes with a number of films using trick photography. In 1907
came The Haunted Hotel, featuring William V. Ranous, in
which objects appeared and disappeared at will. "What pride

I took in carrying out all the weird happenings in The Haunted
Hotel," recalled J. Stuart Blackton. "By means of a stop
mechanism in the lens shutter, I endowed every piece of furniture with airy animation. The knife sawed through the loaf
of bread unassisted, 'in a manner calculated to baffle the
spectators,' as our catalogue might have said."[8]

In 1909 came Princess Nicotine, or The Smoke Fairy,
with Gladys Hulette making her screen debut in a delightful
extravaganza of trick photography, whose chief purpose was
to sell Sweet Caporal cigars and cigarettes. Two fairies,
Miss Hulette being the eldest, appear--in miniature--to a
man seated at a table, and torment him as he tries to smoke
a cigarette and his pipe, by hiding inside the latter and setting
fire to a pile of matches, etc. The film closes with the vic-
tim squirting a soda syphon at the fairies, but succeeding
only in drenching himself. A contemporary reviewer wrote,
"The effect of The Princess Nicotine when thrown upon the
screen is so startling that it defies explanation. The little
fairy moves so realistically that she cannot be explained away
by assuming that she is a doll, and yet it is impossible to
understand how she can be a living being, because of her
small stature."[46]

J. Stuart Blackton must also take credit for a policy
of filming the classics in the early years of Vitagraph. His
ability at condensing a full-length novel or play to ten minutes
of screen time was staggering. Among such films he produced at the Company prior to 1910 were The Story of
Treasure Island (1907), Francesca di Rimini (1907), Romeo
and Juliet (1908), Macbeth (1908), East Lynne (1908),
Richard III (1908), Oliver Twist (1909), and Shakespeare's
Tragedy, King Lear (1909). Even Griffith at Biograph could
not boast such an output of literary adaptations.

Prior to 1910, Blackton, like Smith, had ceased to
direct, but from the early 'teens he did supervise all production at Vitagraph, leaving Albert E. Smith free to handle
the business side of the Company. The main title of a Vitagraph production might read "Albert E. Smith presents" or
"Produced under the Personal Supervision of J. Stuart Blackton and Albert E. Smith," but it was Blackton who should

---

Opposite: Top, a scene from Francesca di Rimini (1907),
with Florence Turner in the center and Paul Panzer as the
court jester. Bottom, Gladys Hulette in Princess Nicotine
(1909).

take absolute credit for the artistic success of the film. It
says much for the man that he never resented Smith's name
appearing on a film which was absolutely the product of his
mind and his ability.

Not that it should be supposed that Blackton spent his
day supervising his productions on the studio floor. The
supervision might very well begin at his office desk, with a
reading and possible rewriting of the script, and end with a
check on the final cut of the film. Vitagraph had too many
good directors under contract for either Blackton or Smith
to have any concern with the mechanics of direction. Karl
Kitchen in a 1915 Photoplay article painted a picture of Blackton as a man with limitless energy: "The Blackton energy
seeking always an outlet in constructive employment, and his
versatility being of the readily adaptable sort, he finds it
possible to direct a secretary and two stenographers in matters of executive detail, give attention to larger phases of
studio policy, turn his ready pen to bringing within scenario
limits such dramatic conceptions as flash across his brain
and still be able to complete in each day the work which
none other than he may do."[64]

Films such as The Battle Cry of Peace or Womanhood, the Glory of a Nation could well be considered to have
been directed by J. Stuart Blackton, even if the director's
credit went elsewhere, so closely did Blackton supervise important productions such as these. Blackton did suddenly
return to direction at Vitagraph in 1917, with a series of
one and two reel shorts, produced by his then-wife, Paula,
and collectively titled "Country Life Series." In 1919, Paula,
herself, directed a five-reel feature for this same series,
The Littlest Scout. From all accounts, the films, none of
which now exist, had little merit, and it is quite possible
that Paula and not her husband directed the entire series.

Blackton was surprisingly easy-going in his attitude
toward his own films. If they turned out well, he was delighted. If they were bad, his daughter recalls, "we'd see
the final cut, and he'd say, 'That's dreadful, isn't it?'"
Blackton would shrug his shoulders, dismiss the film from
his mind, and proceed to the next project.

The producer had one failing, if it may even be considered a failing, and that was his desire for social standing.
James Morrison recalls, "He was a social climber, and we
understood that." Assistant Director Frank Lawrence, the

only member of the Vitagraph Company I found with a word of criticism for Blackton, wrote me, "I knew both Buster and Marian Blackton when they were children and roamed around the Vitagraph costume room, but a common employee, such as me, would never be noticed by the well-to-do and high born Commodore Blackton's other two children [by Paula], Charles and Violet, who knew me as someone to send on errands. The English are a caste-society. They never can, and never will, forget it. When you add wealth to caste, you have the unapproachable condition that calls for a butler to interpret."

Blackton became a commodore of the prestigious Atlantic Yacht Club in the early 'teens, and from thence forth always called himself Commodore Blackton. He owned a large mansion in Brooklyn and an estate, Harborwood, in fashionable Oyster Bay. As his daughter recalls, "My father built Harborwood at a cost of $300,000. The estate stretched over a hill from Oyster Bay to Cold Spring Harbor. Don't ask me how many acres. It was a paradise in which were wooded sections and a spring-fed lake, a large house and the 'Casino' with an enormous room and four loggias, one at each corner of the building, for elaborately furnished guest quarters. Italian architecture, and two brick and concrete arms stretching out into Cold Spring Harbor, where my father's yachts were moored in a channel that was dug in the harbor to accommodate their size. By the way, we had Teddy Roosevelt at Sagamore Hill on one side and [Louis] Tiffany on the other. Where else but in this country could a poor lad find himself in his early forties?"

The Oyster Bay estate was sold in 1920, and Blackton was to spend his last years in semi-poverty. He accepted the loss of his wealth with the same attitude of mind as he had accepted a poor film, with a shrug of the shoulders and a determined attempt at beginning something new.

As might have been expected, J. Stuart Blackton was a conservative in the 'teens and early Twenties, but as he grew older he mellowed into a liberal. His last film, possibly never completed, titled Marching On, was a tribute to a man named Archie Price, who committed suicide in a San Diego park as a protest against the treatment of the poor and underprivileged of America.

In 1917, Blackton resigned from Vitagraph (see Chapter 7) and formed his own independent producing company,

releasing initially through Paramount. He explained, "I
have devoted twenty years of my life to the art of motion
pictures, and I am beginning to learn how little anyone
knows of its marvelous possibilities. I am quite convinced
that great pictures cannot be produced commercially. David
Belasco could not produce fifty-two plays a year and keep
them up to the Belasco standard. Great pictures cannot be
painted, great books cannot be written, nor any great work
of art or literature accomplished in a hurry or on scheduled
time by routine work.

"I am going to apply my experience of long years of
practical work--added to my vision of future possibilities--
to the making of perhaps four artistic productions a year.
They will be produced independently, and from scenario to
finished product every detail will be under my personal supervision. Every production will be built upon the firm foundation of a literary masterpiece. It was literature that changed
the moving photographs of twenty years ago from a nine days'
wonder into the biggest combination of allied art, science,
education and entertainment that the world has ever known."14

Blackton was ambitious in his plans to be an independent producer. He acquired film rights to the popular
novels of Sir Gilbert Parker. He not only directed himself,
but brought in directors to work under his supervision, including James Young (Missing) and George Melford (Wild
Youth). After 1918, Blackton ceased to release his productions through Paramount, but offered them to any distributor
interested, among which were Pathe, Independent Sales Corporation and even Vitagraph.

It was Vitagraph which released--in 1918--Blackton's
most lavish independent production, The Common Cause.
Based on a play by J. Hartley Manners and Ian Hay, the
film urged international unity among the Allies, and warned
of the danger in rearming Germany. Five of America's
leading stage actresses, Julia Arthur, Marjorie Rambeau,
Irene Castle, Effie Shannon and Violet Heming, appeared in
a symbolical prologue to the production; Violet and Charles
Stuart Blackton played war waifs, and Lawrence Grossmith
appeared as an English Tommy. Other Blackton independent
productions include Dawn (1919), The House of the Tolling
Bell (1920), Life's Greatest Problem (1919), My Husband's
Other Wife (1920), Passers-By (1920) and Respectable by
Proxy (1920).

The studios of Blackton Productions, Inc. were, like those of the Vitagraph Company, located in Brooklyn, at 423 Classon Avenue. (It is quite remarkable that Brooklyn, a city not exactly noted for film-making, should at one time have been able to boast of two major studios.) Principal players under contract included Sylvia Breamer, Fanny Rice, Robert Gordon, Eddie Dunn, Lefty Alexander and Harry Davenport. Contracted character players included two long-time members of the Vitagraph stock company, Julia Swayne Gordon and Van Dyke Brooke. Jack Martin was studio manager, and Martin Justice, also from Vitagraph, was art director.

A reporter from The New York Dramatic Mirror visited the Blackton studios in 1919, and the producer talked of his work and his aspirations: "I am learning to paint pictures with my camera; by way of illustration, in a subject I have just completed, Moonshine and Shadow [released as The Moonshine Trail], you will see some absolutely new effects, whereby the effect attained resembles a painting in tone and impression. Of course the figures are moving and are not stationary as in the painting. These results are accomplished by a combination of real painting and photography. I believe that it will be possible to put on the screen a picture that art lovers will recognize immediately as being the style of a Corot, a George Inness, an A. H. Wyant or any of the painters of repute. This cannot be accomplished however by the transferring of realism to the screen. It's my belief that art is nature idealized.

"I do all the cutting of the Blackton pictures myself as well as the printing, as I think that the cutting especially is one of the most important phases of the art itself. I cannot picture authors like Rex Beach or Robert W. Chambers permitting a $25 a week clerk taking any of their novels or books and blue penciling them carte blanche or ad lib, and then turning back the stories with their markings and saying, 'this is what we have done to your novel, etc.' The man who directs the picture knows how to edit it. It is hard work and exacting to be sure, but I don't mind it as long as I get the results I desire."[25]

Blackton's independent productions were not the success he had hoped they would be. Possibly Blackton was too concerned with art and not enough with entertainment, or possibly he overestimated the intelligence of the film-going

public. Or, perhaps the fault lay entirely with J. Stuart
Blackton for failing to realize that he was not a good director.   Blackton tried hard at directing, but somehow he never
really succeeded.   He could not be faulted as a producer or
as a supervising producer, but the instant he decided to
handle the direction himself, a film never quite succeeded.
That is not to say that Blackton was not a competent direc-
tor--the success of some of his films in the Twenties proves
he was--but he was not a great director.   His greatness lay
in producing.

Undaunted by his lack of success as an independent
producer, Blackton announced plans to establish a studio in
England, and on December 29, 1920 he set sail for London,
accompanied by his wife Paula, two of his children, Violet
and Charles Stuart, and Felix Orman, who was to assist the
producer in scriptwriting and publicity.   Marian Blackton
joined her father later.

In England, Blackton produced and directed three fea-
tures, The Glorious Adventure, A Gipsy Cavalier and The
Virgin Queen.   The first, released in England and the United
States in 1922, was filmed in Prizmacolor, and featured
English beauty, Lady Diana Manners, supported by Cecil
Humphreys, Flora Le Breton, and Victor McLaglen.
McLaglen was signed by Vitagraph to star in The Beloved
Brute as a result of his performance in this film.   A Gipsy
Cavalier starred Flora Le Breton and the French boxer,
Georges Carpentier, and was released in England in August
of 1922.   The Virgin Queen was another Prizmacolor pro-
duction, again featuring Lady Diana Manners, with American
actor Carlyle Blackwell and Walter Tennyson, and released
in England in January of 1923.

All three productions were costume pictures, heavy
in English history but light in entertainment value, and all
were stagey.   A Gipsy Cavalier boasted a thrilling last reel,
in which Flora Le Breton is trapped in a coach sinking in
a river flood, with George Carpentier swimming against the
tide to rescue her.   It was obviously J. Stuart Blackton's
answer to Griffith's Way Down East.   The climax of The
Glorious Adventure featured the Great Fire of London, but
even that was dull.   The Blackton family all contributed to
the films, with Paula advising on the costumes, Marian
acting as script girl, and Marian, Violet and Charles Stuart
all playing small roles.

The Glorious Adventure was the most important of
Blackton's English productions. It was the first British
feature to be released in color, and, because the leading
lady was a prominent member of the English aristocracy,
the film created quite a stir. Queen Mary was said to be
considerably displeased that members of Court should have
descended to the depths of acting in motion pictures.

Marian Blackton admits, "The Glorious Adventure
was a very bad film, but there were moments of great
beauty in it, and some of the color was remarkably good
for its time. Especially the close-ups and a few semi-close
shots with Diana, and the improbable bit where Charley II
[William Luft] is about to seduce her, and is so struck by
her purity and innocence--now Marian, don't get catty--that
he sends her home ... still a virgin! But the scenes were
exquisite, the backgrounds marvelous, and my father's artist-
eye created something unforgettable."

In later 1922 or early 1923, J. Stuart Blackton returned to America. Basically he had failed as an independent
producer; his experiments with color, making film stars of
the aristocracy, and innovations in artistic lighting, etc. had
proved unsuccessful, but Blackton could still return to his
alma mater, Vitagraph. This he did, and produced and directed some of the best films released by the Company in
the Twenties.

When Vitagraph was sold Blackton continued directing
films, as an independent, for Warner Brothers, which re-
leased four of his features during 1926, Bride of the Storm,
The Gilded Highway, Hell-Bent for Heaven and The Passionate
Quest. The scripts for all four films were the work of
Marian Blackton, who would usually receive screen credit as
Marian Constance.

After 1926, Blackton retired from direction, a
wealthy man after the sale of Vitagraph, and dabbled in
various schemes and projects, including real estate. As a
businessman, J. Stuart Blackton was a great producer, and
the money soon disappeared. "To my father, money was
stage money, always," commented his daughter. In August
of 1931, Blackton filed a petition in bankruptcy. By a
curious quirk of fate, at the same time Eugene V. Brewster
also filed a petition for bankruptcy. Brewster had been the
first editor, and subsequently publisher, of The Motion Picture

Story Magazine, founded by Blackton in 1911 as a publicity
organ for Vitagraph and the other member companies of
Motion Picture Patents Company. The magazine eventually
became Motion Picture Magazine, and as such is still published today. Brewster's bankruptcy was a result of his
trying to promote his third wife, Corliss Palmer, as a film
star. J. Stuart Blackton had no problem in handling women;
it was handling money which proved his downfall.

J. Stuart Blackton accepted his change in financial
circumstances stoically. He had been poor once, and he
showed little concern at being poor again. He worked on
various film projects, including a short on California mis-
sions for Educational, and a number of abortive schemes for
the W.P.A. He was involved in a social gathering known as
The Breakfast Club, and there is film extant of his greeting
many old Vitagraphers there, including Hughie Mack, Kate
Price, Flora Finch and Florence Turner. As Blackton's
daughter recalls, "Somehow everyone was tremendously impressed by my father, and persisted in acting as if he was
a celebrity, when he was just a real broke chap. A has-
been! But what a happy has-been!"

In the early Thirties, William P. S. Earle, a Vitagraph director who had worked closely with Blackton in the
past, approached him with the suggestion to produce a history
of the cinema. Blackton enthusiastically embraced the idea,
and The March of the Movies, also known as The Film
Parade, came into being. Blackton and Earle gathered together all the early footage they could find, and where film
was no longer extant went ahead and recreated it. The
Blackton family and friends enthusiastically worked on the
production, which included a fascinating re-enactment of The
Battle of Manila Bay, featuring both Blackton and Albert E.
Smith.

As Marian Blackton recalls, "My father and A.E.
seldom met after my father's financial nose-dive, in fact
even before this; though while my father and I had our own
unit at Vitagraph, there were occasional dinners and evening
gatherings when A.E. brought his beautiful wife, Lucille,
formerly Jean Paige, to our home, and these occasions were
reciprocated. But I was amazed when A.E. turned up the
day we made the filming of the Manila Bay scene. My father
must have asked him to join us, but he never told me that he
had. We had a lovely, cosy chat after the filming was
finished. I remember him well, looking around the shabby

loft, above a garage, where we produced the film, and
sighing and then pressing my hand.   I could swear that
there were tears in his eyes."

    The Film Parade played one day, on a double bill
with a Western, at Loew's Theatre, New York, on December 21, 1933.   Variety of December 26, 1933 gave it a
reasonably favorable review.   However, the production did
little business, and Blackton continued to work on it, changing sections, removing others, almost until his death.   In
the late Thirties he would appear, in person, with the film.
The last public performance of The Film Parade appears to
have been in 1957, when it played a couple of Los Angeles
theatres.

    All that appeared to have survived on the film were
a number of 16mm prints and various rolls of 35mm nitrate.
During 1974, Robert Gitt and I, with Marian Blackton's help,
worked on restoring the film, and there is now a complete
negative preserved in the National Film Collection at the Library of Congress.   "Corny" and cliché-ridden as The Film
Parade might seem to modern audiences, this sixty-minute
film should be acknowledged as the last great production of
a great film pioneer.

    About 1937, Blackton co-produced with Ray J. Largay
a film titled Marching On, the story of Archie Price, featuring Sherman J. Bainbridge.   As I have already indicated,
Archie Price committed suicide in a San Diego park as a
protest against poverty and injustice in this country.   No
record exists of this film ever having been released, or
even completed.   Marian Blackton recalls, "My father went
down to San Diego to photograph the announced 'enormous
gathering of people who would come to honor Archie Price.'
He said the turn-out of mourners for poor Archie was pa-
thetically small.   I think my father took some footage of the
event, but the whole thing was a fiasco and badly handled by
Archie's supporters, and, I suspect, hampered by political
maneuvers on the part of office holders in the city of San
Diego, and state officials."

    Death came suddenly and unexpectedly to J. Stuart
Blackton.   He left his Los Angeles home one late afternoon
on a shopping errand.   While crossing Pico Boulevard he
was hit by a bus, and died a couple of days later, on August
13, 1941.   After his death, the nurse gave Marian his
clothes, and, by chance, her hand went into his trouser

pocket, where she found a handful of rubber bands.   The
Commodore always carried them with him, claiming "You
never know when you might need them."   In all the years,
both good and bad, that Marian had been close to her father,
that was the only time she cried.

   Blackton died penniless.   Dear, faithful William P.
S. Earle purchased a plot of land at Forest Lawn cemetery
and had Blackton's ashes interred there.   Later, Earle
married Evangeline Russell Blackton, and when she died,
placed her ashes next to Blackton's.   When I spoke with
Bill Earle in 1972 he was a feeble, old man, whose one
wish was to die and be buried next to his beloved Evangeline
and J. Stuart Blackton, and to be with them forever in the
hereafter.   Death came at last in 1973 for William P. S.
Earle, and for his sake I sincerely hope there is a hereafter.

Chapter 3

ALBERT E. SMITH

Albert E. Smith was the financial genius behind the Vitagraph Company. If J. Stuart Blackton was responsible for the company's artistic achievements, then Smith could take full credit for the company's sound business success. The two partners complemented each other well. Whenever the company went through a financial crisis--as it did in the late 'teens--Smith was there to see it through, while Blackton would effectively handle the film production side, oblivious to Vitagraph's monetary troubles.

One example of Smith's financial care in running Vitagraph was his insistence upon Price, Waterhouse and Company creating a special accounting system for the company. This system became so highly regarded that in 1916, Price, Waterhouse published a book about it for their other clients.

The one failing of Albert E. Smith, and many might argue that it was not anything of the kind, was his lack of personal feeling. In his business dealings Smith saw little, if any, room for sentiment. When Florence Turner tried to sell Vitagraph some stories in 1924, she was curtly turned down by Smith, with no thought for the part she had played in the company's early success. Smith's concern for business before anything else could also be his downfall. In 1916, when Vitagraph had the opportunity to sign Mary Pickford to a contract at $10,000 a week, just before she was about to put her signature to the contract Miss Pickford asked if she might see Smith's new baby. "Let's get this business off our minds first," said Smith. To which Pickford responded, "Well, then I'll never see it," flounced out of the room, and shortly afterwards signed a new contract with Famous Players-Lasky.

Albert E. Smith, the business man, presents no problems to a researcher. His business dealings are all there
in black-and-white among the papers he so carefully preserved, which are now deposited at the University of California in Los Angeles. The private Albert E. Smith is not
so easy to describe, for unlike J. Stuart Blackton, he
shunned publicity. In 1917, Exhibitor's Trade Review, in
one of the few articles ever published about him, wrote as
follows: "Intensely earnest, indefatigable, perfectly even
tempered, wholesome mentally and physically, alive to the
littlest item affecting the industry of which he has a broad
grasp, he is yet a man of few words who knows and applies
the faculty of concentration. This means not that he is dis-
tant, for the fact remains that he is one of the most agreeable of men--the kind of man who, as his employees and
intimates testify, is the kind of man who wears well. Than
which nothing better can be said of a man as a man."[23]

Albert Edward Smith was born in the small town of
Faversham in the county of Kent, England, on June 4, 1875.
His father, who had at least eight other sons and one daughter, was a market gardener. In 1888, the entire Smith
family emigrated to America, for the unlikely reason that--
according to Albert E. Smith--his great grandmother was
seeking a cure for asthma. "By all accounts she was a
sort of latter-day Queen Bess," wrote Smith in his autobiography, "whose demeanor was strong or fierce enough to
provoke a mass migration because of a running nose."[92]

The family not only crossed 3,000 miles of sea to
reach America, but also a further 3,000 miles of land to
California, where they eventually settled in Santa Barbara.
Albert E. Smith left his family in New York, and practiced
various trades, including bookbinding and carpentry, before
entering the world of show business as a prestidigitator.
An early playbill describes him as "The Prince of Entertainers, introducing original experiments in Prestidigitation,
plus character impersonations, ventriloqual dialogues and
polyphonic imitations." A reviewer at the time commented,
"Mr. Smith's repertoire is distinctly unique and original,
being a clever combination of sleight of hand and invisible
mechanical appliances of his own invention."[70]

After formation of the Vitagraph Company, Smith
firmly put behind him all thoughts of a career as an enter-
tainer. He did, of course, assist in direction and production, but, unlike Blackton, never appeared in front of the

camera. By 1912, he was paying little attention to the production side of the business, being too engrossed in its finances. It was not until 1917 that Smith again returned to
production; Exhibitor's Trade Review (August 11, 1917) reported, "Albert E. Smith is an absolutely one-man power in
the corporation and upon him will devolve the duty of making
every final decision connected with the production end of the
business." Amusingly, the same news story noted, "It was
President Smith, according to the directors, who was responsible for making Vitagraph known as the 'producing company
with the beautiful women.' This policy of engaging beautiful
women with histrionic ability is to be continued by Mr. Smith,
who expects to produce a new line of beautiful motion picture
stars in the very near future that will surpass anything here-
tofore seen on the American stage or screen."

   In his younger days Smith had an eye for beautiful
women. After he divorced his first wife, May, about whom
nothing is known, in 1912, in January of 1913 he married
the actress, Hazel Neason. She died of Spanish influenza
on January 24, 1920, and Smith married, for a third and
final time, another actress, Jean Paige.

   When Albert E. Smith first became involved in show
business as a prestidigitator, he was a crew-cut, handsome
young man. By the mid-teens, the crew-cut had been replaced by a well-coiffured head of hair, but aside from the
addition of a pair of spectacles, Smith was still a handsome,
young man, and also a very elegant one. In appearance, he
was very much the prosperous business executive.

   If Albert E. Smith had any failing as a studio head,
it was his insistence upon bringing his brothers into the
company. (Not that nepotism was all that unusual in the
film industry--it was rampant at Universal.) The West
Coast studio of the Vitagraph Company had, among its production staff, Vic, David, W.S., Steve and Ernie Smith.
George Smith was in charge of Vitagraph's London office,
and J. P. Smith was the company's representative in Australia and the Far East. In fact, only one brother, F. J.
Smith, had no direct connection with the Vitagraph Company.

   An amusing incident occurred when Albert E. Smith
arranged a family reunion at the West Coast studio in March
of 1917. Actress Bessie Love, preparing for her day's
shooting, stepped from her dressing room to check a detail
with her director, David Smith. She stood at the head of the

stairway, and called loudly, "Oh, Mr. Smith." Instantly,
from all parts of the studio, there came the reply, "Yes,
Miss Love, what is it you wish?"

Albert E. Smith, to all extents and purposes, retired
after selling the company to Warner Brothers. His wife recalled, "He had a wonderful life after he retired, going
down to the ranch. Mr. Smith loved it. And he had so
many hobbies--photography and collecting things. He col-
lected books, and he was just a great connoisseur of art."

The Academy of Motion Picture Arts and Sciences
presented an Academy Award to Smith in March of 1948.
Also honored at the same ceremony were Colonel William
Selig, George K. Spoor and Thomas Armat. The inscrip-
tion on the base of the "Oscar" reads, "One of the small
group of pioneers whose belief in a new medium, and whose
contributions to its development, blazed the trail along which
the motion picture has progressed, in their lifetime from
obscurity to world-wide acclaim."

In 1952, Smith's autobiography, Two Reels and a
Crank, written in collaboration with Cecil B. DeMille's director of publicity, Phil A. Koury, was published.[92] Much
of the book deals with Smith's adventures in South Africa
during the Boer War, and in Cuba with Theodore Roosevelt
and the Rough Riders. There does appear to be evidence to
support Smith's claim that he and Blackton went to Cuba; it
is mentioned briefly in William Basil Courtney's "History of
Vitagraph," published in 1925.[26] There is no documentation
concerning Smith's adventures in South Africa with a young
Richard Harding Davis, but I, for one, find it hard to doubt
the man. When Phil A. Koury questioned some of Smith's
anecdotes, he replied, "Do you want me to tell you what
history says, or do you want me to tell you what I saw?"

Four years after publication of his autobiography,
Smith decided to hold a party, on October 21, 1956, to
celebrate the 60th anniversary of the foundation of the Vitagraph Company. Among those present were Arline Pretty,
Clara Kimball Young, Mary Anderson, Alice Calhoun, Antonio Moreno, Betty Blythe, Charles Brabin, Anita Stewart
and Paul Panzer. Smith was visibly moved by the occasion:
"For me it is so wonderful to find such a nice group of
people assembled for an event of this kind. Our Vitagraph
organization was in truth a family organization. We worked

Charles Brabin, Anita Stewart, Jean Paige (Mrs. Albert E. Smith) and Albert E. Smith at Vitagraph's 60th Anniversary Party on October 21, 1956.

loyally together, and you only need to meet today the personnel we had to realize what wonderful people they are."

Albert E. Smith died in Hollywood on August 1, 1958. He was a wealthy man--among the real estate he owned was the Chateau Marmont on Hollywood's Sunset Boulevard--but he was also wealthy in the friends in the industry he had made through the years, and those people that had been lucky enough to know and work with him were wealthy because of that privilege.

Chapter 4

FLORENCE TURNER

The first major star of the Vitagraph also happened
to be the screen's first star. Her name was Florence
Turner, and the film star may be said to have been created
when she joined the Vitagraph Company in the Spring of 1907.
"The Vitagraph Girl, " as Florence Turner was affectionately
known, was the first actress to be put under contract by a
film company. She had no competitors; only "The Biograph
Girl, " Florence Lawrence, came anywhere near to approach-
ing her in popularity.

Florence Turner was born in New York City in 1887,
and had an extensive career on the legitimate stage and in
vaudeville before joining Vitagraph. She was known in the
theatre as Eugenie Florence, and her speciality was im-
personating Fay Templeton and Marie Dressler. Miss
Turner claimed that while on a vaudeville tour, a fellow
member of the company, Mabel Crawley, remarked to her,
"You pull such extraordinary faces that you would make your
fortune as a motion picture actress!"[28]

Her work at Vitagraph was not limited solely to
acting when she first joined the company. As she recalled
later, "I had to attend to all the business affairs of the concern as well as act. I was a sort of handywoman! I paid
the staff and artistes, kept the books, and was clerk,
cashier, accountant and actress all rolled into one."[28]
While Florence Turner attended to her various duties, her
mother--like the mothers of Mary Pickford and the Talmadge
Sisters, Mrs. Turner played a very important part in her
daughter's screen career--was also working at the studios
in the capacity of wardrobe woman, script-girl and extra.

Not exactly beautiful, Florence Turner had a petite
body and dark hair and eyes which made her Latin ancestry

34

more than apparent.   Yet, she had no problem portraying
any nationality.   Her liquescent eyes would one moment
beguile an audience with their beauty, and at the next might
be popping out of her head in a hideous comic caricature.
"The distortion of the human face is one of the most interesting studies to me, " she once remarked. [54]

     There was no role that Florence Turner did not play
during her years at Vitagraph.   She appeared in everything
from Shakespeare (King Lear, A Midsummer Night's Dream,
etc.) to Southern melodrama (A Dixie Mother).   Her features
could be transformed from those of a haughty society lady
to the friendly, weather-beaten visage of a servant girl.   On
September 4, 1911, Vitagraph released Jealousy, a one-reel
"study in the art of dramatic expression, " containing no sub-
titles, in which Florence Turner was the sole player.

     Florence Turner was also one of the first--if not the
first--film player to make personal appearances.   During

Florence Turner (center) with James Young (left), James
Morrison and Clara Kimball Young in A Vitagraph Romance
(1912).

1910, she was enthusiastically received at a number of
theatres in Brooklyn. The first of such appearances was
at Saratoga Park, Brooklyn, in April, when she made a
"naive and fetching little speech," and the audience sang of
her charms with a song titled, appropriately enough, "The
Vitagraph Girl." So successful were these personal appearances that other Vitagraph players began engaging in
them; when Maurice Costello, Turner's leading man, appeared on stage at Brooklyn's Fulton Auditorium in November of 1910, 1,600 people turned up for the event.

In 1912, The New York Dramatic Mirror commented
about Miss Turner, "No actress in motion pictures has a
larger following."[47] Her entire career had been with Vita-
graph--no other player, at that time, could claim such devoted service to one producer--and Florence Turner was
considering a change. The Moving Picture World (March 22,
1913) noted, "Her work increased the sale of the Vitagraph
pictures over those of all other makes. She figures that
the Vitagraph Company can spare her now better than it
could before, and therefore she is going out to get some of
the 'good gravy' for herself while she is still in her prime."[56]

Early in 1913, Florence Turner left Vitagraph and
embarked on an ambitious vaudeville tour. Her act consisted of impersonations. First, a Vitagraph one-reeler,
in which she starred, would be screened; then Miss Turner
appeared as a little girl singing. This was followed by a
character study of a young boy in a theatre gallery, following
every move of the villain, hero, and heroine. Other impersonations included an elderly village gossip and a saleswoman in a five-and-ten-cent store.

Florence Turner's next move was a surprising one.
She announced her intention to go to England, to appear at
a number of music halls, and, more importantly, to form
her own company. On March 15, 1913, director Larry
Trimble with his canine star, Jean, and actors Tom Powers
and James Morrison resigned from Vitagraph. It was assumed that they were to join Miss Turner, but in fact only
Trimble and Jean came over to England with her initially.
Tom Powers joined her later, while Morrison never made
the trip.

On May 26, 1913, at the London Pavilion, Florence
Turner made her British debut. Shortly thereafter she
formed Turner Films, with studios at Walton-on-Thames, the

home of British film pioneer Cecil Hepworth.   Larry Trimble, who had directed Florence Turner almost continuously
since 1910, was named head of production, and one of Cecil
Hepworth's most popular male stars, Henry Edwards, was
chosen to be the company's leading man.

     Why did Florence Turner choose to produce in Eng-
land?   In a 1916 interview Larry Trimble explained, "We
located in England because three years ago the power of
large combines in this country [U.S.A.] left slight opportunity for an independent producer with small capital.   Miss
Turner's popularity in Vitagraph pictures was our great asset
in appealing directly to British exhibitors, who, as you know,
were buying in the open market.   But the extent of Miss
Turner's fame on the other side none of us realized until the
night of her first personal appearance in the London Pavilion.
I never saw such a demonstration for any player.   She was
forced to remain on the stage six minutes beyond the allotted
time, and even then the audience was not content."[33]

     Florence Turner was to star in upwards of thirty pro-
ductions in England.   They ranged from one-reel shorts,
such as Creatures of Habit (released in England on April 13,
1914), through two-reel comedies like her first English production, Rose of Surrey (released in England on September 29,
1913), which The Bioscope described as "one of the most
charming English film comedies ever produced," to the five-
reel Far from the Madding Crowd (released in England on
February 28, 1916).   The last was the first in a series of
six Turner productions to be released--on June 23, 1916--by
Mutual in the United States.

     The most important film in which Miss Turner played
in England was the 1915 My Old Dutch, based on the popular
song by Albert Chevalier, who also appeared opposite Florence
Turner in the production.   It was directed by Larry Trimble,
and written by Chevalier and Arthur Shirley.   Like most of
Miss Turner's British films, My Old Dutch was released in
the U.S.--by Universal on November 22, 1915.   The film
was very favorably received.   Commented The Moving Picture
World of November 13, 1915, "My Old Dutch is a rare picture, great in its simplicity, strong in its appeal, and splen-
didly played by its two principals.   It is wholesome.   It is a
story that might have come from between the covers of a
Dickens--with its sunshine and shade, its quaint types, its
Life."   Interestingly, on August 25, 1911, Vitagraph had released a one-reel version of My Old Dutch, featuring Van
Dyke Brooke, Mary Maurice, and Maurice Costello.

A production which showed up Florence Turner's pantomimic genius was a one-reeler titled Florence Turner Impersonates Film Favorites, released in the U.S. by MinA [sic] on November 25, 1915. In it, Miss Turner appeared as Ford Sterling, Broncho Billy Anderson, Mabel Normand, and Sarah Bernhardt in the last scene from Queen Elizabeth.

Possibly Florence Turner might have continued to produce films in England for the international market, but the hardships created by the First World War put an end to her plans. Larry Trimble returned to America in August of 1916, announcing that although he was still director-in-chief of Turner Films, it was his intention to produce only in this country. There were rumors of a rift between him and Florence Turner, and, also, Trimble was having matrimonial problems. On November 12, 1916, Florence Turner also returned to America; Turner Films were no more.

The American film industry to which Florence Turner returned had changed drastically from the days when she was its brightest star. Many of the early producing companies--Kalem, Lubin, Edison, etc.--were going out of business. Many of the early stars had been retired.

Florence Turner was still able to get the occasional starring role, but never in major productions. In October, 1919, Photoplay announced that she was to direct a series of comedies at Universal, in which she was also to play the lead. Then, in the fall of 1920, she was signed to join the stock company of players at Metro.

However, Florence Turner was not happy, and in 1922 she decided to return to England. "So here I am again, glad, and, oh most happy to be in the country where its people have always made me so heartily welcome, and hoping never to leave it again," she wrote. "I can only say most sincerely that coming back to Great Britain has just meant coming home to me."[100]

Of course, on her return to Britain she was no longer the head of her own company. She played leading roles in a number of films, none of which appear to have been released in the U.S., and also made many stage appearances, when she would give impersonations of Pauline Frederick, Nazimova, Mae Murray, Chaplin and Larry Semon. The stars might change, but Florence Turner's impersonations of them remained constant.

Ill-luck, however, overtook Florence Turner yet again.
It was not a World War this time that put an end to her
British filmwork, but a crisis in the British film industry
which, in 1924, closed all studios. She was stranded, penniless, in London, until fellow-actress Marion Davies paid
for her and her mother to return to the States, and gave
Florence a small role in Janice Meredith.

In 1925, Larry Trimble wanted to produce a remake
of My Old Dutch, with Florence Turner recreating her role
of Sal. James Morrison recalls, "Larry Trimble came to
me, and he said, 'Jim, Flotie wants to get back into pictures, and I think she can!' He got a little company to-
gether--the people who were in it worked for nothing, because we loved Flotie--and we did scenes from My Old Dutch."
The screen test was shown to executives at Universal, who
agreed to Trimble's directing the film, but cast May McAvoy,
not Florence Turner, in the lead.

Small roles--usually those of mothers--came Florence
Turner's way for the rest of the Twenties. Many readers
will remember her as Buster Keaton's mother in College
(1927). However, as the decade drew to a close, film roles
became fewer and fewer. Motion Picture Classic (July,
1928) painted a pathetic picture of her: "She waits for the
studio telephone call that will give her a few days' work.
Young-looking and slim, a capable actress, a brilliant pan-
tomimist ... What does she ask? Stardom? No. Meaty
little parts. Character roles. A chance to come back."

In the early Thirties, Florence Turner put together
a stage presentation titled "Pioneer Film Days," in which
she gave impersonations of Mrs. 'Iggins, the charlady, the
Armenian Woman Murderer, and the death of Francesca da
Rimini. The Los Angeles Examiner (October 15, 1933) described the presentation as "a revelation of the humorous and
tragic struggles of the early motion picture period."

Finally, in 1937, Louis B. Mayer offered Florence
Turner a contract as a stock extra at M-G-M. Despite her
many misfortunes and the low ebb her career had reached,
Miss Turner never became dispirited. "Certainly I cling to
pictures," she said, "and why not? I was big once. I can
be big again as a character actress. Experience has taught
me that there's only one way to the top. That is to hang
around, ready to grasp, or fight for, the slightest opportunity. I don't feel humble or ashamed because circumstances

have temporarily whipped me. True success, I believe, is
founded upon determination inspired by failures. I know that
eventually I shall be a 'star' again."

In the early Forties, Florence Turner entered the
Motion Picture Country House, where so many once-famous
stars played their final scenes. Here, in the peace and
quiet of Woodland Hills, California, she died on August 28,
1946. Florence Turner had come a long way--the film industry had come a long way--since she had made her screen
debut in a half-reel comedy, How to Cure a Cold, almost
forty years earlier in a bustling Brooklyn studio.

Possibly the finest tribute to Florence Turner was
paid by Edward Wagenknecht in The Movies in the Age of
Innocence, when he wrote: "Nobody in my generation could
have had any difficulty in understanding the young Norma
Talmadge's enthusiasm for her even before she herself had
become a Vitagrapher: 'I would rather have touched the hem
of her skirt than to have shaken hands with St. Peter.'"[104]

Chapter 5

JOHN BUNNY

Any writing on the Vitagraph Company would, of necessity, have to devote a considerable amount of space to comedian John Bunny. Without a doubt, John Bunny is Vitagraph's chief claim to fame to most people. Bunny's film career--lasting a mere four years--was entirely with Vitagraph, but it was a career that assured him immortality as the early cinema's most famous comedian.

Yet, discussing John Bunny is not an easy matter. He is remembered as a comedian, but those of his films which survive just are not funny, nor would they appear ever to have been funny, or even mildly amusing. His screen personality was that of a jovial fat man, but off-screen, apparently, he was far from jovial. He was pompous, rude, and arrogant, and was actively disliked by his fellow Vitagraphers. "He looked down on anybody who wasn't as great as he was," recalled actor James Morrison. Director William P. S. Earle commented, "Knowing he was a motion picture star, he was something of an s.o.b."

Jan Zilliacus, daughter of Larry Trimble, who directed many of Bunny's films, told me: "He was very bad-tempered, very difficult. He upstaged everyone. He was an old egocentric. He always wanted the camera on him. He wasn't as mean as W. C. Fields, but he was verging on it."

There can be no question of Bunny's popularity with the general public. He was universally adored; in Russia he was known as "Pockson," in France as "Monsieur Cinema," and in Germany, "Herr Kintop." Flora Finch, Bunny's co-star, wrote, "John Bunny was one of the most dearly beloved of the film stars, both in the studio and out, tho' he was funny only when he worked. On the streets, people would follow him for blocks and call out, 'Oh, Bunny!'"[43]

When John Bunny died on April 26, 1915, the newspapers of the world poured forth their tributes. "Was ever
a name so famous?" asked London's Evening Standard on
April 28, 1915.   A headline of the front page of the Dublin
Evening Herald of April 29, 1915 read, "John Bunny Is Dead.
The Best-Known Man in the World."   The British humor
weekly, Punch, in its issue of May 12, 1915, published an
article, headed "The World's Loss," which read, 'Helen's
face may have launched a thousand ships, but Bunny's en-
raptured millions of audiences.   Wherever a picture-palace
exists, whether at Helsingfors or Brindisi, Cairo or Cape
Coast Castle, Vladivostok or Littlehampton, Hobart or
Duluth, Bahia Blanca or Archangel, there the features of
John Bunny are as familiar as household words.   Vast mul-
titudes of human beings who do not yet know what the Kaiser
looks like are intimate with Bunny's every expression."[107]

John Bunny was born in New York City on September
21, 1863; his father came from Cornwall, England, and his
mother from County Clare, Ireland.   At the age of twenty,
he entered show business, working in an obscure minstrel
show, and for the next twenty-five years he played everything from Shakespeare to vaudeville.   As Robert Grau
noted, "John Bunny's twenty-five years on the stage was
much like the average stage career.   That he never reached
stellardom may be due to lack of managerial acumen."[51]

A detailed account of Bunny's stage career would fill
many pages.   In 1897-98, he was manager and director of
the Grand Opera House, Salt Lake City.   From 1898 until
1905, he was stage manager and director for William Brady's
productions, including Way Down East, in which Bunny appeared as Hi Holler.   The period from 1905 until 1908 saw
him with Henry W. Savage's company, appearing in, among
others, Easy Dawson and Tom Jones.   During 1909 and 1910,
John Bunny was with Lew Fields' company in Old Dutch.

Why Bunny chose to enter films, and why he chose
the Vitagraph Company is something of a mystery.

In Motion Picture Acting by Frances Agnew, Bunny,
himself, wrote: "I was one of the foremost comedians on
the stage. I have played good parts with the Shuberts, Chas.
Frohman's productions and all the biggest managers.   However, I awoke to the fact that the stage game was not what
it had been and that the 'movies' were the coming thing. So
I decided I would rather be behind the guns than in front of

them. I wanted to be with the 'shooters' rather than with
the 'shot,' so I cancelled my thirty weeks' contract with the
Shuberts, threw aside all the years of experience and success I had had, and decided to begin all over again. I went
down to the Vitagraph studio, which was then in its infancy,
and frankly told them I wanted to work in pictures."[1]

J. Stuart Blackton recalled, "A very fat man was
leaning against the wall of the studio, like a buttress supporting the wall of Notre Dame. 'We need a new comedy
man,' said Albert, 'maybe this one will be funny.' He saw
us coming. 'Look,' he said, 'can either of you gentlemen
do this?' Springing into the air he clicked his heels together
three times before he hit the ground again. 'I want a chance
at the pictures,' he pleaded, 'just a chance!' He got his
chance."[13]

There is considerable question not only as to why
Vitagraph, but as to when. According to William Basil
Courtney, Bunny's name first graced the Vitagraph payroll
on October 27, 1910.[26] Albert E. Smith claims Bunny's
first Vitagraph film was Doctor Cupid, released on January
10, 1911.[92] Historian Sam Gill, who has undertaken extensive research into John Bunny's career, claims that his first
screen appearance was in Jack Fat and Jim Slim at Coney
Island, released on December 2, 1910. The only subject on
which there is agreement is Bunny's initial salary--$40 a
week.

Bunny was to appear in more than 150 Vitagraph films,
almost all of which were one reel or less in length. In
more than half of his films, Bunny played opposite Flora
Finch, a tall, thin, spinsterish actress, with pinched features. They complemented each other perfectly, and many
who saw them together on the screen believed them to be
man and wife. However, not only were they not married,
but, as Albert E. Smith remembered, "they cordially hated
each other."[93]

One of the most delightful surviving John Bunny shorts
--very few of his films are extant--is The Troublesome Step-
daughters, released on July 6, 1912. In it, Bunny portrays
a middle-aged widower who brings home a new wife and
mother for his five grown-up daughters, whom he still thinks
of as children. The comedy is not in Bunny's performance,
which is a straight-forward characterization, but in the antics
of his daughters, out to make life unpleasant for their new

mother.   One of the charms of The Troublesome Stepdaugh-
ters is that the daughters are played by Edith Storey,
Dorothy Kelly, Lillian Walker, Edith Halleren and Norma
Talmadge, all of whom were to achieve varying degrees of
stardom.

    Directing John Bunny was apparently no easy matter,
for he had a problem in keeping awake, a problem presumably brought on by his obesity.   "The commonest sight
in the yard was Bunny's four-dimension figure standing as
nearly stark upright as such a figure could, and held steady
by one hand resting on the tank railing, while he slept and
snored in peaceful indifference to the hurry and scurry
around him," wrote William Basil Courtney.[26]

    On May 25, 1912, John Bunny, along with director
Larry Trimble and cameraman Arthur Ross, sailed for
England.   The trio shot some six shorts there and in Ireland, including Bunny at the Derby, released on October 29,
1912, and The Blarney Stone, released on March 28, 1913.

    While in England, Bunny also filmed some scenes for
a film adaptation of episodes from Charles Dickens' Pickwick Papers, which apparently the actor had wished to make
for over a year.   A supporting cast of English players was
hired, including Arthur Ricketts and Minnie Raynor, and the
film was released in three parts, the first appearing on
February 28, 1913.   "Mr. Bunny as Pickwick needs hardly
to be described," wrote Hugh Hoffman in The Moving Picture
World (February 15, 1913).   "Nature endowed him for the
part, and one who cannot imagine him as Pickwick must have
imagination poorly developed indeed."

    In London, John Bunny was mobbed by his admirers;
while shooting Bunny at the Derby, a riot almost ensued.
Vacationing in Paris and Berlin, Bunny noted--much to his
satisfaction--"I found myself better known than I had any
right to expect."[55]

    The adulation appeared to have affected Bunny's al-
ready inflated ego.   When he returned to New York on September 21, 1912, J. Stuart Blackton commented, "The trip

---

Opposite, above: John Bunny with Flora Finch in The Subduing of Mrs. Nag (1911); below, John Bunny and Larry
Trimble (center) in Bunny All at Sea (1912).

spoiled him.... He returned with delusions of grandeur and was never the same again."[13]

Bunny was earning over $200 a week at Vitagraph, but offers were arriving for vaudeville appearances at many times that amount. On January 20, 1913, he began an engagement for one week as a monologist at Hammerstein's Victoria Theatre, New York, at a salary of $1,000. Noted Variety (January 24, 1913), "Mr. Bunny is very funny as a Vitagraph comedian."

John Bunny returned to Vitagraph, working with a new director, George D. Baker. A new contract, negotiated in the spring of 1913, was said to guarantee him $1,000 a week for fifty weeks a year.

However, the stage still beckoned. Bunny returned to Hammerstein's Victoria Theatre in October of 1913. Variety (October 3, 1913), described his comedy routine: "In this latest thing Bunny probably believes is an act, the moving picture actor starts off with a film of himself, in bed, having forgotten about the theatre engagement. An announcer first appears before the curtain informing the audience Mr. Bunny cannot be found, but not to become impatient. Then the picture starts. It shows the announcer racing to the Bunny home and getting Bunny out of bed, bringing him to the theatre with Bunny dressing in a taxi en route. As the film ends, Bunny slips through the sheet."

Bunny eventually left Vitagraph in the summer of 1914 to star in his own show, Bunny in Funnyland. It opened at the Academy of Music in Baltimore on September 9. Variety (September 11, 1914) thought it "one of the best 'kid' shows that has come this way for some time." The show, however, did not do well, and Bunny returned to Vitagraph for a while.

In March of 1915, he was back again on the stage with the John Bunny Show, which opened at the Bronx Opera House. Variety (March 19, 1915) had not forgotten what it had said before about Bunny's return to the theatre: "And duly apologizing for the time-worn wheeze, let it be early recorded that as a star of the speaking stage, Funny Bunny is one of the best studio actors extant."

On May 1, 1915, The Moving Picture World reported that John Bunny was seriously ill at his home in Flatbush.

He died before that issue of the magazine had appeared. Bunny's last Vitagraph appearance was in <u>How Cissy Made Good</u>, released on February 2, 1915, in which he played himself being interviewed by a reporter from <u>Motion Picture Magazine</u>. On June 2, 1915, Vitagraph released <u>Bunny in Bunnyland</u>, in which John Bunny appeared as a cartoon character, drawn by Carl Lederer.

Among the many tributes to Bunny was one titled "The Art of John Bunny," which appeared in the English trade journal, <u>The Bioscope</u>, on May 6, 1915. The anonymous writer commented that "our grandchildren may still find delight in John Bunny's genial humour, and we need have no fear that this appreciation will ever be tinged with doubt as to the critical sagacity of their grandfathers."[3]

No writer could have been more wrong. John Bunny is a name in the history books, nothing more. His films have not stood the test of time, nor has the critical praise for them.

Chapter 6

THE VITAGRAPH FAMILY

Looking back on the early film industry, J. Stuart Blackton wrote, "The atmosphere of the studios in those days was that of a big family circle; the women sat around, making over the gowns in the wardrobe for their parts and exchanging recipes; the men talking about their cars and chickens and homes. Temperament as an alibi for tantrums hadn't been discovered yet and the directors didn't wear short pants."[11] Nowhere was this more true than at the Vitagraph studios, where a family atmosphere had existed from the early years of its formation through to the mid-teens, at which time big business began to get involved, and sentiment, friendship and a spirit of comradeship disappeared.

The family atmosphere at Vitagraph was never stronger than at Christmastime, with the annual presentation of turkeys to all members of its staff. Each Vitagrapher would receive his or her turkey; then, as Blackton recalled, "Pop, Albert and I would line up near the door, and as each person started home, it was our very great pleasure to shake hands with them, wish them a Merry Christmas and thank them for their share of the success attained that year by the Vitagraph. Every employee came to us, and I will tell you all that there was no greater thrill in all the world than for each of us, Pop, Albert and myself, to call every solitary employee by name, as each of the three of us could do, and try to make them believe we appreciated their loyalty and friendship."[10] By 1913, Vitagraph was distributing a cash bonus to each employee, in addition to the turkey, with no one receiving less than five dollars. At Christmas, 1913, $24,000 was given away to the staff.

Among other activities at Vitagraph which were conducive to a feeling of belonging to a family were the concert parties, the first of which was held on January 8, 1909,

following a Vitagraph employees' dinner. Over six hundred
guests were entertained by such acts as "A Comedy Sketch"
by Maurice Costello and Florence Turner, "Magic and Mystery" by Albert E. Smith, and "Monologues of Nonsense" by
J. Stuart Blackton. By 1912, Vitagraph employees were
holding their entertainments outside the studio--on July 10
of that year, one such event was held at the Atlantic Yacht
Club--and the entertainment consisted of dramatic sketches,
featuring Ralph Ince, Rose Coghlan and James Morrison,
among others; Miss Zena Keefe, "That Dainty Comedienne";
and Miss Adele de Garde, with "Character Songs." (Interestingly, several of the sketches presented at time were later
adapted, by Vitagraph, into highly successful films.) On
April 7, 1915, one of the last of the Vitagraph family entertainments was held at Stauch's Dancing Palace, Coney Island.

"It was a family; it really was," recalled James Morrison. "The people out there were very fond of each other.
Now in the dressing room which I had were Earle Williams,
Harry Morey and Leo Delaney and myself. And afterwards,
Tom Powers joined us." However, unlike other families,
the members of the Vitagraph family came from many different backgrounds. James Morrison, Tom Powers and
Helen Gardner had all studied acting under Madame Alberti
at the American Academy of Dramatic Arts. Madame Alberti had formed them into a small pantomime company, a
background which proved perfect for an actor in silent films.

J. Stuart Blackton must take credit for bringing into
the Company a large number of old-timers from the legitimate stage. The doyen of such players was Charles Kent,
who joined Vitagraph as an actor in 1906, and soon began
also directing. Honorable mention must also be made of
Louise Beaudet, Cissie Fitzgerald, William Shea, Hector
Dion, Paul Panzer, Mary Maurice, William Humphrey, Hal
Reid, Van Dyke Brooke, George Ober and William V. Ranous.
When Blackton left Vitagraph in 1917, these old-timers still
at the studio also departed.

Among the younger members of the Vitagraph family,
the best-loved by early film-goers were Edith Storey, Clara
Kimball Young, Lillian Walker, Norma Talmadge, Anita
Stewart and Dorothy Kelly. Brooklyn's Erasmus High School
was a constant source of young girls, anxious to enter films.
Norma Talmadge and Anita Stewart both entered films as a
result of their posing for song slides. Norma had posed for
three sets of slides of Scott and Van Altena in 1909. When

Above, Norma and Constance Talmadge.   Opposite, Anita
Stewart.

a fourth set was needed, Norma was sent for, but had already gone to the Vitagraph Studios. She told her schoolmate, Anita Stewart, of the easy money to be made posing, and loaned her the long dress that she had worn in applying for work at both Scott and Van Altena and Vitagraph. Anita Stewart appeared in at least twenty sets of song slides before following Norma to Vitagraph.

At least two Vitagraph actresses entered films through the efforts of relatives. Mary Charleson was persuaded to join Vitagraph by her aunt, Kate Price, a jolly, plump character actress, who usually played opposite Hughie Mack. Jane Novak's description of her entry into films demonstrates just how simple it was to become a star in 1913:

"My aunt, Anne Schaefer, was the star of the Vitagraph Company, and they were at Santa Monica, and she had a photograph of me on her desk. The head of the studio there, Rollin Sturgeon, saw the photograph, wanted to know who it was, and said, 'Why don't you bring her to California?' Of course, I was delighted. I was fifteen or sixteen, and I came out. The day that I arrived, my aunt met me in town, and we had a red car line that used to come right almost in front of her hotel in Santa Monica. She said, 'We'll have breakfast, and then we'll go over to the studio.' Well, Ruth Roland's leading man was in the dining room, and he said, 'Why don't you come over to the Kalem studio?' So, my first day in California, I appeared in a film. Then I went to Vitagraph."

Two of Jane Novak's earliest Vitagraph films were Deception, released on December 9, 1913, and Sacrifice, released on December 11, 1913, both of which "starred" Myrtle Gonzalez.

Vitagraph could boast a number of popular child players as members of its stock company. There was the Vitagraph Boy, Kenneth Casey, and Adele de Garde, who came to the Company from Biograph. Zena Keefe worked at Vitagraph during the summer months, and on the vaudeville circuit in the winter. Four-year-old Bobby Connelly was publicized as "the youngest actor before the camera" in 1914; typical of his films was Sonny Jim in Search of a Mother, released on January 26, 1914. Bebe Daniels appeared in at least one Vitagraph production, Anne of the Golden Heart, released on January 22, 1914.

Then, of course, there was Jean, the Vitagraph Dog, whose popularity was equal to that of any human screen actor. As The Vitagraph Bulletin (October 15, 1910) noted, "Jean is an inspiration; no-one could help making a fine story about her, and no actor could act badly in her support."

The water tank at the Vitagraph studios was a focal point of activity. It was the scene for high jinks, such as the time that Maurice Costello, to celebrate Rollin Sturgeon's elevation to director, threw him into the water, an incident which resulted in a fight, described as "the most memorable fistic encounter in Vitagraph's history."[26] When a film was made of Annette Kellerman diving into the tank, and engaging in other aquatic exploits, a number of good-looking young girls were hired to dive and swim along with the Australian star. One of those girls was Mabel Normand, who was signed to appear in at least seven films for the Company, including Over the Garden Wall, released on June 10, 1910; Betty Becomes a Maid, released on March 14, 1911; and The Subduing of Mrs. Nag, released on July 14, 1911. Mabel became known as "Vitagraph Betty" as a result of her performance in Betty Becomes a Maid, which started a series, not to be confused with some later films, in which "Betty" was played by Edith Storey.

As an example of the affection in which these early players were held, consider the reaction of The Moving Picture World of July 27, 1912, to one film, Aunty's Romance, directed by Maurice Costello. "The appearances of the old-time Vitagraph Girl are so rare these days that to see her is well worth a long walk. If you question this assertion, go to see Florence Turner in Aunty's Romance. If you are an old-time picturegoer this film will have an added interest by reason of the appearance with Miss Turner of the man who for so long played opposite to her--Maurice Costello. That was in the days when the Vitagraph Company was not the great organization it is today--for surely, if any evidence were needed as to the rank of this company it would be furnished in the releases of July 12 and 13. The Foster Child and Aunty's Romance are issued as ordinary, everyday affairs. There is no suggestion in the advance announcements of the company that these two possess unusual merit. Yet they are pictures in which Americans may take justifiable pride--Americans abroad perhaps even more than Americans at home. The former will feel that in black-and-white the home product equals in all cases and in most is superior to the Continental output."

Film-making at the Vitagraph Studios in the years between 1909 and 1913--the heyday of the one-reel production--was a casual affair. As James Morrison recalled, "If they needed extras in a scene, they would use their stock company, anyone who was there. A director could walk through and see you, probably walking out to the gate, going home, and he would nab you for a scene." Lillian Walker remembered an incident for Robert Giroux, indicating the care-free life at Vitagraph. "We often went to the beach from the Flatbush studio, which wasn't far from Sheepshead Bay. I once finished a day's work, and swam out to a raft with Niles Welch, and, a few minutes later, there was a prop boy swimming out, yelling, 'You're wanted at the studio!' I had to go back, my hair wet and so on, put on a wig, and do another scene."

Equally casual was Vitagraph's system of giving its staff pay raises. Again, James Morrison recalled, "I remember we used to get paid in cash, and we never knew when we were going to get a raise. We usually got a raise when the Paris office sent word--Yes, the Paris office. They had great power over there, because we sold so many pictures in Europe. When the raise came, we couldn't count the money. Sometimes it was five dollars, ten dollars or whatever it was. I was going home one evening, and Julia Swayne Gordon was behind some scenery, and she said, 'Jim, will you come over here and count this for me?' And I said, 'Sure, Judy.' She'd gotten a fifteen-dollar pay raise for some picture she'd done. Strange enough, that's the way the business went."

On July 1, 1911, The Moving Picture World announced that Vitagraph was to release four productions a week, one of which was to be a Western. By 1913, Vitagraph was releasing over three hundred films a year. In March of that year, a Western Vitagraph Studio had been established at Santa Monica, California, under the directorship of Rollin Sturgeon. As an indication of the number of persons employed by Vitagraph, the following is a listing of the Western Vitagraph Stock Company in 1914: John Buss (scenic artist), Fred Wade (darkroom man), "Dad" Babcock (carpenter), Dave Smith (assistant manager), Steve Smith (manager), Bill Duncan (wardrobe), Jack Mower (juvenile lead), Jim Brown

---

Opposite: The Vitagraph Studios at 1438 2nd Street, Santa Monica in 1914. (Courtesy of the Bruce Torrence Collection).

(carpenter), Clyde Smith (property man), Ernie Smith (assistant cameraman), Don Clarke (assistant director), Doris Schroeder (editor), George Stanley (leading man), Ulysses Davis (director), Rollin Sturgeon (director), Elisabeth Kendrick (cashier), Alfred Vosburgh (leading man), Otto Lederer (character actor), Albert Chaney (chauffeur), George Holt ("heavy"), Jane Novak (juvenile lead), Anne Schaefer (leading lady), Myrtle Gonzalez (leading lady), Margaret Gibson (ingenue), George Kunkel (character actor), Simmie Sues (camera assistant), and Roy Lederer (child actor).

With so many films being produced, it is difficult to single out one or two films for special mention. However, it would be wrong to ignore The Illumination, released on April 5, 1912, featuring Tom Powers, Rosemary Theby, Harry Northrup, Helen Gardner, Wallace Reid and Rose Tapley. Set at the time of Christ, The Illumination tells of the affect that Jesus' presence has on two very different people: Joseph, a young Jew, and Maximus, a Roman centurion. The Christ is never seen, except as a light passing across the faces of the protagonists. "This picture deserves praise for its method of handling," commented The Moving Picture World (March 30, 1912). "It breathes the atmosphere of Bible times and is carried on with an understanding of those times that is adequate and faithful."

In an entirely different vein was A Vitagraph Romance, directed and written by James Young, and released on September 18, 1912, in which James Morrison and Clara Kimball Young try to crash the movies. Appearing in this behind-the-scenes look at the Vitagraph Company were "Pop" Rock, Albert E. Smith, J. Stuart Blackton, Edith Storey, James Young and Florence Turner. "A dandy offering that we feel sure will please," commented The Moving Picture World (September 28, 1912).

On July 23, 1910, The Moving Picture World summed up the lot of the members of the Vitagraph family. "I should say, then, from what I saw at the Vitagraph studio and have seen elsewhere, that the lot of a stock company of a first-class moving picture making house is preferable to that of the stock company of many great theatrical enterprises. The conditions of the work are more agreeable. It is mostly done in the daytime; there is comparatively little traveling; producers and principals are considerate; the awful ordeal of a public appearance is not to be faced, and there is a touch of the happy family about the whole business."

It was a happy family, but as the movies came of age, conditions and circumstances changed. The film industry became precisely that, an industry, and the old, happy-go-lucky style had to end. If Vitagraph was to continue as a leader in the field, many alterations had to be made. On August 11, 1916, Variety announced, "There is to be a general change in the method of procedure in the matter of players and the stock organization at the Vitagraph studios. Slowly, but surely, the members of the stock organization, which has been one of the Vitagraph's strong points for years, are being dismissed. The new order of things will mean that a 'jobbing system' is to be inaugurated, the company holding only the stars and engaging players for each production as it is put into work."

During 1916, the following players and directors left Vitagraph: Flora Finch, Wally Van, Tefft Johnson, Harry Northrup, Leah Baird, Frank Lloyd, Van Dyke Brooke, L. Rogers Lytton, Harry Davenport, William Humphrey, Donald Hall, Frank Currier, George Baker and Ralph Ince. Only three important additions were made to the contract players and directors in that year: Webster Campbell, Marc MacDermott and Alice Joyce. The Vitagraph family was no more.

Chapter 7

1910 - 1920

Almost symbolizing a new era in the history of the Vitagraph Company was a fire at its Nassau Street offices on July 2, 1910, which destroyed the negatives of all the early Vitagraph productions. The fire seemed to be a sign that the pioneering days were behind it, and everything belonging to those days had to be discarded. The Vitagraph Company was now a leader in its field, entering a new decade, prosperous and powerful. The fire persuaded the Company to expand further its Flatbush studios, with a new three-story office building. "With the accounting department also established at the factory in addition to the scenic and other departments," noted The Moving Picture World of August 27, 1910, "the Vitagraph village takes on an aspect of activity and prosperity that is an imposing tribute to the growth of the moving picture business."

The Company released several important productions during 1910. The Life of Moses, the first of what was supposed to be a series of Biblical pictures, produced in cooperation with the Reverend Madison Peters, was released in five parts, from December 4, 1909 through February 19, 1910. The Moving Picture World (December 18, 1910) considered it "a picture that is deserving of the greatest praise and commendation as a whole." Becket, released on July 9, 1910, and featuring Charles Kent and Maurice Costello, received particular praise. The Moving Picture World (July 16, 1910) commented, "Becket atones for a great deal of ineptitudinous rubbish which unfortunately still finds a place on the moving picture screen. Becket, in short, is bound very materially to enhance the growing reputation of the Vitagraph Company of America." Of Florence Turner's A Dixie Mother, released on December 17, 1910, The Moving Picture World, in a full-page article on November 26, 1910, asked, "Is it to be the photoplay of the year?"

Vitagraph players were now beginning to travel far afield in a quest for authentic locations. Late in 1910, Florence Turner, Charles Kent and Robert Gaillord, together with director Larry Trimble and cameraman Walter Arthur, spent several weeks shooting at Cape Shore, near Portland, Maine.

On July 1, 1911, Vitagraph began publication of a bi-monthly magazine, Vitagraph Life Portrayals, to give exhibitors details of all its new releases. This magazine superseded The Vitagraph Bulletin, the issue of March 15, 1910 of which had explained why Vitagraph used the term, "Life Portrayals." "Vitagraph Life Portrayals describes Vitagraph films better than any other phrase that can be invented. They are more than motion pictures, as you have noticed. They have the vital spark of life itself. The characters you see in Vitagraph dramas and comedies are not artificial and stagey. They act like real people doing things that real people would do in the ways that real people would do them. Do you see the point? This is the secret of the charm of Vitagraph Life Portrayals."

On August 18, 1911, Vitagraph began releasing a monthly newsreel, titled Current Events. Commented The Moving Picture World of August 5, 1911, "This idea of a sort of special picture newspaper is a very excellent one and will prove a valuable illustrative as well as a historical record, besides filling the pleasing object of giving people actual reproductions of events which previously could only be imagined after reading cold type descriptions; surely we are moving at a marvelously progressive rate." Current Events was to become the Hearst-Vitagraph Weekly News Feature, and appear twice weekly. There appears to have been a friendly bond between Hearst and Vitagraph. On December 20, 1914, Mrs. William Randolph Hearst and her three sons came to the studio to make a film, intended as a Christmas surprise for Hearst.

The two major Vitagraph productions of 1911 were A Tale of Two Cities and Vanity Fair. The former, featuring the entire Vitagraph stock company, headed by Maurice Costello and Florence Turner, was released in three parts on February 21, 24 and 25. It was notable for introducing Norma Talmadge, James Morrison and Lillian Walker to the screen, and received lavish praise. The Moving Picture World (March 4, 1911) commented, "The staging is little short of sumptuous. There is shown a care in the attention

Maurice Costello in A Tale of Two Cities (1911).

to details which stamps the picture as an unusually faithful
reproduction and affords opportunity for those who have read
and loved Dickens in the books to see his story move before
them, much, perhaps, as it moved before him during its
composition. Without being an expert upon Dickens, it seems
safe to say that this production of one of his most famous
stories will go down in motion picture history as one of the
most notable of photoplay productions of the beginning of the
year." Interestingly, The Moving Picture World advised
theatre owners to show the three parts of the film together,
a suggestion which possibly persuaded Vitagraph to desist
from splitting up a film into separate parts, issued on different days, for when Vanity Fair was released on December
19, 1911, it was as a three-reel feature. In so doing, Vitagraph moved one important step ahead of its competitors by
accepting that audiences were willing to sit through a film
more than one reel in length.

James Morrison (foreground) in The Seventh Son (1912).
Note the white line at right, indicating the maximum prox-
imity of the action to the camera.

Vanity Fair, featuring Helen Gardner as Becky Sharp,
was the subject of equally impressive reviews. For The
Moving Picture World of December 16, 1911, "It comes
nearer to being a flawless adaptation than anything that has
appeared in moving pictures."

The number of directors at work with the Company
was increasing steadily. In the summer of 1912, Ralph
Ince and James Young were both promoted to directing. Two
stage directors, Robert North and Bert Angeles, were added
to the Vitagraph payroll in January of 1913, and in August of
the same year Ned Finley and Tefft Johnson also became
directors. By 1914, according to Albert E. Smith, Vitagraph
had twenty-nine directors under contract, including Van Dyke
Brooke, Rollin Sturgeon, William Humphrey, Larry Trimble,
Albert W. Hale, Red Thompson, Captain Harry Lambert, L.
Rogers Lytton, Lionel Belmore and Theodore Marston.

The Santa Monica studios of Vitagraph had opened in
March of 1913, under the directorship of Rollin Sturgeon,
and a scenario department was set up there, headed by
Daisy Smith, formerly of Kalem, and David Miles, formerly
of the Kinemacolor Company. There was further expansion
at the Brooklyn studios, where a new glass-covered studio
was erected in the summer of 1913.

"A visit to the Vitagraph plant leaves no doubt as to
its resources," wrote Louis Reeves Harrison in 1912.
"They are ample for the production of a play that will fill an
entire evening's programme. There are several studios in
the main building and they can be operated by natural light
alone or by artificial light alone or by the two in conjunction.
This company was, in fact, the first to use electric light in
taking moving pictures, the experiments being conducted at
the Manhattan Theatre with ordinary arc lights of enormous
amperage furnished by Joe Menchen."

On December 7, 1912, Vitagraph sent a party of
players and technicians on a round-the-world cruise, which
was to take six months. In the party were W. S. Smith,
Clara Kimball Young and her husband, James Young, William
V. Ranous and his wife, Maurice Costello, his wife and two
children, Helene and Dolores, Eugene Mullin, manager of the
Vitagraph scenario department, and cameraman Harry
Keepers. The group went from New York to San Francisco,
sailed from there to Hawaii, and then on to Hong Kong,
India, Burma, Egypt, Italy and France. The Kalem Company, since 1910, had been sending groups of film-makers
to specific locations abroad, but this was the first time a
company of players toured the world, producing films.

Early in 1914, the Vitagraph Company took a step
which must have surprised many of its competitors in film
production, and which shocked many theatre owners. It
leased the Criterion Theatre, on the northwest corner of
Broadway and 44th Street, New York, and renamed it the
Vitagraph Theatre. The Vitagraph opened on February 7,
1914, with a bill consisting of two films and a live sketch.
The two films were Goodness Gracious!, a satire on movie
melodramas, directed by James Young, with Sidney Drew
and Clara Kimball Young, and, appropriately enough, a five-
reel melodrama, A Million Dollar Bid, directed by Ralph
Ince, and featuring Anita Stewart, Julia Swayne Gordon,
Harry Morey, and E. K. Lincoln. Reviewing the evening's
entertainment in the next day's New York American, critic

Alan Dale wrote of A Million Dollar Bid, "This was pic-
turized (isn't that a lovely new Vitagraphic word?) from the
play I once saw, called Agnes, and very thrilling it turned
out to be. In fact, it was undoubtedly the very finest picture I have ever seen. I don't speak of the 'plot,' or the
story, but of the particular episode showing the wreck of
Geoffrey Marshe's yacht. Not since I saw S.O.S. at the
Grand Guignol in Paris had I such cold chills down the
spine."

The sketch, played in mime, was titled The Honeymooners, was written by J. Stuart Blackton, and featured
James Morrison and Mary Charleson. It ran for thirteen
weeks, with the players appearing at every evening performance and at Wednesday and Saturday matinees.

After the opening of the Vitagraph Theatre, "Pop"
Rock declared that "the Vitagraph Company has just begun
to show Broadway what it means in moviedom," and there
was talk that the Company was planning to take over the
leases of a number of other Broadway theatres, including
the Casino and Daly's. In fact, Vitagraph leased only one
additional theatre, the Harris, on 42nd Street, in May of
1914, to which it moved The Christian, featuring Earle
Williams and Edith Storey, after the film's premiere at the
Manhattan Opera House.

Exhibitors became very concerned over Vitagraph's
policy. Variety (February 20, 1914) reported, "If the Criterion is a success, what's to prevent other manufacturers
from going into it and what's to stop them from opening big
theatres in the leading cities of the country, the exhibitors
are asking." Theatre owners were alarmed that film producers might become competitors for their patrons, and a
committee of exhibitors was appointed to talk with the Vitagraph Company. After the meeting it was announced, in
The Moving Picture World of April 11, 1914, that Vitagraph
would acquire no further theatres, and that "the Vitagraph
Theatre benefits all men showing Vitagraph pictures." As
it happened, the film producers were eventually to acquire
whole chains of theatres, from the early Twenties onwards,
actions which were eventually to lead to the motion picture
anti-trust suits of the late Forties.

Film programs changed regularly at the Vitagraph
Theatre, as did the live entertainment. In December of
1914, a speaking playlet was produced for the first time;

it was titled <u>What the Moon Saw</u>, written by Sidney Rankin
Drew, and featuring Mr. and Mrs. Sidney Drew. This was
followed a month later by <u>A Nocturne in A-Flat</u>, a thirty-
four-minute sketch, written by J. Stuart Blackton. According to <u>Variety</u> (January 8, 1915), "On its merits it couldn't
play Corona, Long Island, on a split week at cut salary.
The thing is crude and amateurish to the last degree."

All in all, the Vitagraph Theatre was not a success.
<u>Variety</u> (March 5, 1915) pointed out what it thought was
wrong: "The trouble with the Vitagraph is the Vitagraph.
It's all Vitagraph. After seeing a Strand show at 50 cents
and a Broadway theatre or other picture performance for
25 cents or less, each with an orchestra, not forgetting the
New York Theatre next door at 15 cents, the Vitagraph at
75 cents is all wrong." In December of 1915, it was reported that during the theatre's first year, it had lost
$50,000, and would have lost a lot more had it not been
for the popular success of <u>The Battle Cry of Peace</u>. It
came as no surprise, therefore, when after the performance
of January 30, 1916, the theatre became the Criterion once
again, with a Shakespearian season, featuring James K.
Hackett and Viola Allen.

One of the films which were premiered--on March 7,
1915--at the Vitagraph Theatre was the five-reel melodrama,
<u>The Juggernaut</u>, directed by Ralph Ince, and featuring Anita
Stewart, Earle Williams and Julia Swayne Gordon. The
highpoint of the production was one of the most famous and
spectacular train wrecks ever filmed. The wreck was
staged, under the direction of Victor Smith, at South River,
New Jersey, on Sunday, September 27, 1914. A spur from
the Raritan River Railroad was built to jut seventy-five feet
over a lake, and Engine No. 56, a retired Long Island Railroad locomotive, was wrecked. History records that Edward Wentworth was responsible for building the track and
trestle; Herman Rogers planned the dynamiting, and the entire event was photographed by Walter Arthur. Not content
with a mere wreck, Vitagraph also filmed an exciting rescue
sequence, in which the heroine is dragged through one of
the train windows and rowed to shore, while the other surviving passengers are left to splash around in the water and,
presumably, drown.

As an example of the ethics--or lack of them--in
early film-making, immediately after the wreck had been
staged, Universal sent over a cameraman to film the

wreckage. However, Victor Smith and a sturdy band of
Vitagraph "protectors" were on hand, and Universal's
cameraman soon departed the scene.

From the inception of the General Film Company in
April of 1910, Vitagraph, as a founder member of the Motion Picture Patents Company, had belonged to the organization. All releases of the member-companies were handled
through the exchanges of the General Film Company, but as
Vitagraph gradually expanded its feature-length production
schedule with the "Big V" and "Blue Ribbon" features, the
Company began to release films through its own exchanges.
General Film continued to distribute short subjects for Vitagraph and the other member-companies: Kalem Lubin, Selig,
Edison, Essanay and George Kleine.

By the spring of 1915, it had become apparent to a
number of those companies that a new releasing organization
was necessary to handle only feature-length productions. So,
on April 5, 1915, the Vitagraph-Lubin-Selig-Essanay Motion
Picture Company--V-L-S-E for short--was incorporated, with
Albert E. Smith as President, Siegmund Lubin as Vice-President, William N. Selig as Treasurer, and George K. Spoor
as Secretary. Walter W. Irwin, former general legal counsel
for Vitagraph, became the new concern's general manager.
Each of the four production companies involved guaranteed to
release one feature a month until September of 1915, when
the output was to be doubled. Some twenty branches of
V-L-S-E were established throughout the country. The first
two features to be released through V-L-S-E were Lubin's
The Eagle's Nest and Vitagraph's The Juggernaut. These
and other productions were announced in the organization's
journal, The Big Four Family, which began publication on
June 5, 1915 and continued until May 27, 1916.

V-L-S-E was a successful organization, particularly
as far as the Vitagraph Company was concerned. The stock
and interest of Lubin, Selig and Essanay were eventually
purchased by Vitagraph in September, 1916.

On the whole, 1916 was not a good year for the Vitagraph Company, and for Albert E. Smith it was the beginning of a very trying three-year period. However, a couple
of pleasant things did happen during the year, one of the
nicest of which was Corinne Griffith's entry into films, first
at the Company's Santa Monica studios, and then as a star
with Vitagraph in the East. One of the most glamorous stars

of her day, Miss Griffith remained with Vitagraph until
1922, and was married to actor-director Webster Campbell,
who had joined the Company in February of 1915.   Corinne
Griffith's starring features at Vitagraph include Transgres-
sion (1917), Miss Ambition (1918), The Adventure Shop (1919),
Tower of Jewels (1920), The Whisper Market (1920), What's
Your Reputation Worth? (1921) and Island Wives (1922).

     In January of 1916, Vitagraph opened new studios at
Brightwaters, Long Island, at which, it was announced,
Ralph Ince would direct all his future productions.   However, the number of films Ince was to make there was extremely limited, as he left the Company in November of the
same year.   According to Motography (January 1, 1916),
"The new studio was formerly the Forester's Lodge, two
stories high and with floor space enough to permit deep sets.
It is thoroughly equipped in every detail and a complete
staff of workers have their homes nearby."

     The tragic event of 1916 was the death, on July 27,
of William "Pop" Rock, the President of Vitagraph for almost twenty years.   Just prior to his death, Rock had told
Billboard (October 28, 1916) of some of the projects he still
hoped to bring to fruition: "Personally speaking, I hope to
do some big stunts in the moving picture line before I quit
business, one of which would be a gigantic filming of the
history of America, commencing with the landing of Columbus.
These feature pictures would cost fully a million dollars to
do, and I doubt if it would be a profitable venture from a
strictly dollars and cents standpoint, but I should like to
undertake it with my own capital and leave it behind when I
go on the long journey as my contribution to the moving picture industry."   "Pop" had come a long way since entering
the States as a boy in the 1860s.   Through his own resource-
fulness he had amassed a fortune of one-and-a-half million
dollars by the time of his death.   "Mr. Rock was entirely
a self-made man," J. Stuart Blackton told the New York
Tribune (July 28, 1916).   "He was a fine, convivial fellow,
whom every one liked."

     The "Pop" Rocks were disappearing from the film
industry, and in their place came ruthless business con-
glomerates and ambitious young men, one of whom, Benjamin B. Hampton, was to play an important part in the next
period of Vitagraph's history.

     Hampton is best remembered for his authorship of

A History of the Movies, published by Covici, Friede in
1931. Few people are aware of his ambitious plans in the
mid 'teens to set up a "moving picture consolidation," headed
by Vitagraph, which was to acquire Paramount (including
Famous Players-Lasky), Lubin, Essanay, Selig, Oliver
Morosco Company and Pallas, with financing by the American
Tobacco Company, of which Hampton was secretary.

The first step was the incorporation of a new company,
The Smith-Blackton Corporation, which purchased Vitagraph
on May 17, 1916, at which time "Pop" Rock resigned. Hampton already had a letter, dated March 18, 1916, from Mary
Pickford, authorizing him to form the Mary Pickford Corporation within the consolidation. He had further investigated the
possibility of acquiring the Lubin, Selig and Essanay concerns.
A headline in Variety of March 31, 1916 reported, "Amalga-
mation rumors galore agitating the film industry." However,
Variety was not entirely taken in by Hampton, for the story
under the headline ended thus: "When all the rumors and
reports are traced down, they simply amount to the man in
the middle trying to swing both ends on air in the hope he
can turn the air into currency, if the ends will swing together."

Hampton's financial dealings are, to say the least,
difficult to follow. On behalf of Vitagraph, now The Smith-
Blackton Corporation, he acquired åll the stock in V-L-S-E--
in other words, the L-S and E interests--for $250,000, after
pointing out to Smith that "The trouble with the V-L-S-E
output at the present time being that, while perhaps one-
half of its pictures are good, the other half are mediocre or
poor. This would be obviated if all the pictures were produced under our supervision." Hampton also acquired the
Lubin Company.

Hampton had persuaded Smith and Blackton that he
represented various financial interests, including Percival S.
Hill of the American Tobacco Company, Charles Sabin of
the Guaranty Trust, John Prentiss of Hornblower and Weeks,
and C. A. and George J. Whalen of the United Cigar Stores.
He further persuaded Smith that his consortium wished to
purchase the Vitagraph Company, and use it as a nucleus for
their "moving picture consolidation." It was agreed that the
price to be paid for Vitagraph was $750,000. Various papers
were drawn up, but as Smith wrote in a personal memoran-
dum, "We know nothing of the details of the organization until
the mass of papers are read hurriedly to us at various times

and in various places--the deal being finally closed in the
offices of Hornblower and Weeks or the Guaranty Trust,
downtown. " In order to close the deal, Smith found it
necessary to borrow Hampton's purchase price for V-L-S-E
from the Irving Bank.   The various financiers behind the
deal soon disappeared from view, and Smith found himself
in the unenviable position of a man heading a company,
$250,000 in debt to a not entirely sympathetic bank.

Smith bitterly wrote to Percival S. Hill of the American
Tobacco Company, "When I entered into our arrangement with
yourself and your associates, I did so not for the money involved, of which I had all that I desired, but for the honor
of actively participating and being the head of what I hoped
would be the biggest aggregation of picture talent in the
world.   Before our arrangement was concluded, I was the
head of the Vitagraph Company and the V-L-S-E, and, in
addition, held the respect of all the men that I have been as-
sociated with during the past twenty years.   During the last
three months, the respect has been largely eliminated by the
small methods employed in trying to do a big job.   We have
been handicapped by not being furnished with the finances
that were promised when our deal was negotiated. "

On August 11, 1916, Hampton also had written to Hill
concerning lost opportunities: "In March Mr. Lowry [Ira
M. Lowry, general manager of Lubin, and Siegmund Lubin's
son-in-law] had Charley [sic] Chaplin here for about three
weeks.   During perhaps fifteen days of that time I had an
option on him for one year for $350,000 and $200,000 in
common stock.   We did not close with him.   Re Pickford, I
believe we lost at least a million dollars a year when we
lost her.   Famous Players and Jesse Lasky Company, on
February 22nd, orally agreed to consolidate with us; on our
present capitalization we could have had them with us on a
basis of $6,000,000 of our stock.   Mr. Zukor now states
that he will not consider less than $12,500,000, and de-
clares that a large part of it will have to be in cash. "

Like the tea party in Alice in Wonderland, the financial problems of Vitagraph got curiouser and curiouser.
Benjamin Hampton told Smith that the former postmaster
general, Frank Hitchcock, was representing Dupont, and
might be willing to invest the needed $250,000 in Vitagraph.
Smith left for a tour of the California studios on March 2,
1917, and in his absence various money men including John
Prentiss of Hornblower and Weeks and a Mr. Davenport of

the Finance and Trading Company took control, with the
latter threatening receivership unless all was done according
to his orders.

A special meeting was called, and two employees of
the Finance and Trading Company, Griswold and Lockhart,
were named Cashier and Assistant Cashier respectively. At
the same meeting, Frank Hitchcock was elected Chairman of
the Board. The new officers began to dismiss old employees
out-of-hand, and the contracts with four of the Company's leading stars, Edith Storey, Lillian Walker, Peggy Hyland and
Antonio Moreno, were cancelled. As Smith noted, "I returned to New York on May 2nd, and find the Vitagraph
Company being operated by individuals who, in my opinion,
had no rights on the premises whatsoever.... The business
is being run by Griswold, Lockhart and a bunch of satellites,
and thousands of dollars of the Company's money is being
wasted."

In June of 1917, J. Stuart Blackton resigned from the
Company, to become an independent producer. Possibly the
financial problems at Vitagraph had something to do with his
decision, although his daughter claims that it was because of
a personal vendetta that had arisen between the then-wives of
the two partners.

Much of what was happening at Vitagraph had been
kept out of the trade papers. Indeed, concerning Hitchcock's
election as Chairman of the Board, Smith had told The
Moving Picture World (May 19, 1917), "Mr. Hitchcock is
the very man we need." However, Variety on July 6, 1917
printed a news story which gave most of the details: "The
Vitagraph Co. is about to make some changes in the personnel of its executives. These changes will be dictated by
Finance and Trading Co., a branch of the Guaranty Trust
Co., which loaned Vita $1,000,000 about a year ago, re-
payable at the rate of $200,000 annually. The first note is
due and wasn't met at maturity, with the result the lenders
are assuming a supervision of the direction of the business.
Negotiations have been on for the past fortnight looking to
the turning over of the entire distribution of V-L-S-E through
another channel, but this week it was decided to continue
with the present exchanges. There is a report that in addition to the retirement of J. Stuart Blackton, as reported in
last week's Variety, Walter W. Irwin will also withdraw,
leaving Albert E. Smith in charge of productions and ex-post-
master general Frank H. Hitchcock looking after the business
end."

Irwin did indeed resign, but his resignation did not take effect until January 1, 1919. The Finance and Trading Company suggested to Smith that he, Blackton and "Pop" Rock's son, John, sell their stock in the Company to it, rather than face bankruptcy. Smith appeared at the offices of the Finance and Trading Company in July of 1917, but refused to sign over his stock in the Company, and effectively called its bluff. A meeting was arranged with various bankers and it was agreed that everyone would work together to get Vitagraph out of the red. Hitchcock surrendered his contract with the Company in 1919, and Davenport, Griswold and Lockhart resigned. By 1920, Smith was reasonably victorious, and had fought off what he considered "a conspiracy on the part of the financial crowd to steal the Company."

On March 15, 1919, Smith had been able to report to the directors of his company that "The business at this time is in A1 condition, being in better shape than at any time during the last two-and-a-half years." Despite the

William P. S. Earle directing Gladys Leslie in His Own People (1917). The Moving Picture World (January 12, 1918) described this Vitagraph production as a "thoroughly human portrayal of simple Irish types."

financial problems, Smith and Blackton, and then Smith on
his own had been able to ensure a heavy production schedule.
In 1918 the Company had announced that it would release
fifty-two "Blue Ribbon" features that year, including eight
with Earle Williams, eight with Alice Joyce, nine with
Corinne Griffith, nine with Harry Morey and nine with
Gladys Leslie.

Early in 1919, Vitagraph acquired what was left of
the Kalem Company, a company which Hampton had had his
eye on way back in 1916. William Wright, secretary and
treasurer of Kalem, joined Vitagraph in its sales and pro-
motion department, where he remained until December of
1923, when he joined Yale University's "Chronicles of America" Film Company, which at that time leased the practically
inactive Brooklyn studios of Vitagraph. Phil Lang, Kalem's
Vice-President, also joined Vitagraph as head of its scenario
department, but the Spanish influenza epidemic took his life
on January 24, 1919. The acquisition of Kalem also meant
that Vitagraph took over that Company's very extensive
laboratory facilities and staff.

Despite the advance in film-making over the years,
it is interesting to note that cinema audiences still looked
back with pleasure to Vitagraph's heyday, the years from
1910 through 1914. On June 23, 1917, The Moving Picture
World announced that Vitagraph was to reissue the films of
John Bunny, re-edited and retitled under the series name of
"Favorite Film Features."

Chapter 8

THE BATTLE CRY OF PEACE AND ITS SEQUELS

As far as most of Europe was concerned, the First
World War broke out in the summer of 1914. However,
America was not to enter the conflict until April 6, 1917,
and during the intervening years there were a number of
attempts in this country to sway the American people in
favor of the allied cause and armed intervention, and, above
all, to instill in the American people a need for preparedness. Preparedness implied the need to be prepared
against aggression from any country, but it was understood
that what the American people were expected to prepare for
was attack from Germany and its allies.

During 1916, not only were a considerable number of
books and pamphlets on preparedness published, but several
films on the same subject were produced. Notable among
these were The Flying Torpedo (Triangle-Fine Arts), Defense
or Tribute (Public Service Film Company) and The Fall of a
Nation (Thomas Dixon). There was even a juvenile warning
for preparedness, produced by James A. Fitzpatrick, titled
A World War in Kidland. However, the most influential film
to deal with preparedness was produced by the Vitagraph
Company in 1915; it was titled The Battle Cry of Peace and
its impact on the American film-public was considerable.

The basis for The Battle Cry of Peace was Defenseless America by Hudson Maxim (1853-1927), published by
Hearst's International Library in 1915. As J. Stuart Blackton recalled, "One night at the club I met Hudson Maxim....
We entered into a discussion and finally, knowing my interest
in the problem of national defense, Mr. Maxim asked me to
read his story on this question. This I did the next day,
and was at once struck by the tremendous force of its argument. I was imbued with the desire to put some such patriotic thought into a motion picture, so working with Mr.

Maxim's book as a basis for my facts, I conceived The Battle Cry of Peace.

"I realized shortly that there was a possibility that I might be misunderstood by the same class of citizenry which was aroused against Governor Slaton when he took his courageous stand in the Frank Case.* With this thought in mind, I went personally to prominent men of affairs, and, without exception, I received their hearty and unqualified endorsement."[42]

The most influential person with whom Blackton discussed his idea for The Battle Cry of Peace was Theodore Roosevelt, Blackton's neighbor at Oyster Bay. The producer claimed to have spent three days and nights working on a scenario, which he then read to Roosevelt. "As I finished," wrote Blackton, "he strode to his bookcase and

Norma Talmadge in The Battle Cry of Peace (1915).

---

*A reference to Leo Frank, convicted of murder on questionable evidence, who was lynched by an angry mob after his death sentence had been commuted by Governor Slaton of Georgia.

took out a Bible. I can see him now, the book held close
to his near-sighted eyes, rapidly turning over the pages.
He literally pounced upon the desired passage. 'Here it is, '
he cried in a vibrant tone, 'thirty-third chapter of Ezekial,
third verse. Whosoever heareth the sound of the trumpet,
and heedeth it not, if the sword comes and takes him away,
his blood shall be upon his own head. That's America today.
Heedless! Put that in your picture, Blackton. '"[12]

According to Blackton, a few days later Roosevelt
arranged for the producer to meet at Oyster Bay with
several of his friends: Mayor John Purroy Mitchell of New
York, Brigadier General Cornelius Vanderbilt, Admiral
Dewey, Rear Admiral Blue, the Reverend Lyman Abbott,
Major General O'Ryan, Colonel Plunkett, and Elihu Root.
The film was discussed and endorsed by all present, who
also volunteered their own ideas. "Get every word of that
in your picture," ordered Roosevelt. "Drive it home to the
peace-at-any-price creatures!"[12]

Production got under way immediately, with Blackton
supervising, and Wilfred North nominally "directing." It
was claimed that 25, 000 National Guard troops appeared in
the film, along with 800 members of the Grand Army of the
Republic and 5, 000 horses. As if it were a real army
fighting a real war, Elsie Janis came along to entertain the
troops at the front, and Colonel Roosevelt appeared to give
the men a "pep" talk. The cast of players, all members of
the Vitagraph stock company, was as follows:

John Harrison...............Charles Richman
Mr. Emanon................L. Rogers Lytton
Charley Harrison...........James Morrison
Mrs. Harrison.............Mary Maurice
Mrs. Vandergriff...........Louise Beaudet
Mr. Vandergriff............Harold Huber
Poet Scout.................Captain Jack Crawford
The Master................Charles Kent
Magdalen..................Julia Swayne Gordon
Vandergriff's Son...........Evart Overton
Alice Harrison.............Belle Bruce
Virginia Vandergriff........Norma Talmadge
Dorothy Vandergriff........Lucille Hammill
Butler....................George Stevens
Columbia ....Thais Lawton
The War Monster ....Lionel Brehan

George Washington............Joseph Kilgour
General Grant ....Paul Scardon
Abraham Lincoln..............William Ferguson

At the end of the film, Admiral Dewey, Major
General Leonard Wood, the Reverend Lyman Abbott, Hudson
Maxim and Secretary of War Garrison appeared, and ha-
rangued the audience in sub-titles. Theodore Roosevelt did
not appear in the film, because he was afraid that such an
appearance might be interpreted as a bid on his part for the
1916 Republican nomination.

Apart from a short roll of negative preserved at
George Eastman House, The Battle Cry of Peace is a lost
film. Its content, however, may be clearly gauged from
the following synopsis, published in the program for the
film's premiere:

> Hudson Maxim, international authority on arms
> and ammunition, delivers a lecture at Carnegie
> Hall. In this he graphically describes the defense-
> less condition of the United States, and shows how
> utterly unprepared it is to withstand invasion.
>
> In the audience is a young American--John Harri-
> son. Inspired by Maxim's disclosures and seeing
> in his imagination the awful consequences to which
> our national unpreparedness may lead, he resolves
> to consecrate his every effort to the cause of ade-
> quate defense.
>
> He is engaged to a beautiful girl, Virginia Vander-
> griff, whose millionaire father is an active advo-
> cate of national disarmament and 'Peace at any
> Price.' John makes a fruitless effort to show
> Vandergriff the fallacy of his stand and how not
> only his country but his fortune and even the lives
> and happiness of his wife and children hang in the
> balance.
>
> An intimate friend of Vandergriff and a frequent
> caller at his house is one Emanon--ostensibly a
> peace propagandist, but in reality a foreign spy.
> He is the head of a band of conspirators who are
> plotting the invasion of America; whose agents are
> behind Peace Movements; whose lobbyists have

exerted heavy influence against army and navy appropriations.

The plans are finally completed. The invaders approach New York. The news reaches a huge peace meeting at which Vandergriff is one of the principal speakers. In the midst of this meeting a shell crashes through the walls of the building.

A dramatic moment from The Battle Cry of Peace (1915).

The battleships of the enemy, while out of range of the guns of Forts Hamilton, Hancock and Wadsworth, are able to bombard New York. Submarines approach. Bombs are dropped from aeroplanes.

Shells are devastating the buildings in the downtown district. The Municipal Building is destroyed; entire blocks are burning. Homes are desecrated; citizens slain without mercy. Terror reigns.

John's mother and sister are killed. Vandergriff is shot in the street; John escapes a similar fate

by a miracle and then only to be bayoneted in
defense of the girl he loves. And as a climax to
the horror Virginia's mother, to avoid disgrace at
the hand of the enemy, kills her two daughters and
herself.

In the two parts that follow are shown an allegori-
cal masterpiece contrasting Columbia, crushed,
bleeding and trampled upon by a merciless foe,
with Columbia as she should be--proud, command-
ing, supreme.

Yes, there shall be peace--but peace with plenty--
peace with honor.

The spirit of '76--the spirits of Washington,
Lincoln and Grant are not dead--they live! They
live to inspire the hearts of Americans into a
realization of their duty to their country and of
the great truth that to be peaceful we must be
powerful; to champion the laws of humanity we
must have power to enforce these laws.

Through the country sweeps a wave of patriotism.
In every home men pledge their lives; women
pledge their sons and husbands to the campaign
for peace--a greater army, a mightier navy, and
all that will insure that Peace for which America
so earnestly prays.

The Battle Cry of Peace was first seen at a private
screening at the Vitagraph Theatre on August 6, 1915. On
September 9 it was given its first public showing, again at
the Vitagraph Theatre. The film was accompanied by a full
orchestral score composed by Elliot Schenck, and S. L.
Rothapfel arranged stage effects, consisting of the roaring of
mobs and the screaming of women from behind the screen.
The latter was not appreciated by Photoplay critic Julian
Johnson; he wrote, in the November, 1915 issue, "a mis-
taken idea of producing realism by hammering the bass drum
for every cannon shot and bomb explosion, accompanied by a
weird assortment of other noises, even to the cries of the
scurrying populace and groans of the wounded by a mob behind the screen, made the general effect so confusing that it
was impossible to concentrate the mind upon the serious
matter presented."

The audience, packed with celebrities, from Thomas Dixon to Rex Beach, first heard Captain Jack Crawford, poet scout of the Grand Army of the Republic, denounce the popular song, "I Didn't Raise My Boy to Be a Soldier." J. Stuart Blackton then read a letter from Colonel Roosevelt, which stated, "Every man worth being called a man should realize that if he has the right to vote, then it is his duty to bear arms.... The duty of military service should be as widespread as the right to vote."[75]

Blackton also announced that--in August--he had become an American citizen. The reason for this, of course, is obvious. Pro-German factions--"the cowardly Germans of New England," as Roosevelt referred to them--quickly pointed out Blackton's British citizenship, and the anti-German nature of The Battle Cry of Peace. It was even suggested that the British Embassy had secretly channeled funds to Blackton to help pay for the production.

The producer had gone to great pains to explain that the aggressors in The Battle Cry of Peace wore a uniform unlike any other. "I defy anyone to find in it the slightest resemblance to the uniform of any power," said Blackton. "I spent a great deal of time in designing the helmet and it is absolutely original."[7] However, as Variety (August 13, 1915) pointed out, "Vitagraph does not point in any way to one foreign nation, but there can be no doubt in the minds of any one who witnesses the screen presentation that Germany is pointed out."

Reviews of the film were extremely favorable. In each city in which it played it was endorsed by civic and religious leaders. The Daughters of the American Revolution arranged a special screening for Congress; President Wilson declined the invitation. The Battle Cry of Peace opened in England in March of 1916 under the title, An American Home; the London Daily Mail thought it "lurid," but "produced with that eye for effect which the Americans possess."

One major opponent of The Battle Cry of Peace was Henry Ford, who attacked Hudson Maxim's Defenseless America and the film in an article titled "Humanity and Sanity," published in May of 1916. Ford suggested that the film had been financed by various munition manufacturers, and was a calculated attempt to drag the United States into the War. It was a complaint he had voiced earlier in the

New York Mail of December 11, 1915, when he was quoted
as saying, "all militant propagandists are simply doing what
they are doing because they are financially connected with
munition plants." Vitagraph sued for libel, and on April 23,
1917, judgment in its favor was handed down in the New York
Federal District Court.

When America did enter the First World War, The
Battle Cry of Peace was re-edited and retitled The Battle
Cry of War. Certain subject matter was eliminated, and
the film was then, according to The Moving Picture World
(May 5, 1917), "even a greater lesson to show men of the
United States why they should hasten to enlist in one of the
three branches of the Service."

The Battle Cry of War was also the working title for
the sequel to The Battle Cry of Peace, on which Blackton
began work almost as soon as the latter was released. The
story, written by Cyrus Townsend Brady and Blackton, again
dealt with the invasion of America, the destruction by air-
ships of the lower half of Manhattan, and the setting-up of
enemy headquarters at the Woolworth Building. Most importantly, it illustrated the role that women might play in
the war effort.

William P. S. Earle was the director of the film,
with Blackton again closely supervising, and Blackton's eldest
son serving as assistant director. Leading roles in the eight-
reel feature were played by Alice Joyce, Harry Morey,
Joseph Kilgour, Peggy Hyland and James Morrison; Theodore
Roosevelt and Woodrow Wilson also appeared. Exterior
scenes were shot at Fort Wadsworth, New York, and on
Staten Island. The production was ready for release by
February of 1917, and then exhibitors throughout the country
were asked to name the new film. The title eventually
chosen was Womanhood, the Glory of a Nation, as which the
film premiered at the Chestnut Street Opera House, Philadelphia, on March 19, 1917.

It was reported that within twenty-four hours of that
screening, the Daughters of the American Revolution, the
National Preparedness Society, the American Defense League,
the National Security Society and the Navy League had made
plans for a nation-wide campaign to assure the attendance of
every able-bodied man at every theatre screening Womanhood, the Glory of a Nation. The star of the film, Harry
Morey, was later asked by the navy to tour the country, to

stimulate enlistment.   Another player in the production,
James Morrison, took part in a one-reel propaganda short,
showing what life in the navy would be like for a raw re-
cruit; it was probably directed by Vitagraph's Wilfred North.

On April 1, 1917, Womanhood, the Glory of a Nation
opened at the Broadway Theatre, New York, before an
audience which included Enrico Caruso, E. H. Sothern,
William Fox, Thomas Dixon, Carl Laemmle and Daniel
Frohman.   Blackton spoke to the audience and introduced
Burr McIntosh, who denounced William Jennings Bryan as
"the arch traitor of the history of our country."   When
Theodore Roosevelt appeared on the screen, Exhibitor's
Trade Review (April 14, 1917) reported that "the audience
cheered for a period of fully three minutes."

Again, as in The Battle Cry of Peace, the invaders
of the United States were thinly disguised Germans, preach-
ing "Might Makes Right" and "War Knows No Necessity."
However, with America's entry into the World War only days
away, no one protested.

Reviews were mixed.   Louis Reeves Harrison in The
Moving Picture World of April 21, 1917 wrote, "Womanhood
is an inspiring appeal to chivalry, to manhood, to ennobling
sentiments which lie deep and strong in the American heart,
though almost smothered by material prosperity."   To Julian
Johnson in Photoplay (June, 1917), "Womanhood is simply a
wholesome melodrama in none of whose phases has there
been much ingenuity, and in some things too little care....
I am not saying that Womanhood won't entertain; perhaps it
will give you the Spring's thrilling evening, but don't look for
another Intolerance."   Motion Picture Magazine (June, 1917)
really summed up everything: "I would not call it a remarkable drama, but it is great because of its timeliness and the
sincerity of its motives."

There is an interesting footnote to add to the saga of
Womanhood, the Glory of a Nation.   A projectionist named
George Hann, at the Windamere Theater, East Cleveland,
Ohio, attempted to set fire to a print of the film.   He was
arrested, and a warning was issued "to the motion picture
interests of the country to take every precaution to safeguard
films against damage by persons in the employ of the German
government."

Prior to the release of Womanhood, the Glory of a

Nation, Cyrus Townsend Brady and J. Stuart Blackton had written Whom the Gods Destroy, a story of an Irish patriot named Sir Denis Esmond, who is arrested as a traitor for his conspiracies against England, and is saved from hanging at the last minute through the personal intervention of King George V.

Whom the Gods Destroy was directed by William P. S. Earle, photographed by Clark Nickerson--who also photographed Womanhood, the Glory of a Nation--and starred Alice Joyce, Harry Morey and Marc MacDermott. At its release on December 18, 1916, the public was quick to note the similarity to the case of Sir Roger Casement, Irish patriot, hanged in 1916 for encouraging Germany to intervene in Ireland's fight for independence from Britain. The production was seen as an attempt to whitewash Britain's handling of the Casement affair and the Easter Rebellion, both of which had created considerable anti-British sentiment in this country. Rioting broke out at a number of cinemas showing the film, and the Sons of Irish Freedom declared the production "slanderous and degrading" and claimed the film was an attempt to discredit the Irish race.

The critics were not so sure that it was anti-Irish. Exhibitor's Trade Review (December 16, 1916) wrote, "The theme is timely.... To the Irish it is vivid; and to those of English descent any tale connected with the tragedy of the Sinn Fein revolt will be interesting. Vitagraph has chosen a neutral path in presenting this story by taking the attitude that while the freedom of Ireland from English sovereignty may be a good thing, it is best accomplished by other means than violence at a time when Britain is facing a great crisis."

However, to most people, Whom the Gods Destroy was further evidence of Vitagraph's and, particularly, J. Stuart Blackton's close links with Britain, and the company's desire to promote the British cause. Interestingly, Whom the Gods Destroy was considered too pro-Irish by the British, and was banned.

One should not underestimate the importance that these three films played in encouraging the American people to enter the First World War in support of Britain and her allies. Blackton here demonstrated the propaganda value of the motion picture in a way that no other producer had previously done. As a political weapon, the motion picture film might well be said to have come of age with The Battle Cry of Peace.

J. Stuart Blackton had been the guiding light behind these three major productions; Albert E. Smith was very much in the background. William P. S. Earle recalls that "He [Smith] didn't want to put out money, and when Blackton decided to do Battle Cry of Peace, Smith was against it, but when he found out how profitable it was, he was more than interested because it meant money."

By the summer of 1917 Smith was firmly back in control of Vitagraph production, and Blackton had become an independent producer for Paramount. In Motography of September 1, 1917, Smith announced: "With these two features [The Battle Cry of Peace and Womanhood, the Glory of a Nation], Vitagraph, I think, has partially done its duty toward awakening the nation to a sense of its obligation to itself and civilization. Now, I feel, the policy of Vitagraph and of every other motion picture manufacturer should be to make pictures that will take the minds of the people off the war and their troubles, make them laugh, and in that way, make them happy. That is to be our policy.... My idea is to produce romances--not problem plays, but clean stories with a light atmosphere and a laugh lurking here and there in their literary folds."

Chapter 9

THE COMEDIANS

The most famous of Vitagraph comedians was John Bunny, but there were also a number of lesser, together with two major, comedy players whose careers were closely linked to the Vitagraph Company. Hughie Mack and Kate Price were enchanting audiences at the same time as John Bunny and Flora Finch were doing likewise. Wally Van, also, was a Vitagraph comedy star of the early 'teens, with his character, "Cutey."

In the late 'teens, Earl Montgomery and Joe Rock, both of whom entered films with Vitagraph, were a popular comedy team. In the Spring of 1920 the Company tried unsuccessfully to star them separately as heads of their own comedy units, with Charles "Chuck" Reisner directing Montgomery and Grover Jones directing Rock. Montgomery faded from films fairly quickly, but Joe Rock went on to produce a series of Stan Laurel comedies in the mid-Twenties, was active as a producer in England in the Thirties, and in 1968 was responsible for the highly successful Cinerama feature, Krakatoa, East of Java.

English-born comedian, James Aubrey, who had been one of the original players in Fred Karno's A Night in an English Music Hall, was also working at Vitagraph at the same time as Montgomery and Rock. On March 12, 1923, Albert E. Smith noted, "Aubrey is very passé as a comedian," and did not renew his contract, but Aubrey continued to work as a comedian with other companies throughout the Twenties.

Montgomery and Rock and James Aubrey were in the minor league as comedians; their films were basically crude and lacking finesse. The two Vitagraph comedians whose popularity was almost on a par with that of John Bunny, and whose productions were generally well-constructed, written and directed, were Larry Semon and Sidney Drew. The two had decidedly different comedy styles, yet both were active in the film industry during roughly the same years.

In the early 'teens, Sidney Drew, with his second wife, Lucille McVey, introduced to the screen, and became the chief exponent of, polite, domestic comedy. It was a comedy style totally opposite to the slapstick humor perfected by Mack Sennett, and, with the passing of the silent film, as practiced by Sidney Drew and his imitators--in particular Mr. and Mrs. Carter De Haven--it disappeared completely. The nearest equivalent to domestic comedy in sound films was the screwball comedy genre of the Thirties,

Mr. and Mrs. Sidney Drew

featuring Cary Grant, Irene Dunne, Myrna Loy and Carole Lombard. Today, if it exists at all, it is in television programs such as All in the Family and Maude, which in content are aeons removed from the simplistic, straightforward approach of the Drew comedies. Audiences enjoyed domestic comedy, but some critics were not so enthusiastic. Writing

of Mr. and Mrs. Sidney Drew in his The 7 Lively Arts,
Gilbert Seldes noted, "In them there was nothing offensive,
except an enervating dullness." Seldes continued, "And
apart from the agreeable manners of Mr. and Mrs. Sidney
Drew nothing made them successful except the corrupt
desire, on the part of the spectators, to be refined."

Sidney Drew was born in New York City on August 28,
1864; his mother, Mrs. John Drew, was one of America's
foremost comediennes, and he was to be the uncle of Ethel,
Lionel and John Barrymore. After education at New York's
Episcopal Academy and the University of Pennsylvania, Sidney
Drew embarked on a stage career, making his debut, with
Leonard Grover, in Our Boarding House at Philadelphia's
South Broad Street Theatre. According to contemporary
critics, his recognition as a master of light comedy was in-
stantaneous. Drew, in association with his mother, organized
his own company, presenting such comedy successes as The
Rivals, The Road to Ruin and A Jealous Wife. In 1896 he
turned his attention to vaudeville, and was a pioneer in presenting legitimate drama on the vaudeville stage, with his
sketch, "When Two Hearts Are Won," at Keith's Union Square
Theatre, New York.

In the spring of 1913 Sidney Drew embarked on a new
phase of his career and joined the Vitagraph Company. He
made his screen debut in The Still Voice, released on May 24,
1913, and quickly rose to prominence within the company.
Drew was starred with John Bunny for the first and only time
in The Feudists, a two-reel comedy directed by Wilfred North
and released on August 23, 1913. He began to direct his own
productions almost a year after joining Vitagraph; the first
film for which he received directorial credit was Never Again,
released on March 28, 1914.

By this time Sidney Drew had his own company of
players, including Edith Storey, Ethel Lloyd, Ada Gifford,
Lillian Burns and Lucille McVey. These players accompanied Drew to Florida in April of 1914 for a stay of some
six weeks.

Sidney Drew's first wife, Gladys Rankin, who had
gained some fame as a dramatist under the name of George
Cameron, had died in January of 1914. It was the first Mrs.
Drew who had written the play upon which her husband's first
film, The Still Voice, was based. While in Florida, Drew
became attracted to one of his players, Lucille McVey, who,

in films, used her grandmother's name of Jane Morrow.
Born in Sedalia, Missouri, on April 18, 1890, Miss McVey
had spent some six years on the concert stage, and was
recognized as one of the foremost "child dialect readers"
before joining Vitagraph early in 1914. She and Sidney Drew
were married on July 25, 1914, and their marriage led to
the creation of the Mr. and Mrs. Sidney Drew Comedies.

In Florida, Sidney Drew produced what was possibly
his finest feature-length comedy, A Florida Enchantment,
starring himself and Edith Storey. This five-reel "farcical
fantasy," released in September of 1914, had Edith Storey
(as Lillian Travers) discover a seed which could change
women into men and vice versa. She takes one, with the
result that she adopts all the mannerisms and the behavior
of a man, including growing a beard, kissing women friends
on the lips, smoking cigarettes, sporting a moustache, etc.
Deciding that she needs a valet rather than a maid, Edith
Storey then forces her maid to eat a seed. Finally, she
reveals what has taken place to her fiancé, Dr. Fred Cas-
sadene (played by Sidney Drew), who, in disbelief, also eats
one of the seeds, thus becoming effeminate to the point of
wearing women's clothes. The end of the film reveals that
it was all a dream on Miss Storey's part.

Sidney Drew's direction draws from Edith Storey a
quite remarkable performance. The actress gives one of
the finest male impersonations I have ever seen onscreen or
off. Drew, himself, makes the best of a unique opportunity
for transvestism. Surprisingly, A Florida Enchantment drew
little enthusiasm from the critics at the time. "A farcical
fantasy, eh?" commented Variety (August 14, 1914). "Yes,
it is, and besides that it is the most silly inane 'comedy'
every put on the sheet. The thing started off like a comic
opera, but it lapsed into a weary, dreary, listless collection
of foolish things that drove several of the few people at the
Vitagraph Tuesday night out of the theatre before the third
reel had been run through.... The picture should never have
been put out, for there's no one with any sense of humor
whatsoever, or intelligence either, who can force a smile
while watching this sad 'comedy.'"

More favorable critical response was given to a
thirty-eight minute playlet, What the Moon Saw, written by
Sidney Drew's son, S. Rankin Drew, and produced at the
Vitagraph Theatre in December of 1914. 'What the Moon
Saw ought to reach vaudeville," noted Variety (December 18,

1914). "Big time has need of such material. It stands up
well among the best half dozen sketches the variety entertainment has ever seen.... Mr. Sidney Drew played in his
best style. The others (members of the Vitagraph players)
were mediocre."

S. Rankin Drew appears to have joined the Vitagraph
Company around the same time as his father. He entered
films, he claimed, at the urging of his cousin, Lionel
Barrymore. A dapper-looking young man, Drew was a
popular member of the acting contingent at Vitagraph, one
of his first successes being in An Unwritten Chapter (released on July 4, 1913), playing opposite Dorothy Kelly.
S. Rankin Drew later turned to writing and directing, with
equal success. Sadly, his career was all too short. He
was killed in France in the spring of 1918 while serving
with the French Flying Corps.

One of the first big successes of the Drews as a
husband and wife team came in 1915 with Playing Dead, a
five-reel "human interest drama" based on a story by
Richard Harding Davis. Aside from playing the leading
roles, Sidney Drew directed and Mrs. Drew wrote the
screenplay. Playing Dead was not a comedy, per se. It
concerned a feminist (played by Donald Hall), who preaches
female emancipation, which provokes one of his fellow club
members to comment, "The things that fellow Maddox says
should exclude him from the society of law-abiding, money-
making millionaires." Viewed today, the production is somewhat boring, with endless subtitles and a number of actors
all too obviously playing more than one role.

In January of 1916 the Drews departed from Vitagraph
and signed a contract with Metro to produce a one-reel
comedy a week, at a yearly joint salary of $90,000. It was
at Metro that the couple perfected the Henry and Polly characters, who were to be the central players in their productions from this point on. Contemporary writers give Mrs.
Drew much of the credit for the success of the Mr. and Mrs.
Sidney Drew comedies. Interviewing the Drews in 1917,
Frederick James Smith wrote, "Mrs. Drew is definite in her
ideas about screen comedy. Just between ourselves, I give
Mrs. Drew 75 per cent of the credit for the conception of
the Drew comedies. That is, she is the team member who
selects an idea and builds on it. Mr. Drew has the actor's
discernment to understand her mental process and to perfect
it on the screen. To him goes the credit for putting the idea
over."[96]

There can be no question as to the popularity of the
Drew comedies produced at Metro. Writing in The Moving
Picture World of August 19, 1916, Epes Winthrop Sargent
noted, "In these days of knockabout, the Metro-Drew
comedies stand for the best of real comedy; the sort of
comedy that made Mr. Drew's mother, Mrs. John Drew,
beloved by a nation that still holds her in affectionate re-
membrance."

At the expiration of their Metro contract the Drews
announced their retirement from the screen, and returned
to the stage in a lightweight comedy titled Keep Her Smiling.
In August of 1918 the couple signed a contract with J. Van
Beuren to produce a series of two-reel comedies, for release through Paramount. Between working on these comedies, Mr. and Mrs. Sidney Drew continued to tour in Keep
Her Smiling.

The death of his son had been a great shock for
Sidney Drew, and the comedian's health began to deteriorate
rapidly. While playing in Detroit on April 4, 1919, he col-
lapsed. He was brought back to New York by his wife, and
died there on April 9, 1919.

Mrs. Drew remained active in films for a number of
years, and in 1921 directed a five-reel feature, Cousin Kate,
for the Vitagraph Company. Starring Alice Joyce in the title
role, the film, based on a novel by Hubert Henry Davis, had
much of the simple charm of the Mr. and Mrs. Sidney Drew
comedies. "This picture offers a very simple story told in
a simple fashion, yet possessing decided charm and unde-
niably attractive from a strictly artistic standpoint," commented Exhibitor's Trade Review (April 2, 1921). "It is
light entertainment, but Mrs. Sidney Drew has made excellent use of the material at hand, and, thanks to her wise
direction and the sympathetic work of a well-chosen cast,
the interest holds to the end."

Sidney Drew's passing was noted with lengthy and
sympathetic obituaries in all the leading newspapers and
magazines. The tribute which appeared in the July, 1919
issue of Photoplay is well worth quoting: "The best of
Sidney Drew is immortalized on the screen. When the
history of motion picture comedy is written, years from now,
Mr. Drew will occupy a great fundamental place in it, for
his celluloid jests were veritable transcripts from the life of
the American people. He will endure as the first genuine

exemplifier of the comedy of situation and character in
pictures. "

The genuine grief and sorrow at the death of Sidney
Drew was not apparent at the passing of another famous
Vitagraph comedian, Larry Semon. Semon presented the
exact opposite to Drew in screen comedy, but unlike Drew's,
those of his films which have survived do little to help historians appreciate his one-time appeal. Larry Semon's
place in the hierarchy of screen comedians, it has been suggested, is somewhere just below that occupied by the big
four, Chaplin, Lloyd, Keaton and Langdon. However, a
viewing of his extant productions suggests a position far,
far below that occupied by the masters of screen comedy.

Lawrence Semon was born in West Point, Mississippi
on July 16, 1889, the son of a professional magician, "Zera
the Great. " Semon's earliest known professional appearance
was as a cartoonist in vaudeville at New York's Fifth Avenue
Theatre in November of 1913. The following review of his
twelve-minute act appeared in Variety (November 14, 1913):
"With all due respect to Lawrence Seamon's [sic] ability and
cleverness to entertain with the chalk and crayon and inci-
dentally make the gift of drawing pay, a sigh of relief will
go up when all of the New York newspaper artists have made
their debut on the local vaudeville stage. A likable chap,
with a pleasing voice, Seamon is able to make himself heard
without tripping up any of the footlights. He's regularly employed on the Evening Sun and daily contributes baseball
players' heads to its sporting sheet. In this 'act' he makes
only heads of diamond heroes best known to New York fans. "

In 1916, Semon joined the Vitagraph Company as a
comedy writer and director. Apparently, many producers
at that time believed cartoonists were ideally suited to the
production of comedy films--an idea which was generally
proved incorrect. Albert E. Smith recalled, in answer to
a letter of inquiry in 1953, that he had first met Semon
when he was a cartoonist on the Brooklyn Daily Eagle. "He
submitted some comedy scripts to us. We found his ideas
were of a comic nature and finally gave him a position in
our scenario department. From this he graduated to producing one-reel comedies. " However, it should be pointed
out that the 1916 Motion Picture Studio Directory indicates
that Semon had previously directed Palace Players comedies
at Universal before joining Vitagraph.

Larry Semon

Semon began his career at Vitagraph directing other comedians, including Frank Daniels, Hughie Mack and James Aubrey. In January of 1917 he was sent out to Vitagraph's Western studio to produce a series of "Big V" comedies there, but returned to New York in May of the same year. (It is perhaps worth noting at this point that Vitagraph was one of the few early companies which concentrated its production on the East Coast. The Western studios of Vitagraph, at first located at 1438 2nd Street, Santa Monica, and later at Talmadge Street and Prospect Avenue, Hollywood, were relatively unimportant. It was only in the Twenties that Vitagraph moved production to the West Coast, and virtually closed down the Flatbush studios. An employee who was assigned to the West Coast in the 'teens, therefore, might very well be considered of little importance. That same employee's return to New York, in the same way, could be construed as a recognition of his value to the Company.)

In July of 1917, Larry Semon stepped before the camera for the first time in a one-reel comedy titled Boasts and Boldness. His good looks were completely obscured by the heavy white make-up which was to become his stock-in-trade. From this point on he starred in more than twenty one-reel comedies, bearing titles such as Slips and Slackers, Plans and Pajamas, Tough Luck and Tin Lizzies (all 1917), and Babes and Boobs, Romans and Rascals, Hindoos and Hazards, Big Boobs and Bathing Beauties (all 1918).

Semon began producing two-reel comedies in 1918 with Huns and Hyphens. His comedies were favorably received by the public and the critics. Typical of the latter's response is the following review of Frauds and Frenzies (released on November 11, 1918) in Exhibitor's Trade Review (November 16, 1918): "This two-reeler, produced and written by Larry Semon and in which he plays the leading role, is packed full of the sort of slapstick stuff that will amuse the representative audience. It contains plenty of laughs worked up in a more or less legitimate way and is on a par with other comedies produced by Semon." Frauds and Frenzies also holds interest today because of the performance by Semon's co-star, Stan Laurel.

As Semon's fame grew, so did his ego. He began to suffer from a malaise which was to affect a number of silent comedians, that of over-confidence. The cost of his productions rose astronomically; the quality did not. On December 6, 1919, The Moving Picture World announced that Semon

had renewed his contract with Vitagraph, and had been
promised $3,600,000 to produce an average of ten two-reel
comedies over the next three years.   One of the first comedies to be produced under the new contract, School Days, a
grotesque slapstick comedy with adults playing children's
roles, was particularly well received.   Major Bowes, managing director of New York's Capitol Theatre, booked it for the
week of May 9, 1920, and featured it prominently in all his
advertising.   School Days boasted many of the regular Semon
company, including leading lady Lucille Carlisle (later to be
replaced by Semon's wife, Dorothy Dwan), fat man Frank
Alexander, and female impersonator Frank Hayes.   Norman
Taurog and Mort Peebles assisted Semon in the direction.

        Larry Semon's lavish spending on his productions
soon became a major headache for Albert E. Smith.   His
brother, W. S. Smith, had reported that not only was Semon
wasting a good deal of Vitagraph's money, "with a great
show of industry but not accomplishing much," but was also
plotting to move to another studio.   Furiously, Smith, in
September of 1920, sued Semon for $407,338.22 in damages,
claiming that "the defendant deliberately increased the cost
of his productions through delays, carelessness and waste to
an unreasonable figure, with the aim of forcing the Vitagraph
Company to release him from his contract."

        The case appears to have been settled out of court,
but Smith was far from happy with Semon's expenditure of
Vitagraph's money.   He became highly critical of Larry's
films.   Of The Sawmill, one of the most famous and in-
genious of Semon two-reelers, Smith wrote on October 26,
1921, "We have all seen The Sawmill, and no one is able
to engender any enthusiasm over it.   Of all the pictures
Larry has made to date, I think it is the least satisfactory,
from a comedy standpoint, and when the cost is taken into
consideration, it makes one regard it an atrocity." (Amusingly, some two years earlier, Smith had placed an adver-
tisement in Exhibitor's Trade Review of March 29, 1919,
advertising Semon's comedy, Well I'll Be --! thus: "Albert
E. Smith, President of Vitagraph, told Larry the lid was off
the cash-box and Larry spent 93% of what was in the till on
this one.")

        The one solution to the Larry Semon problem for
Smith was to contract for the comedian to produce ten two-
reel pictures a year, to be released through Vitagraph, for
which Vitagraph would pay forty-five thousand dollars for

each of the first five films, and fifty thousand dollars for
the last five. Semon was allowed the use of the Vitagraph
studios but expected to provide his own staff. A contract
between the two parties was drawn up and signed on May
12, 1922.

For a year things went fairly smoothly, with Semon
wasting his own money rather than Vitagraph's. However,
on September 17, 1923, Smith was forced to reject a Semon
comedy titled Moonshines (presumably never released) as "a
palpably cheap picture." The end of the Larry Semon-Vita-
graph relationship was near. It was easier for the Company
to lose Semon than to put up with his antics. Semon moved
over to Chadwick Pictures, while Smith, with typical business acumen, had his staff check through Larry Semon's out-
takes to see if there was any footage that, with the help of
a few sub-titles, could be put together to make a number of
two-reel comedies.

After leaving Vitagraph, Semon went downhill rapidly.
In 1925, for release through Chadwick, he produced a crude
feature-length version of The Wizard of Oz, featuring himself, Oliver Hardy and Dorothy Dwan. By February of
1928, Semon was appearing in the Los Angeles debtors'
court, confessing himself not only penniless but also owing
$80,000. To try to repay the money he owed Semon em-
barked on a national vaudeville tour, but in August of 1928
he suffered a complete nervous and physical breakdown. He
died, of tuberculosis, at a health ranch near Victorville, on
October 8, 1928. His death might very well be considered a
blessing in disguise, for undoubtedly he could not have survived any longer as a screen comedian.

Chapter 10

THE SERIALS

Vitagraph was a late entrant into the serial field, one of the silent screen's most popular genres. What the serial lacked in artistic values it made up in box office appeal. By the time the company produced its first one, all the most famous serials--What Happened to Mary?, The Adventures of Kathlyn, The Exploits of Elaine, The Hazards of Helen and The Perils of Pauline--had been released.

Delightfully, Vitagraph's first foray into serial production was a parody of Thanhouser's The Million Dollar Mystery, released in June of 1914, and its sequel, Zudora, released in November of the same year. Both serials had created sensations with their ludicrous plots and lurid advertising. Vitagraph named its parody, The Fates and Flora Fourflush or The Massive Ten Billion-Dollar Vitagraph Mystery Serial. The script was credited to "the great (but unknown) Scandinavian author, Kjarl Brown, S. H. (Square Head), in collaboration with a number of other alleged humorists. The serial featured Clara Kimball Young, a dramatic actress who was seldom given the opportunity to display her talent as a comedienne, and Charles Brown; Wally Van was the director. The first episode, "Treachery in the Clouds," was released on January 4, 1915; Episode Two, "The Treasure Temple of Bhosh," followed the next week; and the finally episode, naturally titled "A Race for Life," was released on January 18, 1915.

Wally Van directed one other serial for Vitagraph, The Scarlet Runner, featuring Earle Williams, and released in the autumn of 1916. William P. S. Earle was credited with direction of two episodes of this serial, which he started, but which Van completed. The Scarlet Runner is noteworthy for including among its players Adolphe Menjou in one of his first screen roles. Wally Van went on to

direct many more serials, in particular The Evil Eye, released in the spring of 1920 by Hallmark, for which company
Wally Van was director-general for some five years.

Vitagraph's first true serial was The Goddess, released in fifteen two-reel episodes, beginning on May 10,
1915.   Ralph Ince was the director, and the stars were
Vitagraph's popular romantic team of Earle Williams and
Anita Stewart.   Simultaneous with the serial's release, the
story was published in the Hearst newspapers.

"The conventional series, with its dependence upon
dime novel situations, is being done to death," explained
Albert E. Smith in The Moving Picture World of May 1,
1915, "and we are not falling into line at this late date to
make another version of incidents that have been presented
times without number.   If we didn't have something new we
would not think it worth while to enter the serial field.   The
Goddess will have no more in common with the ordinary
melodrama than has a story in the Century magazine with the
fiction prepared for circulation among messenger boys."

"The Serial Beautiful," as Vitagraph liked to consider
The Goddess, was scripted by Gouverneur Morris and Charles
W. Goddard.   It concerned a modern Joan of Arc, reared on
a desert island in the belief that she was a goddess.   Es-
caping from the island, she meets a friendly human and is
persuaded to go about the earth, spreading the gospel of
kindness and love.   In her travels the goddess faced the
problems of anarchism, socialism, labor, and modern Chris-
tianity.

Reasonably successful, The Goddess did not run to the
twenty episodes that Smith had hoped for.   The "superior
tone" of the production was not entirely to the liking of 1915
audiences.

Aside from The Scarlet Runner, Vitagraph did not release another serial until 1917.   The company's first serial
of that year was The Secret Kingdom, directed by Theodore
Marston and Charles Brabin, the first episode of which was
released on January 1, 1917.   The Secret Kingdom featured
Charles Richman, Dorothy Kelly and Arline Pretty, who had
come to Vitagraph from Universal.

"The Universal was very crude, but the Vitagraph
was not," recalls Miss Pretty--her real name!   "I did to

some extent enjoy making serials, because they were in the theatres--they were sixteen episodes or whatever--and you were in the theatres sixteen whole weeks. They were like the series on television today, except they didn't give you the end of it. They left me always in some awful position, and they'd all come back to see how I got out of it, so it was really very good. However, I don't think they were ever regarded as important, naturally, as the feature pictures I did also at Vitagraph.

"I worked every single day, of course, on these things until they were over. We'd be there at eight o-clock in the morning and work all day. We made one episode a week. We'd have as many rehearsals as were necessary; some were easier than others. Some we could almost go in and do; we'd got so used to these crazy things. To do two reels a week, we couldn't take too long in rehearsing."

Miss Pretty recalls one harrowing experience she had while making The Secret Kingdom, which illustrates the lengths to which actresses were expected to go for the sake of their art.

"You know, I was always being kidnapped, and taken somewhere, and Charles [Richman] was always rescuing me. So they took me to a place in Brooklyn, on the top floor of one of these brownstone-front houses. Charles was to come and get a room in the next house, and let a rope down to me. I was to jump out, and he was to take me across. Naturally I was a little nervous about it! I'd never jumped out of a four-story place in my life before--and never expected to!

"I had an evening dress on, and they did make a belt to go under the dress, with a hook on it. Then everybody left me for some reason--can you imagine that? Leaving me there to decide when I was to jump out! The cameras were all down in front of the building; Teddy Marston was down there. A man whose name was Eddie Wentworth had charge of the stunts, and he said, 'Don't jump out until I call all right.'

"I thought I heard 'All right,' and I went, and jumped out. And I went zooming down to the first floor, where I was stuck. I'd be smashed to pieces if I'd gone all the way. Charles and Eddie came down, and they were as white as sheets, because when I jumped out, nobody had a hold of the

rope on the roof. They had put it around the chimney, so
it wouldn't fall off, and fortunately they were looking at it.
They saw it start to go, and they ran as fast as they could,
and stopped it as I got down to the second floor. Eddie
came down, and said, 'Why did you jump before I called all
right?' And I said, 'Well, you did call all right.' He almost fainted, because he realized he'd called 'hold tight,'
and it sounded like 'all right' to me, and I jumped!'"

Vitagraph released two other serials in 1917: The
Fighting Trail and Vengeance and the Woman, both directed
by and starring William Duncan, supported by Carol Holloway. Duncan and Holloway were to be mainstays of Vitagraph's serial production.

William Duncan had been a leading man, and later a
director, with the Selig Company before joining Vitagraph
in 1915. Aside from the aforementioned, he directed and
starred in some five serials for Vitagraph: A Fight for
Millions (1918), Man of Might (1919), Smashing Barriers
(1919), The Silent Avenger (1920) and Fighting Fate (1921).
He left Vitagraph in 1922. He had been much liked; W. S.
Smith wrote to his brother, Albert, on February 5, 1920,
"Duncan ... is working like a trojan, and is very lovely to
get along with." Carol Holloway had come to Vitagraph
after working at a number of studios. She was starred in
two further serials for the company: The Iron Test (1918)
and The Perils of Thunder Mountain (1919).

One of the players in The Fighting Trail was Joe
Ryan, who graduated to stardom in Vitagraph serials. The
first of his starring roles was opposite Jean Paige in
Hidden Dangers, directed by William Bertram, the first
episode of which, "The Evil Spell," was released on July 5,
1920. In it, Ryan portrayed a double role, which led Vitagraph News (June 7, 1920), somewhat tongue-in-cheek, to
dub Hidden Dangers "The Jeckyll [sic] and Hyde serial."

By 1920 the Vitagraph company was beginning to re-
consider the value of continuing serial production. It was
having considerable problems with one of its serial stars,
Antonio Moreno, who was refusing to appear unless directed
by William J. Bowman, a director whom the company would
dearly have liked to be rid of. (Bowman, while shooting the
1920 serial, The Invisible Hand, accidentally exploded a
dynamite charge, blowing up a rented horse and its rider.

The latter was not seriously hurt, but Vitagraph, grudgingly, had to agree to pay for another horse.)

Vitagraph's last serial, <u>Breaking Through</u>, directed by Robert Ensminger and starring Carmel Myers and Wallace MacDonald, went into release on September 25, 1921. Thereafter, Vitagraph left serial production to the two experts in the field, Pathe and Universal.

Chapter 11

BLACK BEAUTY AND CAPTAIN BLOOD

In the Twenties, the Vitagraph Company released a considerable number of program pictures of little merit, usually featuring Alice Calhoun, one or two quality productions directed by J. Stuart Blackton, and two major features, Black Beauty and Captain Blood. Both starred Jean Paige, whom Albert E. Smith had married in December of 1920, and on whose productions it was only natural that Smith should lavish all the attention and money that Vitagraph could provide.

Jean Paige was born Lucille O'Hare in Paris, Illinois, in 1896. She was a beautiful woman when she entered films with the Vitagraph Company in 1917, and she was still beautiful when I talked with her in 1971 at her Los Angeles home. It was her Aunt Emmy who was responsible for her film career, after Lucille had studied at Dr. Byron C. King's School of Drama in Pittsburgh.

"My mother sent me a letter from my aunt, saying, 'Where is Lucille? Martin Justice has just started to direct for Vitagraph, and I have finally persuaded him to say he'll give Lucille a test.' So I went down, and Aunt Emmy and her daughter, who was the only sister I ever had, met me at the train on Friday. And Saturday, Mr. Justice took me out, and Monday they made a test, but I didn't see it, and they didn't either. They cast me immediately. Mr. Justice was making two-reel comedies from the O. Henry stories, so they cast me in one, and I played the lead in the rest of them. I played every day from then on."

Jean Paige's screen debut was in The Discounters of Money, released on July 26, 1917, and featuring Carlton King and Catherine Charleton. It was followed by Blindman's Holiday, a four-reel feature released on September 15, 1917,

99

Jean Paige at the height of her popularity.

and The Indian Summer of Dry Valley Johnson, released on
October 13, 1917; both again featuring Carlton King. In
1918, Jean Paige--William P. S. Earle claimed to have so
named her--was featured in several five-reel productions
directed by Paul Scardon: The Desired Woman, The Golden
Goal, Tangled Lives, The King of Diamonds and Hoarded
Assets. On July 6, 1918, Motography announced that Jean
Paige had become a star; "Miss Paige is one of the youngest
of Vitagraph's stars and affords another splendid good example of Mr. Smith's ability as a judge of stellar material."

        Jean Paige recalls how she came to go out to Cali-
fornia: "Mr. Smith's brother called me to the office, and
wanted to know if I'd come. And I said, 'Well, I don't
know....' He said, 'We have someone down in Florida we
are considering.' I said, 'That's fine--you get her.' I
went home that night, and Aunt Emma was living with me
at the hotel--the St. George Hotel, Brooklyn--and I said,
'Aunt Emma, how would you like to go to California?' I
told her about it, and she was very excited. Oh, she was
a lovely person; the finest aristocrat I ever knew, a wonder-
fully broad mind, and interested in everything.

        "The next morning when I got in--I was playing oppo-
site Earle Williams in The Fortune Hunter--Vic Smith sent
for me. He said, 'Well, Miss Paige, what do you think
about going to California?' I said, 'What's the matter,
couldn't you get the other girl?' He said, 'No, she's busy.'
So I said, 'Well, I don't know how I can refuse again.' He
was just delighted, and I cried.

        'I got home, and told Aunt Emma, and we came out
here--got out there Christmas Eve fifty-two years ago. I
said, 'Aunt Emma, as soon as the picture's over I'm going
right back.' The next day was the loveliest day you ever
saw! No smog in those days. We got a car and a driver,
went all over the city, and I've never wanted to live any
place else from that time to this.

        "Well, then Mr. Smith's wife passed on--in the flu
epidemic, and Mr. Smith came out with the children and the
nurse. We all went to meet him, and he said, 'Well, Miss
Paige, how do you like California.' I said, 'I simply love
it. I get to ride horseback and do all the things I love to
do.' He said, 'I ride every morning, and maybe you could
ride with me sometime.' So I went home and told my aunt
about it, and she said, 'Well, I've always understood Mr.

Smith was a very fine gentleman, and there's no reason why
you shouldn't. ' That was the way it started.

"You know, Mr. Slide, I had been interviewed by
other companies, but something always held me to Vitagraph.
I never was with any other company; everybody was so
wonderful to me. I didn't care how hard I worked or how
long, I loved every minute of it. As soon as I was married,
I was so happy! Of course, I had responsibility for the
children, and I just lost interest in films. I had a contract
with them, and so I had to make The Prodigal Judge and
Captain Blood. The Prodigal Judge was the only picture that
I never cared for; I mean I didn't like myself in it. I loved
Captain Blood.

"I had this contract with Vitagraph. I had to finish
it, and I did those pictures, but I really wasn't interested in
pictures any more. I look back on my life. Here I was a
young girl in Illinois, and my aunt for some reason or another is pushing me. Then, when Mr. Smith and the children
needed me, I was there, and we had such a wonderful and
happy life. You look back on it, and it sort of falls into
place. It's like a plan."

The Prodigal Judge, an eight-reel feature released on
February 10, 1922, was a lurid melodrama, involving errant
wives and abduction. Directed by Edward José, it featured
Jean Paige, along with Maclyn Arbuckle, Ernest Torrence,
and Earle Foxe. As Photoplay (April, 1922) noted, "It's a
curious fact that the most satisfying photoplays are seldom
the ones involving vast expenditure and grave warnings about
leaving the children at home."

Jean Paige might remember The Prodigal Judge with
distaste, but she had good reason for pleasurably recalling
Black Beauty, for it was during its production that she was
married. Unlike the book by Anna Sewell, which told the
story of Black Beauty through what the horse saw, Mr. and
Mrs. George Randolph Chester, who adapted the novel, had
the film present the story through the eyes of both the humans
and the horse. As Photoplay (April, 1921) commented,
"There is, therefore, the 'inside' story of the humans and
the 'outside' story of the horses, and they dovetail so well
there is no break in the interest and no resentment at the
frequent changes from one to the other." The Chesters also
resorted to the technique popular in the cinema around 1913;

J. Warren Kerrigan and Jean Paige in Captain Blood (1924).

that of having a curtain part to reveal a new scene in the drama.

Albert's brother, David, directed the production competently, if with a somewhat heavy hand.   Former Vitagraph juvenile James Morrison was brought to the Coast to play opposite Jean Paige, and the finished film was released, in seven reels, in January of 1921.

Exhibitor's Trade Review (January 22, 1921) commented, "With a charming star and a splendid cast, coupled with a story so very human that few people will fail to

Jean Paige in Black Beauty (1921).

admire it, Black Beauty looms large on the horizon of 1921 with promise of outliving this year and other years on the exhibitor's books." Sadly, the only surviving nitrate print of

Black Beauty was donated by Mrs. Smith to the Academy of
Motion Picture Arts and Sciences, and was not copied onto
modern safety film stock. When Mrs. Smith and I asked to
view the film in 1972, all that remained were three reels.

Interestingly, when Ingmar Bergman was asked by
Stig Björkman to tell of the genesis of his interest in films,
he replied, "I know the first film I ever saw--it must have
been some time in 1924, when I was six or so, at the Sture
Cinema in Stockholm--was Black Beauty. I still recall a
sequence with a fire. It was burning, I remember that
vividly. And I remember too how it excited me, and how
afterwards we bought the book of Black Beauty and how I
learned the chapter on the fire by heart."*

On November 28, 1923, Albert E. Smith wrote to his
brother Frank in Los Angeles: "We have bought the picture
rights to Captain Blood. Hope you have read the story, in
fact, I hope everyone connected with the California organization has read it. If not, they should all do so in the near
future, as this will be one of the most important productions
we have made."

Albert E. Smith claimed to have paid $30,000 for the
film rights to Rafael Sabatini's popular novel of swashbuckling
and piracy, a novel which Smith considered "a rip snorting,
rapid fire melodrama that will please any red blooded audience."92 (In 1923, a film version of Sabatini's Scaramouche
had proved a huge success for its stars, Alice Terry and
Ramon Novarro, and its director, Rex Ingram.)

Production did not get underway until the Spring of
1924, when J. Warren Kerrigan was signed to play the title
role, and James Morrison contracted for the juvenile lead of
Jeremy Pitt. It was no wonder that Morrison should be
dubbed "the perennial juvenile" by a Los Angeles newspaper,
a title which prompted him to quit films the following year.
Smith wanted John Barrymore for the title role, but as he
was unavailable, Smith was forced to sign Kerrigan, whom
he considered "a little too effeminate for the role."

The most expensive aspect of the production was the
purchase of three three-masted schooners. Vitagraph tried,

*Bergman on Bergman (New York: Simon and Schuster,
1974).

without success, to hire the fleet of ships used by First
National for its production of another Sabatini story, The
Sea Hawk. Eventually, the company had to buy two ships
for $7,000, and rent a third from Charles Ray, which had
been used in the latter's production of The Courtship of
Miles Standish. Vitagraph also built a fleet of model ships,
which unfortunately are only too obvious on the screen as
being a fleet of model ships.

David Smith is credited as director of Captain Blood
but, quite clearly, Albert E. Smith was responsible for much
of the direction; during part of the production, David Smith
was in fact sick. Another Smith, Steve Jr., was the cameraman, and the script was by a Vitagraph regular, Jay Pilcher.

Captain Blood (1924) in production. David Smith is at far
right in the straw hat, and Steve Smith is at the camera.

Captain Blood premiered--as an eleven-reel feature--
at New York's Astor Theatre on September 8, 1924, and ran
there for four weeks. It was released nationwide on

September 21, 1924. The day of the premiere, J. Stuart
Blackton cabled David Smith, "On my arrival here I told you
that I intended trying to make better Vitagraph pictures than
you and if you could make them better than myself, it would
please me immensely. From all accounts you have made the
best Vitagraph production ever made and I congratulate you
and wish you every success."

    Unfortunately, others did not share Blackton's en-
thusiasm. Variety (September 10, 1924) thought the actors
gave meaningless and listless performances, commenting,
"It is more than regrettable that the acting personnel fails
to equal the staging, as Vitagraph would then have had something of which it might feel proud." Photoplay (November,
1924) noted "the sea battle in which miniatures are sunk with
awe-inspiring abandon," but went on to say, "this version,
although it is obviously handicapped by a lack of money in
production, has considerable color and vitality."

    Captain Blood, however, did make money for the
company, and it was a success. It proved that Vitagraph
could still make productions on a par with those of the new
giants of the industry, Metro, Paramount, First National,
Universal and Fox. It gave credence to Smith's yearly message to his staff: "Let every member of the Vitagraph
organization realize that this company goes into its twenty-
eighth year armed with the biggest and best pictures it has
ever made. Vitagraph has kept its pledge to exhibitors and
public. It has made clean, wholesome, action pictures with
a real entertainment punch."

Chapter 12

THE END OF AN ERA

Vitagraph entered the Twenties decade in something of a unique position. It was the oldest surviving film company in America; indeed, except for the French Pathe Company, it was the oldest extant film company in the world. It had a small roster of major stars, including Alice Calhoun, Corinne Griffith, Alice Joyce, Antonio Moreno, Jean Paige, Larry Semon and Earle Williams, under contract. The company possessed major studio complexes on the East and West Coasts, and in 1920 had added a further ten acres of land to its Hollywood studio at Talmadge Street and Prospect Avenue.

With its acquisition of Kalem in 1919, Vitagraph now controlled a considerable number of important literary properties, including plays by Dion Boucicault, David Belasco and Charles Klein. Two plays by Klein, The Third Degree and The Lion and the Mouse, proved important productions for Warner Brothers in the late Twenties. David Belasco's The Heart of Maryland was the basis for an important Vitagraph production of 1921, directed by Tom Terriss and featuring Catherine Calvert, Crane Wilbur and Ben Lyon. (It was remade by Warner Brothers in 1927.) Most of the Kalem films acquired by Vitagraph had little commercial value, but the Company did reissue Kalem's best-known feature, From the Manger to the Cross, with a fair amount of success.

The Vitagraph Company's distribution set-up with exchanges throughout the United States, was without equal among releasing organizations. In the summer of 1919, Vitagraph had purchased outright the Ruffell's system of film exchanges in the North of England, one of the oldest established exchange systems in Europe, which virtually controlled film distribution to 800 theatres in England. Vitagraph,

of course, still had its large Paris office, which distributed
Vitagraph releases not only throughout Europe but also
throughout Latin America.

Between 1921 and 1925, Vitagraph released ninety-
five features, a sizable number but still considerably less
than the other major studios, Metro, Paramount, Fox and
Universal. With Albert E. Smith keeping tight financial
control, production costs were low. Vitagraph's operating
expenses for January through March, 1921 were $505,000;
for the same period in 1922 the figure was $487,000.
Vitagraph production was headed by two directors, David
Smith and J. Stuart Blackton, both of whom maintained semi-
independent production units within the company, and both of
whom operated out of the West Coast studios.

Smith directed four important features for Vitagraph:
The Little Minister (1922) with Alice Calhoun and James
Morrison; My Wild Irish Rose (1922) with Pat O'Malley and
Pauline Starke; Masters of Men (1923) with Earle Williams,
Alice Calhoun and Cullen Landis; and Pampered Youth (1925)
with Cullen Landis and Alice Calhoun. The last was the
first screen version of Booth Tarkington's novel, The Mag-
nificent Ambersons, and some historians--in my opinion mis-
takenly--have claimed that it influenced Orson Welles in his
1942 production of the story.

J. Stuart Blackton directed nine features for Vitagraph
in the Twenties, plus one film produced for Vitagraph, but
released by Warner Brothers. He had returned to the Company by 1923, as an equal partner with Smith again, but
occupying the position of Vice-President. Blackton's first
film after his return to Vitagraph was On the Banks of the
Wabash, released in October of 1923 and starring Mary Carr,
Burr McIntosh and James Morrison.

In 1924, Blackton directed Let No Man Put Asunder,
Between Friends, Behold This Woman, The Clean Heart and
The Beloved Brute. The Clean Heart, released on October
26, and adapted from A. S. M. Hutchinson's novel by
Marian Blackton, featured Percy Marmont, Marguerite de la
Motte and Otis Harlan. It was one of Blackton's best films,
as his daughter recalls: "A few changes were made as the
book was much too lengthy to film in its entirety, but we
kept, always, the spirit of the story, the power of love, and
how Wriford [Percy Marmont] was finally forced to accept
it. It was really a sensitive and lovely picture. All the

J. Stuart Blackton and Patsy Ruth Miller study the script of
<u>Hell-Bent for Heaven</u> (1926).

seaside sequences were photographed at La Jolla. We used
this section of coast for several pictures, among them The
Beloved Brute, much of which was done in the famous Torrey
Pines section, overlooking the ocean, where we built a charming cottage later for the filming of an unusual story based on
a book called In the Garden of Charity. The New York office
screamed for a sensational title, and one evening, on loca-
tion, we were dining in a group and I recall saying sarcas-
tically, 'If they want something sensational, we ought to give
them, oh, something like Tides of Passion.' The story was
passed on, and to my horror, and my father's disgust, they
insisted upon using that ghastly title. But it was a good film
and the critics were most enthusiastic in their praise all
over the country. Of course, The Clean Heart got one of
the greatest unanimous receptions from the press of almost
any film made up to that time. Our clipping service did not
turn up with a single poor review. Even Louella Parsons,
who consistently panned all Vitagraph films, gave it a splendid review, albeit a sloppily sentimental one. "

Tides of Passion, starring Mae Marsh and Ben Hen-
dricks, was not released until April 26, 1925. It was pre-
ceded by The Redeeming Sin, also scripted by Marian Blackton, and featuring Nazimova, Lou Tellegen and Otis Harlan.
Of Nazimova, Marian paints a somewhat out-of-character
picture: "A gem to know, easy to direct, one of the least
troublesome, most lovely stars. If only The Redeeming Sin
had been a greater story--I did my best with the script. It
was almost a really fine movie. "

Blackton's last two films for Vitagraph were The
Happy Warrior, released on July 5, 1925, and Bride of the
Storm. The latter, featuring Dolores Costello, was re-
leased by Warner Brothers on February 20, 1926.

Albert E. Smith worked long and hard for the Company. He leased his New York home to Laurette Taylor and
her husband, and operated out of his Oyster Bay residence.
Each day he would leave at eight in the morning, and on the
two-hour, chauffeur-driven ride to the Brooklyn studios would
read proposed and accepted scripts. He would remain at the
studio until six in the evening, closely supervising production
in person at Brooklyn, and through detailed telegrams and
letters to his brother, W. S. Smith, manager of the Western
Vitagraph. Each winter, Albert E. Smith, with family, would
journey out to Los Angeles, to personally supervise production
there.

In the 'teens, Albert E. Smith had faced many problems, particularly of a financial nature. In the Twenties he faced only one problem, but it was a major one--a deliberate attempt by a competitor, Paramount, to force Vitagraph out of business. It was Paramount which released a version of The Little Minister only a month prior to Vitagraph's release of their version of the J. M. Barrie story. Vitagraph owned the rights to the novel, but had neglected to tie up the rights to the play, a fact which any unscrupulous competitor could, and did, seize upon. The Paramount version, directed by Penrhyn Stanlaws and starring Betty Compson and George Hackathorne, may have been the better of the two versions, but that was not the point. Paramount was quite clearly guilty of unfair competition.

Not since the days of the Vitagraph Theatre had the Company considered going into the business of owning theatres, and thus ensuring an outlet for their product. Now, Vitagraph found itself in the position of having theatres closed to it. Paramount and other companies with more films, bigger stars and bigger productions could easily persuade theatre owners to block-book their features and ignore those of Vitagraph, particularly when their rental terms were lower than Vitagraph could possibly hope to offer. Albert E. Smith saw no alternative but to file an anti-trust suit against his competitors. Will Hays, on behalf of the Motion Picture Producers and Distributors Association, tried to persuade Smith to withdraw the suit, but he refused, and on January 29, 1925, Vitagraph severed its connections with the Association.

It was obvious to Smith that if Vitagraph was to survive, it would have to become involved in the exhibition side of motion pictures, and start a theatre chain. The alternative was to dispose of the Company. The choice was made not by Smith but by his doctors, who warned him of failing health and advised immediate retirement.

The total estimated value of the Vitagraph Company in 1925 was $4,200,000. The Company's indebtedness to the Guaranty Trust Company ended on Friday, March 13, 1925, with the payment of a check for $43,000. Vitagraph now belonged solely to Albert E. Smith, J. Stuart Blackton, and "Pop" Rock's son, John.

One of the groups which had been interested in Vitagraph for some time was Warner Brothers, an expanding

production company which lacked a solid distribution set-up.
Early in 1924 there had been talks between the Warners and
Smith, but nothing had materialized, and on April 30, 1924,
Smith wrote to a New York employee of Vitagraph, "I do not
think we have much chance of working anything out in common with any of our Hebraic brethren." Smith's letter reveals a typical attitude among the early film pioneers towards
the Jews, who from 1912 onwards had begun to take over the
film industry.

In February of 1925, Sidney Cohen, ex-president of
the Theatre Owners Association of America, offered to buy
the distribution end of Vitagraph and to make a five-year
contract to produce twenty special features. John Rock urged
Smith, in a letter, to accept the offer as "our only salvation."

On January 25, 1925, Ronald Reader wrote to Albert
E. Smith from Paris, "I am willing personally to help Vitagraph, and could let you have 30,000 francs of my own
money if that would help you.... Don't bother about me, I
owe a lot to you as you have always been a good friend and
I must thank you for being as well off as I am."

Smith did not accept the offers from either Cohen or
Reader. Instead, he resumed discussions with Warner
Brothers. As Mrs. Smith recalled for me, "This was just
before Ronald, my youngest son, was born, so Mr. Smith
had to go back to New York alone, and while he was there--
he was gone about six weeks--Harry Warner called him and
wanted to know if he would sell. And Mr. Smith said, well,
he would not sell a part of it but he would sell the whole
thing. So Harry Warner came over to the hotel, and they
sat up the entire night, and worked the whole thing out that
night."

On April 20, 1925, an agreement was signed whereby
Warner Brothers purchased Vitagraph in its entirety for
$735,000. In the New York Times, Harry Warner was
quoted: "Hitherto we have lacked personal touch with the
exhibitors. Now we are taking over Vitagraph to distribute
our future product throughout the world by means of its
branches. We will go ahead with the work Vitagraph has
planned for this year, finishing their productions, taking over
their contracts and players."[79]

Albert E. Smith cabled to the Vitagraph staff on the
West Coast on April 22, 1925: "We have sold control of

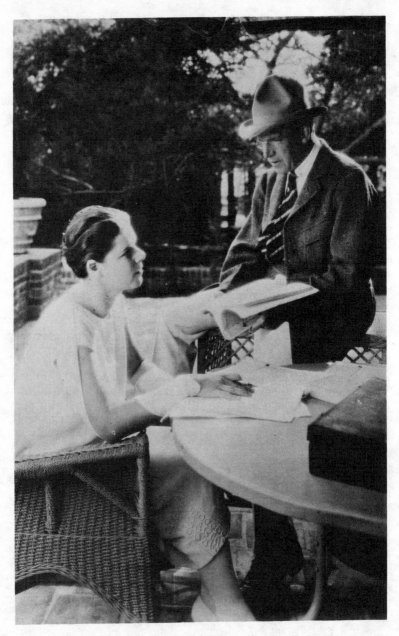

J. Stuart Blackton and his daughter Marian in the Twenties.

Vitagraph to Warner Bros.   Albert Warner is president.   I
remain as Chairman of the Board.   Everything will continue
as formerly.   I hope everyone will cooperate with the new
management as they did with me for success.   Will arrive
Monday.   Jack Warner will be glad to help you in any way."
On April 27, J. Stuart Blackton resigned as Vice-President.

It was all over.   After twenty-nine years of existence
the Vitagraph Company was no more.   A sizable portion of
film history was ended.   John Bunny, Flora Finch, Florence
Turner, Maurice Costello, The Battle Cry of Peace, Princess
Nicotine--they all became part of the past.   It was, perhaps,
fitting that Vitagraph should be taken over by Warner
Brothers, a company which was to be the pioneer in sound
motion pictures, and that the Vitagraph studios in Brooklyn
should become the home of the first talkies.   J. Stuart
Blackton summed up Vitagraph's contribution to film history:
"Biograph has been called 'the cradle of the movies.'   If
that is so, Vitagraph was certainly the movie nursery and
kindergarten.   Its list of debutantes and juveniles, its array
of directors, writers and technical men are today--on the
one hand, stars; on the other, leaders in film construction
and creation.   A few of Vitagraph's pioneers are dead, and
perhaps an equal number have retired, but a greater number
are in this hour kings and queens of the great international
art in which America leads the world."[9]

Most of the Vitagraph staff were pleased with the
sale; their positions and futures seemed secure.   The three
partners, Smith, Blackton and Rock, split equally the profits
from the sale.   Yet there must have been many who shared
George Smith's sentiments when he cabled his brother,
Albert, from Vitagraph's London office, "Seventh May and
still raining.   Guess the skies are weeping at the passing of
the Olde Pioneers of Vitagraph."

BIBLIOGRAPHY

1. Agnew, Frances. _Motion Picture Acting._ New York: Reliance Newspaper Syndicate, 1913.

2. Anderson, Mary. "How I Got In," _Motion Picture Magazine_ (December, 1917).

3. "The Art of John Bunny," _The Bioscope_ (May 6, 1915).

4. Bartlett, Randolph. "Dorothy Kelly Her Own Columbus," _Photoplay_ (January, 1916).

5. _____. "Madonna of the Movies," _Photoplay_ (March, 1916).

6. Blackton, J. Stuart. _The Battle Cry of Peace: A Call to Arms against War._ New York: The Motion Picture Publishing Company, 1915.

7. _____. "Awake America!" _The Theatre_ (September, 1915).

8. _____. "A Glimpse into the Past," _The Moving Picture World_ (March 10, 1917).

9. _____. "Yesteryears of Vitagraph," _Photoplay_ (July, 1919).

10. _____. "Winding Backwards with J. Stuart Blackton," _The Director_ (July, 1924-December, 1924).

11. _____. "The Movies Are Growing Up," _Motion Picture Magazine_ (February, 1925).

12. _____. "Theodore Roosevelt, Police Commissioner to Bull Moose." Unpublished manuscript in the

Library of the Academy of Motion Picture Arts
and Sciences.

13. _____. Untitled and unpublished manuscript in the
Library of the Academy of Motion Picture Arts
and Sciences.

14. "Blackton to Produce for Paramount," Paramount
Progress (July 26, 1917).

15. Blaisdell, George. "Making Screen's Initial Feature--
in Miniature," Exhibitor's Trade Review (December 15, 1923).

16. Bodeen, DeWitt. "Wallace Reid," Films in Review
(April, 1966).

17. Botsford, A. M. "Camera, Brush and Pencil," Photo-
Play Journal (November, 1918).

18. Brodie, Allan Douglas. "Mrs. Mary Maurice, 'The
Sweet Mother of the Movies,'" Motion Picture
Supplement (October, 1915).

19. Brownlow, Kevin. The Parade's Gone By. New York:
Alfred A. Knopf, 1968.

20. Bunny, John. Bunnyisms. New York: Kraus Manu-
facturing Company, 1914.

21. _____. "How It Feels To Be a Comedian," Photoplay (October, 1914).

22. Burness, Jessie Niles. "Albert E. Smith--Torch
Bearer," Film Fun (August, 1920).

23. "Captains of the Industry: Albert E. Smith," Exhibitor's
Trade Review (April 7, 1917).

24. "Captains of the Industry: Walter W. Irwin," Exhibitor's Trade Review (July 21, 1917).

25. "A Close Up of Blackton and His Studios," The New
York Dramatic Mirror (August 14, 1919).

26. Courtney, William Basil. "History of Vitagraph,"
Motion Picture News (February 7, 1925-April 11,
1925).

27.   Craig, Marion. "Frapped in Flatbush," Motion Picture
      Magazine (January, 1919).

28.   Crocombe, Leonard. "The Girl of the Film: Florence
      Turner," Pictures and the Picturegoer (June 6,
      1914).

29.   Dale, Alan. "Great Reels at New Vitagraph," New
      York American (February 8, 1914).

30.   Darnton, Charles. "The Battle Cry of Peace," The
      Evening World (September 10, 1915).

31.   Davis, Henry R., Jr. "Clara Kimball Young," Films
      in Review (August-September, 1961).

32.   "Death of William T. Rock, Pioneer Picture Man,"
      The Moving Picture World (August 12, 1916).

33.   Denig, Lynde. "Larry Trimble Brings Turner Films,"
      The Moving Picture World (August 19, 1916).

34.   Douglas, Harvey. "Brooklyn Was Cradle of Film
      Industry," Brooklyn Daily Eagle (February 15,
      1933).

35.   _____. "Movie Exhibitors Once Doubled in Brass,"
      Brooklyn Daily Eagle (February 16, 1933).

36.   _____. "Movie Stars Got Start on Flatbush Lots,"
      Brooklyn Daily Eagle (February 17, 1933).

37.   _____. "Cost $400 to Turn out a Movie in 1911,"
      Brooklyn Daily Eagle (February 20, 1933).

38.   _____. "Movie Stock Stars of 1907 Got $30 Per
      Week," Brooklyn Daily Eagle (February 21, 1933).

39.   _____. "Brooklyn Was Eldorado for Movie Pioneers,"
      Brooklyn Daily Eagle (February 22, 1933).

40.   Dunham, Harold. "John Bunny," The Silent Picture
      (Winter, 1968).

41.   Ennis, Bert. "Then Were the Happy Days," Motion
      Picture Classic (October, 1926).

42. Fairservis, Walter Ashlin. "The Battle Cry of Peace,"
    Photoplay Vogue (September 5, 1915).

43. Finch, Flora. "Close-Ups of Cut Backs," Motion
    Picture Magazine (February, 1925).

44. Fletcher, Adele Whitely. "Sick-a-Bed Lady," Motion
    Picture Magazine (April-May, 1920).

45. Flynn, Hazel. "Bill Earle's Step Still Firm at 80,"
    Los Angeles Citizen News (February 13, 1963).

46. Gardette, L. "Some Tricks of the Moving Picture
    Maker," The Nickelodeon (August, 1909).

47. Gates, Harvey H. "Florence Turner Talks about
    Acting," The New York Dramatic Mirror (October
    30, 1912).

48. Gill, Sam. "John Bunny Checklist," The Silent Picture
    (Summer, 1972).

49. _____. "John Bunny: America's First Comedy Star
    in Moving Pictures." Unpublished Manuscript.

50. Glover, Katherine. "Vitagraph Plays Serious Part in
    Business, Educational and Scientific World,"
    Brooklyn Daily Eagle (September 9, 1906).

51. Grau, Robert. The Theatre of Science. New York:
    Broadway Publishing Company, 1914.

52. _____. "Old Timers of the Stage," Moving Picture
    Stories (July 7, 1916).

53. Hampton, Benjamin B. A History of the Movies. New
    York: Covici Friede, 1931.

54. Hoffman, Hugh. "Florence Turner Comes Back," The
    Moving Picture World (May 18, 1912).

55. _____. "John Bunny Abroad," The Moving Picture
    World (September 21, 1912).

56. _____. "Florence Turner Going to England," The
    Moving Picture World (September 21, 1912).

57. How and Why Moving Pictures are Made. New York:
    Vitagraph Company, undated.

58. "An Interview with J. Stuart Blackton, " The Moving
    Picture World (December 19, 1908).

59. "Interviews with Manufacturers, " The Moving Picture
    World (February 8, 1908).

60. "J. Stuart Blackton, Producing Genius, " Moving Picture
    Stories (April 6, 1917).

61. James, Arthur. "Drawing Straws with the Interesting
    Sidney Drews, " Photo-Play Journal (March,
    1917).

62. "Jimmy Morrison, Versatile Vitagrapher, " The Moving
    Picture World (May 6, 1916).

63. "Julia Swayne Gordon, Vitagraph Woman of Moods, "
    The Moving Picture World (July 11, 1914).

64. Kitchen, Karl C. "Running the Art Business, " Photo-
    play (December, 1915).

65. Kruh, Regina B. "Jean Paige Tells Us What She Loves
    Best, " Photo-Play Journal (February, 1919).

66. La Roche, Edwin M. "The Battle Cry of Peace, "
    Motion Picture Magazine (October, 1915).

67. Lachmund, Marjorie Gleyre. "The One and Only
    Dorothy Kelly, " Motion Picture Magazine (June,
    1917).

68. Lawrence, Florence. "Tom Likes 'Heroics' on Stage, "
    Los Angeles Examiner (February 19, 1933).

69. "Miss Florence E. Turner: The Vitagraph Girl, " The
    Moving Picture World (July 23, 1910).

70. "Mr. Albert E. Smith, the Popular Lyceum Prestidigi-
    tateur, " Mahatma (February, 1899).

71. Moen, L. C. "Florence Turner Returns to America, "
    Motion Picture News (May 24, 1924).

72. "A New Belasco," Blue Book (June, 1914).

73. A New Era in Vitagraph. Brooklyn: Vitagraph Com-
         pany, 1918.

74. Ogilvie, Jack W. "A Tribute to Frank Lawrence,"
         The Cinemeditor (July, 1960).

75. Orman, Felix. The Pioneer of the Photoplay. Pri-
         vately published, undated.

76. Patterson, Ada. "Blackton Measures Upward Career
         by Landings," The New York Dramatic Mirror
         (November 17, 1918).

77. Peltret, Elizabeth. "The Return of Florence Turner,"
         Motion Picture Classic (February, 1919).

78. "Picture Personalities: Miss Florence E. Turner,"
         The Moving Picture World (July 23, 1910).

79. "Pioneer Vitagraph Sold to Warner," The New York
         Times (April 23, 1925).

80. Pollock, Arthur. "James Morrison on the Tricks of
         the Screen Actor's Trade," Motion Picture Maga-
         zine (November, 1916).

81. Ramsaye, Terry. A Million and One Nights. New
         York: Simon and Schuster, 1926.

82. Reel, Oren Clayton. The Life of Earle Williams.
         New York: The Shakespeare Press, 1915.

83. Richardson, F. H. "The Home of the Vitagraph,"
         The Moving Picture World (January 24, 1914).

84. "Rock, Smith and Blackton Were Pioneer Exhibitors,"
         The Moving Picture World (July 15, 1916).

85. Sargent, Epes Winthrop. "New York Holds Record for
         Earliest Exhibiting," The Moving Picture World
         (July 15, 1916).

86. Schaefer, Fred. "A Reel Battle Is Perilously Similar
         to a Real One," Photo-Play Journal (July, 1917).

87. "Scope of the V-L-S-E," The Moving Picture World
     (May 1, 1915).

88. Shea, William. "Barnstorming in the Movies," Moving
     Picture Stories (November 2, 1917).

89. _____. "Twelve Years in One Studio--a Record,"
     The Moving Picture World (March 10, 1917).

90. Slide, Anthony. Early American Cinema. New York:
     A. S. Barnes, 1970.

91. Smith, Albert E. "Screen Test Set for Photoplay's
     Ibsen," The Moving Picture World (February 1,
     1919).

92. _____ and Phil A. Koury. Two Reels and a Crank.
     New York: Doubleday, 1952.

93. _____ and Phil A. Koury. "Two Reels and a Crank."
     Unedited manuscript in the possession of Mrs.
     Smith.

94. Smith, Frederick James. "The Evolution of the Motion
     Picture," The New York Dramatic Mirror (April
     23, 1913).

95. _____. "The Story of Edith Storey," Photoplay
     (September, 1917).

96. _____. "Seeking the Germ," Photoplay (September,
     1917).

97. Spears, Jack. "Norma Talmadge," Films in Review
     (January, 1967).

98. "The Story of the Film--a Faversham Pioneer,"
     Faversham and North East Kent News (March 8,
     1924).

99. T. B. "Vitagraphica: A Brooklyn Reverie," Exhibi-
     tors' Times (September 13, 1913).

100. Turner, Florence. "Putting 'Move' into 'Movie,'"
     Motion Picture Studio (April 15, 1922).

101. "The Vitagraph Company Is About to Make Some
        Changes in the Personnel of Its Executives,"
        Variety (July 6, 1917).

102. "Vitagraph Studio in Flatbush, a Cradle of Movies, Is
        Closing," The New York Times (August 31, 1957).

103. "Vitagraph's History Is History of World's Greatest
        Industry," Exhibitor's Herald (December 29, 1923).

104. Wagenknecht, Edward. The Movies in the Age of In-
        nocence. Norman: University of Oklahoma
        Press, 1962.

105. White, Rex Grover. "The Last Interview," Motion
        Picture Magazine (July, 1919).

106. Who's Who in V-L-S-E Plays. New York: V-L-S-E,
        undated.

107. "The World's Loss," Punch (May 12, 1915).

A VITAGRAPH WHO'S WHO

The following biographies are devoted to fifty of the most prominent members of the Vitagraph Company. Persons whose careers are covered in the text are not included here.

MARY ANDERSON. Born Brooklyn, June 28, 1897.
An actress who made her screen debut with Vitagraph, circa 1913, at the suggestion of her friend, Anita Stewart. Her films during the five years she spent with the company, as an ingenue, include: Father's Flirtation (1914), A Train of Incidents (1914), The Old Maid's Baby (1914), Buddy's Downfall (1914), Buddy's First Call (1914), Cal Marvin's Wife (1915), Getting Rid of Aunt Kate (1915), The Hoyden (1916), and My Official Wife (1916). Retired from the screen in 1923.

LEAH BAIRD. Born Chicago, June 20, 1887. Died Los Angeles, October 3, 1971.
After a brief stage career, joined Vitagraph as a leading lady in November of 1911, making her screen debut in Chumps, playing opposite Marshall P. Wilder. Joined Universal in June of 1913, but returned to Vitagraph in 1915, only to rejoin Universal in September of 1916. Appeared in several important Universal releases, including Ivanhoe (1913), Absinthe (1913) and Neptune's Daughter (1914); she also starred in the first Universal three-reeler, Leah the Forsaken. As The Moving Picture Weekly (September 30, 1916) noted, "Her French type of beauty, wonderful liquid eyes, and lovely smile, showing a remarkable set of 'dining-room' furniture, lost nothing on the screen." Remained active in films throughout the silent era.

GEORGE D. BAKER. Born Champaign, Illinois. Died
   Hollywood, June 2, 1933.
       Extensive stage career as actor and director, plus
newspaper work as cartoonist and writer. Joined Vitagraph
as a director in 1913; his first film probably being The
Pickpocket, starring John Bunny. Baker directed Bunny in
all but four of his films from then on, a total of 39 productions. When Bunny left Vitagraph to return to the stage,
Baker tried to introduce Jay Dwiggins as the new John Bunny,
beginning with The Rocky Road of Love, released on November 13, 1914, but failed. In July of 1915, Baker joined
Metro as Viola Dana's director. He continued to direct
until 1924.

MARGUERITE BERTSCH. Born New York City, December
   14, 1889. Date and place of death unknown.
       Brief career as a playwright, before joining Vitagraph
as scenarist circa 1913. Among the films she wrote are:
The Wreck (1913), Captain Alvarez (1914), A Million Bid
(1914), and My Official Wife (1916). Co-directed, with
William P. S. Earle, The Law Decides, released on May 1,
1916. First film as solo director, The Devil's Prize, released on November 6, 1916. She was the subject of article,
"A Charming Directress," in Moving Picture Stories (November 24, 1916), and author of How to Write for Moving Pictures, published by George H. Doran in 1917. Screen career
appears to end in 1918.

CYRUS TOWNSEND BRADY. Born Pittsburgh, 1861. Died
   Yonkers, N.Y., January 24, 1920.
       The author of more than one hundred books, including
For Love of Country and For Freedom of the Seas. Dr.
Brady was an Episcopalian minister who wrote many scenar-
ios for Vitagraph from 1914 onwards, including The Little
Angel of Canyon Creek (1914), The Chalice of Courage (1915),
The Hero of Submarine D-2 (1916), and By the World Forgot
(1918). Also scripted many serials, including The Fighting
Trail (1917), Vengeance and the Woman (1917), A Fight for
Millions (1918) and The Perils of Thunder Mountain (1919).
His brother, Colonel Jasper Ewing Brady, also scripted a
number of films for Vitagraph, and at the time of Cyrus'
death was under contract to Metro.

MRS. BETA BREUIL. Date and place of birth and death unknown.

The first head of Vitagraph's scenario department. Nothing is known or has been written about Mrs. Breuil except for the following news item from The Moving Picture World of January 15, 1916: "Mrs. Beta Breuil, the woman who organized and brought to a point of great efficiency the scenario department of the Vitagraph Company of America, has been engaged by the Mirror Films, Inc., to do special work on several feature pictures which the Mirror management has in mind for the coming year. Mrs. Breuil, after much travel throughout the world, had been thrown on her own resources at an age past thirty and had tried the stage before she sought and got the position of scenario writer for the Vitagraph Company. From that she rose to the position of editor and headed the department which she organized herself. Some time ago she left the Vitagraph Company, vowing that she would not again undertake such a position as editor of any company. Until she was approached by the Mirror, Mrs. Breuil did free lance writing of scenarios or writing to order."

VAN DYKE BROOKE. Born Detroit, 1859. Died Saratoga Springs, N.Y., September 17, 1921.
      Joined Vitagraph in 1909 after a lengthy stage career. Brooke acted in, directed and wrote many Vitagraph productions, and was a respected member of the company until he was dismissed, along with many other old-timers, in August of 1916. Continued as an actor in films until his death.

ALICE CALHOUN. Born Cleveland, Ohio. Died Los Angeles, June 3, 1966.
      Joined Vitagraph in the late 'teens after working with a number of other companies. In October of 1920, Albert E. Smith announced that she was to be elevated to stardom, and from then until 1925 she was featured in more than twenty Vitagraph releases, including The Charming Deceiver (1921), The Little Minister (1922), Makers of Men (1923), Between Friends (1924) and Pampered Youth (1925). She continued to appear in films until 1932.

KENNETH CASEY. Born New York City, 1899. Died Cornwall, N.Y., August 10, 1965.
      Child actor who made screen debut with Vitagraph in 1909. In 1913 went to England to appear in vaudeville, and after a successful tour returned to the U.S. in November of

1914. He made his American stage debut, billed as "The
Vitagraph Boy," in February of 1915. Variety (March 5,
1915) commented, "The boy is possessed of marked musical
ability, playing the piano, cornet and violin, all well. Good
Scotch jokes are used and also an English coster song."
Returned briefly to the screen in 1917, working for Metro.
In later years became a songwriter, whose works include
"You'll Find a Bit of Gay Paree in Dear Old Montreal,"
"The President Eisenhower March," and "Sweet Georgia
Brown."

GEORGE RANDOLPH CHESTER. Date and place of birth
    and death unknown.
        In February of 1916 became editor-in-chief of Vita-
graph's scenario department. Scripted a number of Vitagraph features, sometimes in conjunction with his wife. In
1921 co-directed, with Mrs. Chester, The Son of Wallingford.
To Universal in 1922. Active in film industry until 1927.

MAURICE COSTELLO. Born Pittsburgh, February 22, 1877.
    Died Hollywood, California, October 28, 1950.
        After eighteen years on the legitimate stage and in
vaudeville, Costello joined Vitagraph in 1907, to become the
company's first major star. He remained with Vitagraph
until December of 1915, appearing in dozens and dozens of
films, the most famous being A Tale of Two Cities (1911).
From 1911 onwards, also directed many Vitagraph shorts,
usually featuring himself: His Wife's Secret (1911, with
Van Dyke Brooke), Cupid versus Women's Rights (1913), The
Adventures of the Counterfeit Bills (1913), What a Change of
Clothes Did (1913), Getting a Practice (1913, with William
V. Ranous), The Perplexed Bridegroom (1914), The Woman
in Black (1914, with Robert Gaillord), The Man Who Couldn't
Beat God (1915, with Robert Gaillord), etc. On December 7,
1912, Costello, with his family, embarked on a six-month
tour of the world, making films en route. In the early 'teens,
a theatre at 159 Street and Broadway, New York City, was
named after him. Costello continued to act in films until the
early Forties, but from the Twenties onwards appeared in
supporting roles and eventually was reduced to working as an
extra. From 1946 until his death he was a resident of the
Motion Picture Country House. In 1902, Costello married
his first wife, Mae, by whom he had two daughters, Dolores
and Helene, both of whom appeared, as children, in Vitagraph
productions. The couple were divorced in 1927, and in 1939

Costello married Ruth Reeves, but they were divorced in
1941. An article on Costello in The Moving Picture World
of December 17, 1910 commented, "People call him 'Dimples' in recognition of his good nature. Mr. Costello is
still fortunately a very young man, and he has a handsome
stage presence, and is a finished and experienced actor; he
probably has before him, and we at any rate hope and believe that he has, many years of successful work in the
picture drama."

WILLIAM P. S. EARLE. Born New York City, 1884. Died
        Los Angeles, 1973.
        One of Vitagraph's most important directors during
the 'teens. The first film which Earle both directed and
wrote was For the Honor of the Crew, released on November 9, 1915. At Vitagraph, Earle also directed Within the
Law, Womanhood, the Glory of a Nation, His Own People and
Who Goes There (all 1917), etc. It was Earle's boast that
he invented back-lighting and the use of stand-in dummies to
replace the leading players while the set was being lit. In
1918, Earle left Vitagraph to join Selznick as Clara Kimball
Young's director. He retired in 1923; lost all his savings
in the Wall Street crash, and in the Thirties was selling
vacuum cleaners from door to door. He worked with J.
Stuart Blackton on The Film Parade in the Thirties, and
after Blackton's death married his widow, Evangeline. (For
more information, see Chapter 2). Ferdinand Pinney Earle,
the artist and sometime film director, was his brother.

FLORA FINCH. Born England, 1869. Died Hollywood,
        January 4, 1940.
        Many years on the stage before making her screen
debut with the Biograph Company in 1909. Joined Vitagraph
circa 1910, and achieved screen immortality as John Bunny's
thin, spinsterish partner in countless Vitagraph one-reel
comedies. The pair first appeared together in The New
Stenographer, released on February 19, 1911. Left Vitagraph in March of 1916, and began the long fade-out with a
series of comedies opposite Nat Goodwin, produced by Mirror
Films. She was able to obtain reasonable supporting roles
during the Twenties, but by the Thirties Miss Finch was
working as an extra at M-G-M. In 1925 she reminisced,
"Many of the old stars are now no longer heard from. Some
have died but more have simply dropped out. Those who
have remained are among the leading actresses and actors in

the world and their success is, I feel, due in no small degree to the talent of Mr. Griffith. He discovered many hidden talents.... My own talents lay in comedy, for which no
doubt my physical appearance has fitted me. Although I am
about five and a half feet tall, I weigh only one hundred
pounds, and from the start I have been in comedy. Some
have said that I played in custard-pie comedies, but that is
not true. I have never in all my days had a pie thrown at
me, and that in itself is a distinction few actors in old
comedies can claim. "

HELEN GARDNER. Date and place of birth unknown. Died
    Florida, November 20, 1968.
        After attending the American Academy of Dramatic
Arts, was persuaded by James Morrison to join Vitagraph in
1911. That year, she gave a widely-praised performance as
Becky Sharp in Vanity Fair. The Moving Picture World
(December 16, 1911) commented, "We might ramble on for
hours in ecstasies over the superb work of Miss Gardner
and at the end of that time have given but a faint idea of
what we saw her do. " In June of 1912, Helen Gardner announced she was forming her own company to produce a
series of five-reel features, under the direction of her husband, Charles Gaskill (born 1869, died Los Angeles, December 9, 1943). The most famous of Miss Gardner's independent features was Cleopatra. In 1915 she returned to
Vitagraph, appearing, under her husband's direction, in The
Still Small Voice and Miss Jekyll and Madame Hyde, among
others. The latter, a three-part Broadway Star feature,
told how "a woman's Better Self unconsciously dominated by
Her Worse Self, leads men to ruin. " Shortly thereafter,
Helen Gardner retired from the screen, although she does
appear to have returned to films briefly in the early Twenties.

JULIA SWAYNE GORDON. Born Columbus, Ohio, October
    29, 1881. Died Hollywood, May 28, 1933.
        After a lengthy career on stage and in vaudeville, and
a brief spell with the Edison Company, Julia Swayne Gordon
joined Vitagraph circa 1909, at the persuasion of William V.
Ranous. "Judy" was a great favorite with her fellow actors
and the public. The Moving Picture World (July 11, 1914)
noted, "Miss Gordon's popularity is of the kind which must
taste particularly sweet to those players who are permitted
to enjoy it. So long has she been doing excellent work that

those who know her and note her first appearance on the
screen settle back comfortably with the feeling that the role
she is handling will be well interpreted no matter what else
happens." One of Julia Swayne Gordon's first important
parts was as Julia Ward Howe in The Battle Hymn of the
Republic, released on June 30, 1911. She left Vitagraph in
1918, but continued to be active in films almost until her
death. Miss Gordon gives a particularly moving performance as Richard Arlen's mother in Wings (1929).

ALFRED HOWARD HERMAN. Born Brooklyn, New York,
    September 6, 1889. Date and place of death unknown.
        Art director at Vitagraph's Brooklyn studios from
1910 until America's entry into the First World War, at
which time he was drafted. In September of 1919, appointed
art director at Vitagraph's West Coast studios. Active in
film industry until the late Forties. Not to be confused with
Al Herman, the director.

GLADYS HULETTE. Born Arcade, New York, July 21,
    1896.
        Gladys Hulette worked at many early film companies,
including Biograph, Edison and Thanhouser. Her most famous Vitagraph appearance was the title role in Princess
Nicotine (1909), but she also appeared in a number of other
Vitagraph productions in the 'teens. Hulette is best remembered for her performance opposite Richard Barthelmess
in Tol'able David (1921). Her brother Frank, along with
"Clay" Davis and Frank Heath, was an assistant director with
Vitagraph for many years.

WILLIAM J. HUMPHREY. Born Chicopee Falls, Mass.,
    January 2, 1874. Died Hollywood, October 4, 1942.
        Lengthy stage career before joining Vitagraph as an
actor and director in 1910. James Morrison recalls,
"Humphrey couldn't play a scene without trying to direct
it." Although Charles Kent is generally credited with the
direction of A Tale of Two Cities (1911), it is possible that
Humphrey was at least co-director, if not solo director.
He was a memorable Napoleon in Incidents in the Life of
Napoleon and Josephine (1909). In January of 1917, Humphrey left Vitagraph to join Ivan Productions as a director. He
soon returned to acting, and became a competent character
player in the Twenties.

RALPH INCE. Born Boston, January 16, 1887. Died
    London, England, April 10, 1937.
        Brother of Thomas H. Ince. Stage career before
joining Vitagraph as a prop boy in 1907. Later graduated
to actor and director. He was famous for his characteriza-
tions of Abraham Lincoln. Important Vitagraph productions
directed by Ince include A Million Bid (1913) and The Juggernaut (1915). Directed all the films of his sister-in-law,
Anita Stewart, from 1912 through 1916. Ince was married
to the minor Vitagraph actress, Lucille Lee Stewart. He
left the company in November of 1916, to become an independent producer, and remained active in films until his
death.

REX INGRAM. Born Dublin, Ireland, March 24, 1892.
    Died Hollywood, July 21, 1950.
        Prominent American silent film director--The Four
Horsemen of the Apocalypse, Scaramouche, Mare Nostrum,
etc.--who in his formative years worked at Vitagraph as an
actor, under his real name of Rex Hitchcock. Vitagraph
films include: The Upper Hand, The Circus and the Boy,
The Evil Men Do, Eve's Daughter, Her Big Scoop, The
Spirit and the Clay, His Wedded Wife, Fine Feathers Make
Fine Birds and The Moonshine Maid and the Man (all 1914).

WALTER W. IRWIN. Born Pittsburgh. Date and place of
    death unknown.
        When V-L-S-E was incorporated in April of 1915,
Walter Irwin became its treasurer, secretary and general
manager. Prior to that he had been general counsel for
Vitagraph, and was a noted specialist in corporation law.
Irwin was forced to resign from V-L-S-E, despite the pro-
tests of Albert E. Smith, effective January 1, 1919.

ZENA KEEFE. Born San Francisco, June 26, 1896.
        Child actress who made her first public appearance
at the age of three in Palmer Cox's Brownies in Fairyland.
Worked at Vitagraph, during the summer months, from 1909
through 1916; during the winter Miss Keefe appeared in
vaudeville. Vitagraph films include The Long Shirt (1911),
The Cabin Boy (1911), Captain Jenk's Diplomacy (1912), The
Light That Failed (1912), The Autocrat of Flap Jack Junction
(1913), Hearts Ablaze (1915) and The Island of Surprise
(1916). Of her 1914 Broadway debut, Variety (December 11,

1914) wrote, "Miss Keefe is growing and improving at the same time. She's an attractive miss and handles herself well, a splendid impression on her Broadway showing." From Vitagraph, Miss Keefe went to World, Ivan and Selznick. She retired in 1924.

DOROTHY KELLY. Born Philadelphia, February 12, 1894.
    Died Minneapolis, May 31, 1966.
        Without any prior experience, joined Vitagraph as an actress circa 1911. Films include: Vanity Fair (1911), The Line-Up (1913), The Flirt (1913), Dorothy Danebridge, Militant (1914), Artie (1916) and The Maelstrom (1916). Miss Kelly was usually starred opposite James Morrison. She was an attractive, little actress, but not as talented as Edith Storey. Married nonprofessional Harvey Hevenor on August 28, 1916, and shortly thereafter retired from the screen.

CHARLES KENT. Born London, England, June 18, 1852.
    Date and place of death unknown.
        Distinguished stage career from 1875 until 1906. For more information, see interview with Kent in The New York Dramatic Mirror of January 1, 1898. Losing his voice, he joined Vitagraph in 1906, and remained with the company until the late 'teens. Kent began as an actor, but soon advanced to directing and was responsible for many of the company's first major successes, including Launcelot and Elaine and The Life of Moses (both 1909). After 1913, he ceased to direct and returned to acting. Active in films until 1923.

FRANK LAWRENCE. Born New York City, June 15, 1883.
    Died Los Angeles, circa 1960.
        Entered film industry in 1901 as a projectionist at a nickelodeon operated on 125 Street by William "Pop" Rock. In 1903, Lawrence joined the Vitagraph Company as its first film cutter. In December of 1916 he was appointed Vitagraph manager in charge of the company's negative room, cutting room, printing department, stills department, etc. In 1917, Lawrence joined Universal and became head of its editorial department. A prominent film editor, Frank Lawrence cut Hell's Angels, and was credited with originating the Tarzan yell by running the soundtrack backwards through his movieola. In 1911, Viola Mallory joined Vitagraph as an errand girl. Lawrence taught her editing, and the couple

were married in 1918.   Viola Lawrence died on November
20, 1973.

L. ROGERS LYTTON.   Born New Orleans, 1867.   Died
    August 9, 1924.
        Real name: Oscar Legare Rogers.   Veteran Vita-
graph actor and director, who joined the company pre-1910
and was let go in August of 1916.   Continued to work as an
actor in films until his death.

MARY BIRCH MAURICE.   Born Morristown, Ohio, Novem-
    ber 15, 1844.   Died Pennsylvania, May, 1918.
        Mother Maurice was known as the "Perfect Mother of
the Screen" and the "Grand Old Lady of the Films."   She
was originally a teacher, before embarking on a stage career with the Pittsburgh Stock Company in 1868.   Mrs.
Maurice joined Vitagraph in the latter part of 1910, and remained with the company almost until her death.   She played
mother to practically every Vitagraph player, and, like
James Morrison, her favorite film was The Seventh Son
(1912).

ANTONIO MORENO.   Born Madrid, Spain, September 26,
    1888.   Died Beverly Hills, California, February 15, 1967.
        To U.S.A. at the age of fourteen.   Stage career be-
fore entering films with the Vitagraph Company in 1914.   To
Pathe in 1917, but returned to Vitagraph in 1919 to star in
serials--The Perils of Thunder Mountain (1919), The Invisi-
ble Hand (1920) and The Veiled Mystery (1920)--and features
--A Guilty Conscience, The Secret of the Hills and Three
Sevens (all 1921)--until 1921.   Active in films until the mid-
Forties.

JAMES MORRISON.   Born Mattoon, Illinois, November 15,
    1888.   Died New York City, November 15, 1974.
        The perennial juvenile at Vitagraph, James Morrison
was under contract with the company from November of
1910 through 1916, and then appeared in many Vitagraph
productions on a free-lance basis.   Morrison made his
screen debut in A Tale of Two Cities; his favorite Vitagraph
films were The Seventh Son (1912) and Over the Top (1918).
When this writer first met him in November of 1970, Morrison was crippled with arthritis and living by himself in a

small Greenwich Village apartment. He had no great love
for his film career. When I remarked how marvelous it
was, he commented, "I don't think so. Most of my pictures
made me sick. I wanted to do more with them, but the material wasn't there." He left films in 1925 because "I was
fed-up with them. Everyone thought I was so old as I'd
been in films so long. A Los Angeles newspaper called me
'the perennial juvenile,' and I decided that was my exit line."
After leaving films, Morrison wrote two novels, and for
seventeen years taught speech and drama at the Parker Col-
legiate Institute in Brooklyn.

WILFRED NORTH. Born London, England, 1863. Died
        Hollywood, June 3, 1935.
        Also known as Wilfrid North. After a number of
years in the theatre, directing and managing, joined Vitagraph in late 1912 as a director. During 1913, North directed most of John Bunny's comedies. A leading director
with the company, North was well liked by both Smith and
Blackton. In 1915, under Blackton's supervision, he directed
The Battle Cry of Peace. In August of 1917, Smith appointed
North Supervising Director at Vitagraph's Brooklyn studios.
North remained with Vitagraph in that position until 1920,
when he joined Select as a director. He returned to Vitagraph in the early Twenties as its West Coast Production
Manager. In the Twenties, he also began to act in films,
at first for Vitagraph--Captain Blood (1924), The Happy Warrior (1925), etc.--and then for other companies. Remained
in films, as an actor, until the Thirties.

HARRY NORTHRUP. Born Paris, France, July 31, 1877.
        Died Los Angeles, July 2, 1936.
        Began his stage career in the 1890s with the Frawley
Stock Company in San Francisco. Screen debut with Vitagraph in 1911. Vitagraph films include: Vanity Fair (1911),
The Illumination (1912) and The Christian (1914). To Metro
in 1916. Northrup was a competent, heavy actor, at his
best in supporting roles during the Twenties.

PAUL PANZER. Born Wurtzberg, Germany, 1872. Died
        Hollywood, August 16, 1958.
        American stage career with the Augustin Daly Musical
Company, appearing in The Geisha, The Runaway Girl,

Floradora, etc. Screen debut in 1905 with the Edison
Company. Then to Vitagraph, as one of the original members of its stock company, along with Hector Dion, William
V. Ranous and G. M. Anderson. Panzer left Vitagraph
circa 1911, and was to remain active in the film industry,
usually in a very minor capacity, until the Forties.

EDWARD R. PHILLIPS. Date and place of birth unknown.
Died New York City, August 29, 1915.
After many years on the legitimate stage, Phillips
joined Vitagraph as an actor in 1905, and was one of the
original members of the Vitagraph stock company. Eventually, he became a director, but ill-health forced him to
retire from the company in 1914. Phillips claimed to have
brought John Bunny to Vitagraph, but there is no proof of
this.

TOM POWERS. Born Owensboro, Kentucky, July 7, 1890.
Died Manhattan Beach, California, November 9, 1955.
After attending the American Academy of Dramatic
Arts, joined Vitagraph as a juvenile lead in 1911, at the
suggestion of James Morrison. Remained with the company
until 1913. Shortly thereafter, he went to England, and remained there for three years, acting in films and on the
stage. May be seen at his best in The Illumination, released on April 5, 1912. Did not return to screen until
1944, when he began to appear in innumerable films, including Double Indemnity (1944), Two Years before the Mast
(1946), Up in Central Park (1948) and Julius Caesar (1953).
Powers was also the author of a number of novels, plays
and short stories. As Florence Lawrence observed, reviewing a stage play in which Powers appeared in the Thirties, "Tom Powers may well be called a versatile chap."

ARLINE PRETTY. Born Philadelphia, September 5, 1893.
After a brief stage career, Miss Pretty made her
screen debut in 1913 with a small company based in Tampa,
Florida. From there, she joined Universal, working for
King Baggot, and then in 1915 joined Vitagraph. Arline
Pretty appeared in several Vitagraph features, including The
Thirteenth Girl (1915), The Surprises of an Empty Hotel
(1916), Mrs. Warren's Brother (1916) and The Dawn of
Freedom (1916), and the serial, The Secret Kingdom (1917).
In 1915, Miss Pretty was elected Miss Brooklyn. She left

Vitagraph in 1917, and continued to work in films until the Sixties, although after the coming of sound her work was that of an extra at M-G-M. For further information, see also Chapter 10.

KATE PRICE. Born Cork, Ireland, February 13, 1872. Died Hollywood, California, January 4, 1943.

Fourteen years in vaudeville before joining Vitagraph in 1910, making her debut in Jack Fat and Jim Slim at Coney Island, released on December 2, 1910. Her fat, jovial appearance made her a popular Vitagraph player, and by 1915 she was starring in her own series of one-reel comedies. In 1916, Kate Price joined Keystone, and by 1917 was playing opposite "Babe" Hardy in Vim comedies. By the Twenties she had become a seasoned character actress in features, specializing in Irish landladies.

WILLIAM V. RANOUS. Date and place of birth unknown. Died Santa Monica, California, April 1, 1915.

With J. Barny Sherry, Ranous was the first member of the Vitagraph stock company, formed in 1905, when the Flatbush studio opened. He became a director shortly thereafter. According to William Basil Courtney, "Ranous celebrated his ascension by immediately becoming temperamental --in the form of secretiveness as to what his current activities might be. To the day of his death any inquisitor of Ranous as to what he was at the moment engaged in directing was solemnly told that the name of the picture was The Lost Hunter." Ranous remained active with Vitagraph, on and off, until his death at the age of fifty-three. In 1913, he directed Treasure Island for Warner's Features.

WALLACE REID. Born St. Louis, Missouri, April 15, 1891. Died Los Angeles, January 18, 1923.

After a very brief stage career, Reid joined the Selig Company in 1909, with his father, Hal Reid. Wally was employed as an actor, and Hal as a scenario writer. Father and son joined Vitagraph in 1911, and Wally remained there until 1912. Vitagraph films include: Jean Intervenes, An Indian Romeo and Juliet, The Seventh Son and The Illumination (all 1912). He may be seen at his best in Every Inch a Man, released on October 14, 1912. From Vitagraph, Reid went on to stardom and became one of the silent cinema's most popular leading men. He died at the height of his

fame. Hal Reid had died on May 22, 1920, at the age of
fifty-seven.

PAUL SCARDON. Born Melbourne, Australia, May 6, 1875.
    Died Fontana, California, January 17, 1954.
        Several years of stage experience in Australia before
coming to the States in 1905. Screen debut with the Majestic
and Reliance companies. Joined Vitagraph as an actor in
1914, and soon graduated to directing. Acted in the first
Vitagraph serial, The Goddess (1915). Acted in and directed:
The Island of Surprise, The Redemption of Dave Darcy, The
Hero of Submarine D-2 and The Dawn of Freedom (all 1916).
Directed: A Game with Fate (1918), Tangled Lives (1918),
Fighting Destiny (1919), etc. Left Vitagraph in 1919. Active
in film industry until 1924.

WILLIAM SHEA. Born Scotland. Died Brooklyn, November
    5, 1918.
        Bill Shea joined Vitagraph in 1905, and claimed to
have appeared in the first production shot at Vitagraph's
Flatbush studio, Julius Caesar. Prior to joining the company, he had been on the stage for many years. In the
early days he was responsible for hiring fellow actors to
appear in Vitagraph productions, and also doubled as painter,
property man, messenger, carpenter and electrician. In the
'teens, he was a popular comic character actor with the company.

S. M. (SAM) SPEDON. Date and place of birth and death
    unknown.
        On September 11, 1909, The Moving Picture World
announced, "S. M. Spedon, formerly of Talent, and an
author of note, has been added to the staff of the Vitagraph
Company of America. He will be connected with the producing department, passing upon and revising manuscripts
of stories, a task for which he is eminently well fitted."
Spedon became head of Vitagraph's publicity department, and
it was he who gave Adele Whitely Fletcher, later editor of
Motion Picture Magazine, Movie Weekly and Photoplay, her
first job. In January of 1917 he joined the staff of The
Moving Picture World.

ANITA STEWART. Born Brooklyn, New York, February 7,
    1895. Died Beverly Hills, California, May 4, 1961.

Joined Vitagraph at the suggestion of her brother-in-law, Ralph Ince. First known film, Her Choice, released on September 30, 1912. Originally billed under her real name of Anna, but owing to a printer's error became Anita. Ralph Ince directed all her films until 1916, including The Wood Violet (1912), The Wreck (1913), The Shadow of the Past (1914), and His Phantom Sweetheart (1915). Late in 1914, she began to be teamed with Earle Williams. Miss Stewart left Vitagraph in the autumn of 1917, after signing a contract with Louis B. Mayer. This resulted in a lawsuit, as her contract with Vitagraph was not due to expire until January of 1918. Vitagraph won the suit, which set an important precedent in terms of players' contractual obligations. Miss Stewart retired from the screen in 1928.

EDITH STOREY. Born New York City, March 18, 1892.
    Date and place of death unknown.
        Began her stage career at the age of ten, and entered films with Vitagraph circa 1911. She was briefly with the company before joining Gaston Melies' concern, but after a few months she returned to Vitagraph, with whom she remained until March of 1917. Edith Storey was a highly talented actress, who may be seen at her best in A Florida Enchantment (1914). She appeared in innumerable Vitagraph productions, her last film for the company being Aladdin from Broadway, released on March 19, 1917. In October of 1913, Edith Storey was one of the seventeen members of the Vitagraph Company who journeyed to North Carolina, to produce a series of films there. However, the bulk of her films were shot at Vitagraph's West Coast studio. Miss Storey retired from the screen in 1921.

NORMA TALMADGE. Born Jersey City, New Jersey, May
    26, 1897. Died Los Angeles, December 24, 1957.
        Joined Vitagraph in November of 1910. Created considerable public interest with her role as a girl accompanying Sidney Carton to the guillotine in A Tale of Two Cities (1911). Other Vitagraph films include The Troublesome Stepdaughters (1912), His Official Appointment (1913), Sawdust and Salome (1914), The Crown Prince's Double (1915) and The Battle Cry of Peace (1915). She left Vitagraph in the summer of 1915, and became one of the silent screen's greatest dramatic stars. Her performance in An Old Man's Love Story (1913) hints at the great things ahead. Miss Talmadge retired from the screen in 1930.

ROSE TAPLEY. Born Petersburg, Virginia, June 30, 1883.
Died Woodland Hills, California, February 23, 1956.
     Made stage debut in 1900. Screen debut in 1905 with
the American Mutoscope and Biograph Company; from there
to Edison, and then to Vitagraph circa 1908. Rose Tapley's
most famous Vitagraph film was Vanity Fair (1911). She
remained with Vitagraph until 1917, when she embarked on
a national lecture tour, promoting better pictures. Active
in films until the early Thirties.

FREDERICK A. THOMSON. Born Montreal, Canada. Date
and place of death unknown.
     Vitagraph director for many years, after a stage
career as actor, producer and manager, spanning a twenty-
year period. Exact date of joining Vitagraph unknown, but
he was with the company in 1911, and, although he would
occasionally leave to direct films for other producers, was
still with Vitagraph in 1917. He came by the nickname of
"Bing" Thomson because, when he was ready to shoot a
scene, he would yell, "All right now--Let's go--Bing." In
later years, in order to avoid confusion with the cowboy
star of the same name, spelt his surname Thompson.

LARRY TRIMBLE. Born Robbinston, Maine, February 15,
1885. Died Los Angeles, February 8, 1954.
     Circa 1908, Trimble sold an animal story to a New
York magazine, which then sent him to Vitagraph to write a
story on film-making. Trimble appeared on the Vitagraph
lot with his dog, Jean, just as the Company was in need of
a dog to play a scene with Florence Turner. Both were
asked to stay, and both became leading members of the
Vitagraph stock company. Jean was equal in popularity to
Vitagraph's human stars, Florence Turner and Maurice Costello. Larry Trimble was a leading director with the
Company until 1913, directing most of the films of John
Bunny and Florence Turner, and, of course, all of Jean's
productions. On March 15, 1913, Trimble and Jean left
Vitagraph and went with Florence Turner to England, where
Trimble remained until August of 1915. He continued to
direct until 1925, and in the Twenties developed another dog
star, Strongheart. In 1941, Trimble married J. Stuart
Blackton's daughter, Marian Constance. It was a second
marriage for both of them but it proved a loving and constant relationship. Jean gave birth to six puppies in December of 1912. She died in 1916. After Jean's departure,

Vitagraph unsuccessfully tried to develop a new animal star,
"Shep, the Vitagraph Dog. "

LILLIAN WALKER.   Born Brooklyn, New York, April 21,
    1888.   Died Trinidad, October 10, 1975.
        Brief stage career.   While appearing in The Follies
of 1910 her photograph was seen by J. Stuart Blackton.
Screen debut in The Inherited Taint, released on March 31,
1911.   Miss Walker became one of Vitagraph's most popular
female stars, and was known throughout the world by the
nickname of "Dimples. " In September of 1913, she was
named Queen to John Bunny's King at the Coney Island Mardi
Gras.   Early 1917, she left Vitagraph; Miss Walker's last
film there was The Star Gazer, released on April 2, 1917.
She remained active in films until 1922.   In 1933 it was reported that Miss Walker was working as a saleswoman at a
Brooklyn department store.

EARLE WILLIAMS.   Born Sacramento, February 28, 1880.
    Died Los Angeles, April 25, 1927.
        First encounter with the theatre at the age of fourteen
as an usher at Oakland's McDonough Theatre.   Several years
with stock companies before being given a letter of introduc-
tion to Frederick A. Thomson at Vitagraph by New York's
Packard Theatrical Exchange.   Screen debut in The Thumb
Print, released on September 1, 1911.   Popular Vitagraph
leading man, usually paired with Anita Stewart.   Williams'
most famous Vitagraph films were The Christian (1914) and
The Juggernaut (1915).   He threatened to quit in January of
1916, but agreed to stay with Vitagraph when given a salary
raise, and remained with the company until 1923.   In the
early Twenties he also directed.   Active in films until his
death.

CLARA KIMBALL YOUNG.   Born Chicago, September 6,
    1891.   Died Woodland Hills, California, October 15, 1960.
        Stage career from the age of three.   Joined Vitagraph
in 1912 with her husband, director James Young (divorced
1919).   An extremely talented actress, equally at home in
comedy and drama.   Her most famous Vitagraph film was
My Official Wife (1914), shortly after the release of which
she and her husband joined World.   Continued to appear in
films until 1938.

THE FILMS OF THE VITAGRAPH COMPANY, 1910-1915

The following checklists give the titles, release dates, lengths, and, where known, directors for all Vitagraph productions between 1910 and 1915, a period which might be described as the "golden era" of the Vitagraph Company.

Certain films lack lengths, indicating these were not published. However, it is reasonably safe to assume that the films in question were approximately one reel or 1,000 ft. in length. In the early years, directorial credits were not always published. In cases where the author, through his researches, has assumed that a certain director was responsible for a particular film, the director's name is followed by an asterisk. Also, there were discrepancies in the title of a film from one source compared to another, and, in certain cases, the author has been obliged to accept the most probable title.

1910

CUPID AND THE MOTOR BOAT (alternative title A SUMMER IDYL). January 1. 940 ft.

THE LIFE OF MOSES. January 4. 868 ft. Charles Kent.*

RICHELIEU, OR THE CONSPIRACY. January 8. 992 ft.

CALL BOY'S VENGEANCE. January 11. 320 ft.

THE OLD MAID'S VALENTINE. January 11. 575 ft.

A SISTER'S SACRIFICE. January 15. 970 ft.

THE TOYMAKER'S SECRET. January 18. 969 ft.

A PAIR OF SCHEMERS. January 22. 743 ft.

FIVE MINUTES TO TWELVE. January 22. 162 ft.

THE LIFE OF MOSES. January 25. 976 ft. Charles Kent.*

THE GIRL AND THE JUDGE. January 29. 980 ft.

CAUGHT IN HIS OWN TRAP. February 1. 503 ft.

THE SKELETON. February 1. 440 ft.

TWELFTH NIGHT. February 5. 970 ft.

THE PASSING SHADOW. February 8. 996 ft.

THE LIFE OF MOSES. February 12. 955 ft. Charles
    Kent. *

THE WAYSIDE SHRINE. February 15. 930 ft.

MURIEL'S STRATAGEM. February 18. 655 ft.

BEAUTIFUL WINDERMERE (alternate title TRIP THROUGH
    THE NORTH OF ENGLAND). February 18. 320 ft.

THE LIFE OF MOSES. February 19. 990 ft. Charles
    Kent. *

PAID IN FULL. February 22. 930 ft.

THE LESSON BY THE SEA. February 25. 963 ft.

THE SOUL OF VENICE. February 26. 950 ft.

AN EYE FOR AN EYE. March 1. 930 ft.

ON THE BORDER LINE. March 4. 920 ft.

THE BEAUTIFUL SNOW. March 5. 426 ft.

THE HISTORY OF A SARDINE SANDWICH. March 5. 478 ft.

A BROTHER'S DEVOTION. March 8. 950 ft.

THE COURTING OF THE MERRY WIDOW. March 10.
    833 ft.

"CONSCIENCE" OR THE BAKER BOY. March 11. 941 ft.

TAMING A GRANDFATHER. March 12. 950 ft.

VICTIMS OF FATE. March 15. 963 ft.

THE MYSTERY OF TEMPLE COURT. March 18. 969 ft.

CAPITAL VS. LABOR. March 22. 949 ft.

THE HAND OF FATE. March 25. 971 ft.

A BROKEN SPELL. March 26. 975 ft.

THE INDISCRETIONS OF BETTY. March 29. 948 ft.

THE TONGUE OF SCANDAL. April 1.

THE FRUITS OF VENGEANCE. April 2.

FROM SHADOW TO SUNSHINE. April 5. 903 ft.

ELEKTRA. April 8. 942 ft.

THE CONQUEROR. April 9. 928 ft.

THE GIRL IN THE BARRACKS. April 12. 908 ft

THE CALL OF THE HEART. April 15. 959 ft.

THE MERRY WIDOW TAKES ANOTHER PARTNER. April 16. 981 ft.

LOVE'S AWAKENING. April 19. 977 ft.

HER SWEET REVENGE. April 22. 987 ft.

ST. ELMO. April 23. 927 ft.

THROUGH THE DARKNESS. April 26. 981 ft.

THE PORTRAIT. April 29. 983 ft.

THE MINOTAUR. April 30. 983 ft.

THE LOST TRAIL. May 3. 972 ft.

ONE OF THE FINEST. May 6. 985 ft.

MARIO'S SWAN SONG. May 7. 842 ft.

THE THREE WISHES. May 10. 945 ft.

THE CLOSED DOOR. May 13. 922 ft.

THE SPECIAL AGENT. May 14.

MUSIC HATH CHARMS. May 17. 563 ft.

A FUNNY STORY. May 18. 356 ft.

OUT OF THE PAST. May 20. 990 ft.

THE WINGS OF LOVE. May 21. 888 ft.

CONVICT NO. 796. May 24. 977 ft.

AUNTIE AT THE BOAT RACE. May 27. 977 ft.

THE LOVE OF CHRYSANTHEMUM. May 28. 990 ft.

THE PEACEMAKER. May 31. 960 ft.

DAVY JONES' PARROT. June 3. 922 ft.

THE MAJESTY OF THE LAW. June 4. 972 ft.

A MODERN CINDERELLA. June 7. 977 ft.

OVER THE GARDEN WALL. June 10. 973 ft.

THE ALTAR OF LOVE. June 11. 995 ft.

THE RUSSIAN LION. June 14. 948 ft.

JAMES J. CORBETT. June 15.

DAVY JONES' LANDLADIES. June 17. 935 ft.

ITO, THE BEGGAR BOY. June 18. 962 ft.

LITTLE MOTHER AT THE BABY SHOW. June 21. 975 ft.

A FAMILY FEUD. June 24. 998 ft.

BY THE FAITH OF A CHILD. June 25. 885 ft.

WHEN OLD NEW YORK WAS YOUNG. June 28. 950 ft.

SAVED BY THE FLAG. July 1. 570 ft.

WILSON'S WIFE'S COUNTENANCE. July 1. 427 ft.

OLD GLORY. July 2. 945 ft.

A BOARDING SCHOOL ROMANCE. July 5. 998 ft.

BETWEEN LOVE AND HONOR. July 8. 917 ft.

BECKET. July 9. 998 ft.

NELLIE'S FARM. July 12. 995 ft.

HER UNCLE'S WILL. July 15. 995 ft.

A BROKEN SYMPHONY. July 16. 993 ft.

TWA HIELAND LADS. July 19. 933 ft.

DAVY JONES AND CAPT. BRAGG. July 22. 935 ft.

HAKO'S SACRIFICE. July 23. 995 ft.

UNCLE TOM'S CABIN (Part One). July 26. 935 ft.

UNCLE TOM'S CABIN (Part Two). July 29. 1,000 ft.

UNCLE TOM'S CABIN (Part Three). July 30.

AN UNFAIR GAME. August 2. 990 ft.

THE WOOING O'T. August 5. 980 ft.

HER MOTHER'S WEDDING GOWN. August 6. 1,015 ft.

THE DEATH OF MICHAEL GRADY. August 9. 935 ft.

MRS. BARRINGTON'S HOUSE PARTY. August 12. 977 ft.

THE TURN OF THE BALANCE. August 13. 980 ft.

DAISIES. August 16. 995 ft.

BACK TO NATURE. August 19. 970 ft.

UNDER THE OLD APPLE TREE. August 20. 995 ft.

THE THREE CHERRY PITS. August 23. 995 ft.

THE MEN HATERS' CLUB. August 26. 985 ft.

ROSE LEAVES. August 27. 995 ft.

JEAN AND THE CALICO DOLL. August 30. 970 ft.
    Larry Trimble.*

A LIFE FOR A LIFE. September 2. 995 ft.

THE WRONG BOX. September 3. 985 ft.

CHEW CHEW LAND. September 6. 600 ft.

A ROUGH WEATHER COURTSHIP. September 6. 400 ft.

HOW SHE WON HIM. September 9. 980 ft.

THE THREE OF THEM. September 10. 985 ft.

THE SEPOY'S WIFE. September 13. 990 ft.

TWO WAIFS AND A STRAY. September 16. 985 ft.

A LUNATIC AT LARGE. September 17. 997 ft.

JEAN, THE MATCH-MAKER. September 20. 1,000 ft.
    Larry Trimble.*

A MODERN KNIGHT ERRANT. September 23. 967 ft.

RENUNCIATION. September 24. 999 ft.

A HOME MELODY. September 30. 907 ft.

THE BACHELOR AND THE BABY. October 1.

RANSOMED; OR, A PRISONER OF WAR. October 4. 998 ft.

THE LAST OF THE SAXONS. October 7. 1,007 ft.

THE SAGE, THE CHERUB AND THE WIDOW. October 8.

BROTHER MAN. October 11.

THE ACTOR'S FUND FIELD DAY. October 11.

ON THE DOORSTEPS. October 14.

THE LEGACY. October 15.

AULD ROBIN GREY. October 18. 991 ft.

DAVY JONES' DOMESTIC TROUBLES. October 21. 1,000 ft.

CLOTHES MAKE THE MAN. October 22. 983 ft.

A DAY ON THE FRENCH BATTLESHIP JUSTICE.   October
     22.   335 ft.

JEAN GOES FORAGING.   October 25.   1,006 ft.   Larry
     Trimble.*

CAPTAIN BARNACLE'S CHAPERONE.   October 28.   994 ft.

THE TELEPHONE.   October 29.   665 ft.

A DOUBLE ELOPEMENT.   November 1.   999 ft.

THE CHILDREN'S REVOLT.   November 4..   992 ft.

IN THE MOUNTAINS OF KENTUCKY.   November 5.   978 ft.

A TALE OF A HAT.   November 8.   954 ft.

THE NINE OF DIAMONDS.   November 11.   990 ft.

JEAN GOES FISHING.   November 12.   988 ft.   Larry
     Trimble.*

DRUMSTICKS.   November 15.   998 ft.

A MODERN COURTSHIP.   November 18.

THE BUM AND THE BOMB.   November 18.

FRANCESCA DA RIMINI.   November 19.

SUSPICION.   November 22.

A FOUR-FOOTED PEST.   November 25.

THE STATUE DOG.   November 25.

LOVE, LUCK AND GASOLINE.   November 26.

A WOMAN'S LOVE.   November 29.

JACK FAT AND JIM SLIM AT CONEY ISLAND.   December 2.
     951 ft.

THE PREACHER'S WIFE.   December 3.   1,001 ft.

A TIN-TYPE ROMANCE.   December 6.   996 ft.

HE WHO LAUGHS LAST.   December 9.   927 ft.

THE COLOR SERGEANT'S HORSE.   December 10.   978 ft.

PLAYING AT DIVORCE.   December 16.   655 ft.

THE INTERNATIONAL MOTOR BOAT RACES.   December 16.
     368 ft.

A DIXIE MOTHER.   December 17.   997 ft.

THE LIGHT IN THE WINDOW.   December 20.   997 ft.

CLANCY. December 23. 995 ft.

JEAN AND THE WAIF. December 24. 989 ft. Larry
    Trimble.*

IN NEIGHBORING KINGDOMS. December 27. 995 ft.

CRAZY APPLES. December 30. 986 ft.

WHERE THE WINDS BLOW. December 31. 987 ft.

1911

ALL IS FAIR IN LOVE AND WAR. January 3. 973 ft.

THE MISSES FINCH AND THEIR NEPHEW, BILLY.
    January 6. 979 ft.

THE OLD WATER JAR. January 7. 984 ft.

DOCTOR CUPID. January 10. 987 ft.

WATER-LILIES. January 13. 991 ft.

COWARD OR HERO. January 14. 975 ft.

THREE MEN AND A GIRL. January 17.

THE GIRL IN THE FILM. January 20.

CAST UP BY THE DEEP. January 21.

IT DID LOOK SUSPICIOUS. January 24.

FIREMEN'S PARADE. January 24.

GIRL OF THE MOUNTAINS. January 27.

DAVY JONES IN THE SOUTH SEAS. January 28.

JEAN RESCUES. January 31. Larry Trimble.*

SOCIETY AND THE MAN. February 3.

A QUEEN FOR A DAY. February 4.

THE DELUGE. February 7. 978 ft.

THE LEAGUE OF MERCY. February 10.

AT THE WHITE MAN'S DOOR. February 11.

CONSUMING LOVE. February 14.

WHEN THE LIGHT WANED. February 17.

THE NEW STENOGRAPHER. February 18.

A TALE OF TWO CITIES (Part One). February 21.
1, 014 ft.

A TALE OF TWO CITIES (Part Two). February 24.
1, 013 ft.

A TALE OF TWO CITIES (Part Three). February 25.
994 ft.

CAPTAIN BARNACLE'S COURTSHIP. February 28.

BERTHA'S MISSION. March 3.

MAMMY'S GHOST. March 4.

THE WILD CAT WELL. March 7.

THE BRIDEGROOM'S DILEMMA. March 10.

RED EAGLE. March 11.

BETTY BECOMES A MAID. March 14.

AN ACHING VOID. March 17.

DAVY JONES, OR HIS WIFE'S HUSBAND. March 18.

THOUGH THE SEAS DIVIDE. March 21.

THE WIDOW VISITS SPRIGTOWN. March 24.

A LITTLE LAD IN DIXIE. March 25.

BILLY'S VALENTINE. March 28.

THE INHERITED TAINT. March 31.

A REPUBLICAN MARRIAGE. April 1.

AN UNEXPECTED REVIEW. April 4.

HOP PICKING. April 4.

FOR HIS SAKE. April 7.

THE SPIRIT OF THE LIGHT. April 8.

WINSOR McCAY. April 8. 650 ft.

BOB SLEDDING. April 8. 350 ft.

WOOING OF WINNIFRED. April 11.

THOUGH YOUR SINS BE AS SCARLET. April 14.

EASTER BABIES. April 15.

THE LEADING LADY. April 18.

THE TROUBLESOME SECRETARIES. April 21.

THE SPIRIT OF THE LIGHT. April 22.

A KLONDIKE STEAL. April 25.

THE PEACE OFFERING. April 28.

PICCIOLA. April 29.

THE DERELICT REPORTER. May 2. 975 ft.

SOLDIERS THREE. May 5. 1,000 ft.

HUNGRY HEARTS. May 6. 985 ft.

HIS MOTHER. May 9. 995 ft.

THE WELCOME OF THE UNWELCOME. May 12. 1,000 ft.

THE PREJUDICE OF PIERRE MARIE. May 13. 985 ft.

WHEN A MAN'S MARRIED. May 16. 1,000 ft.

THE SHOW GIRL. May 19. 990 ft.

SUNSHINE AND SHADOW. May 20. 990 ft.

A DEAD MAN'S HONOR. May 23. 1,000 ft.

TIM MAHONEY THE SCAB. May 26. 1,000 ft.

THE FIRES OF FATE. May 27. 1,000 ft.

CUPID'S CHAUFFEUR. May 30.

THE ENDS OF THE EARTH. June 2.

A CLEVER FRAUD. June 3.

FOR HER BROTHER'S SAKE. June 6.

THE SACRIFICE. June 9.

THE CHANGING OF SILAS MARNER. June 10.

THE TRAPPER'S DAUGHTER. June 13.

PROVING HIS LOVE. June 16.

TEACHING McFADDEN TO WALTZ. June 17.

THE STUMBLING BLOCK. June 20. 993 ft.

THE SLEEP WALKER. June 23.

TWO OVERCOATS. June 24. 519 ft.

BARRIERS BURNED AWAY. June 24. 485 ft.

A QUAKER MOTHER. June 27.

COURAGE OF SORTS. June 28. 1,000 ft.

THE BATTLE HYMN OF THE REPUBLIC.   June 30.
1,000 ft.   Larry Trimble.*

TESTED BY THE FLAG.   July 1.   1,000 ft.

THE LATENT SPARK.   July 4.   946 ft.

IN NORTHERN FORESTS.   July 5.   1,000 ft.

THE WOES OF A WEALTHY WIDOW.   July 7.   1,000 ft.

SNOW BOUND WITH A WOMAN HATER.   July 8.   1,000 ft.

THE OLD FOLK'S SACRIFICE.   July 11.   1,000 ft.

IN THE ARCTIC NIGHT.   July 12.   1,000 ft.

THE SUBDUING OF MRS. NAG.   July 14.   1,000 ft.

A GERANIUM.   July 15.   1,000 ft.

THE LURE OF VANITY.   July 18.   1,000 ft.

ON A TRAMP STEAMER.   July 19.   1,000 ft.

THE SKY PILOT.   July 21.   1,000 ft.

THE RETURN OF "WIDOW" POGSON'S HUSBAND.   July 22.
1,000 ft.

TREASURE TROVE.   July 25.   1,000 ft.

SHE CAME, SHE SAW, SHE CONQUERED.   July 26.
1,000 ft.

THE QUEST OF GOLD.   July 28.   1,002 ft.

THE STRATEGY OF ANN.   July 29.   1,000 ft.

TWO WOLVES AND A LAMB.   July 31.   1,000 ft.

THE CLOWN AND HIS BEST PERFORMANCE.   August 1.
991 ft.

THE PRICE OF GOLD.   August 2.   1,000 ft.

THE $100.00 BILL.   August 4.

THE DEATH OF KING EDWARD III.   August 5.   1,000 ft.

INTREPID DAVY.   August 7.   1,000 ft.

THE LONG SKIRT.   August 8.   1,000 ft.

BILLY THE KID.   August 9.   1,000 ft.

THE BELL OF JUSTICE.   August 11.   1,000 ft.

BIRDS OF A FEATHER.   August 12.   1,000 ft.

FOR LOVE AND GLORY.   August 14.   1,000 ft.

CAPTAIN BARNACLE'S BABY. August 15. 1,000 ft.

MAN TO MAN. August 16. 995 ft.

VITAGRAPH MONTHLY OF CURRENT EVENTS. First issued August 18.

THE SECOND HONEYMOON. August 19. 1,000 ft.

WAGES OF WAR. August 21. 1,000 ft.

HOW BETTY WON THE SCHOOL. August 22. 1,000 ft.

THE SHERIFF'S FRIEND. August 23. 1,000 ft.

MY OLD DUTCH. August 25. 1,000 ft.

A HANDSOMER MAN. August 26. 1,000 ft.

THE GENERAL'S DAUGHTER. August 28. 1,000 ft.

THE WRONG PATIENT. August 29. 551 ft. (released on the same reel with QUEER FOLKS).

QUEER FOLKS. August 29. 448 ft. (released on the same reel with THE WRONG PATIENT).

THE THREE BROTHERS. August 30. 1,000 ft.

THE THUMB PRINT. September 1. 1,000 ft.

THE PRINCE AND THE PUMP. September 2. 1,000 ft.

JEALOUSY. September 4. 1,000 ft.

A FRIENDLY MARRIAGE. September 5. 1,000 ft.

THE WILLOW TREE. September 6. 1,000 ft.

CHERRY BLOSSOMS. September 8. 1,000 ft.

JIMMIE'S JOB. September 9. 1,000 ft.

FORAGING. September 11. 1,000 ft.

HER CROWNING GLORY. September 12. 1,000 ft.

THE CHILD CRUSOES. September 13. 1,000 ft.

BY WOMAN'S WIT. September 16. 1,000 ft.

ONE FLAG AT LAST. September 18. 1,000 ft.

HOW MILLIE BECAME AN ACTRESS. September 19. 1,000 ft.

BEYOND THE LAW. September 20. 1,000 ft.

FORGOTTEN; OR, AN ANSWERED PRAYER. September 22. 1,100 ft.

OVER THE CHAFING DISH. September 23. 491 ft.

THE TIRED, ABSENT-MINDED MAN. September 23.
    511 ft.

BY THE CAMP FIRE'S FLICKER. September 25. 1,000 ft.

HER SISTER'S CHILDREN. September 26. 1,000 ft.

A WESTERN HEROINE. September 27. 1,000 ft.

THE NINETY AND NINE. September 29. 1,000 ft.

HER HERO. September 30. 1,000 ft.

OUR NAVY. October 2. 1,000 ft.

THE WAGER. October 3. 1,000 ft.

THE MATE OF THE JOHN M. October 4. 1,000 ft.

CARR'S REGENERATION. October 6. 1,000 ft.

UPS AND DOWNS. October 7. 1,000 ft.

DADDY'S BOY AND MAMMY. October 9. 1,000 ft.

THE MISSING WILL. October 10. 1,000 ft.

THE INDIAN FLUTE. October 11. 1,000 ft.

THE ANSWER OF THE ROSES. October 13. 1,000 ft.

BY WAY OF MRS. BROWNING. October 14. 1,000 ft.

THE FIGHTING SCHOOLMASTER. October 16. 1,000 ft.

SELECTING HIS HEIRESS. October 18. 1,000 ft. William
    Humphrey. (This was the first film of which Vitagraph
    announced the director.)

THE CABIN BOY. October 20. 1,000 ft. J. Hunt.

LADY GODIVA. October 21. 1,000 ft. Charles Kent.

THE FOOLISHNESS OF JEALOUSY. October 23. 1,000 ft.
    E. R. Phillips.

WIG WAG. October 24. 1,000 ft. Larry Trimble.

AUNT HULDAH, MATCHMAKER. October 25. 1,000 ft.
    E. R. Phillips.

KITTY AND THE COWBOYS. October 27. 1,000 ft.
    Frederick Thomson.

REGENERATION. October 28. 1,000 ft. Charles Kent

CAPTAIN BARNACLE, DIPLOMAT. October 30. 1,000 ft.
    Van Dyke Brooke.

MADGE OF THE MOUNTAINS. October 31. 1,000 ft.
Charles Kent.

A SOUTHERN SOLDIER'S SACRIFICE. November 1.
1,000 ft. William Humphrey.

THE GOSSIP. November 3. 1,000 ft. Frederick Thomson.

A MESSAGE FROM BEYOND. November 4. 1,000 ft.
William Humphrey.

HER COWBOY LOVER. November 6. 1,000 ft. Rollin S.
Sturgeon.

AULD LANG SYNE. November 7. 2,000 ft. Larry Trimble.

ARBUTUS. November 8. 1,000 ft. Charles Kent.

WHO'S WHO. November 10. 1,000 ft. Van Dyke Brooke.

AN AEROPLANE ELOPEMENT. November 11. 1,000 ft.
William Humphrey.

SUFFER LITTLE CHILDREN. November 13. 1,000 ft.
Charles Kent.

THE GIRL AND THE SHERIFF. November 14. 1,000 ft.
Charles Kent.

THEIR CHARMING MAMMA. November 15. 1,000 ft.
Frederick Thomson.

THE LITTLE SPY. November 17. 1,000 ft. Charles Kent.

HEROES OF THE MUTINY. November 20. 1,000 ft.
William V. Ranous.

WISTARIA. November 21. 1,000 ft. E. R. Phillips.

THE HALF-BREED'S DAUGHTER. November 22. 1,000 ft.
Rollin S. Sturgeon.

AN INNOCENT BURGLAR. November 24. 1,000 ft. Van
Dyke Brooke.

THE LIFE BOAT. November 25. 1,000 ft. Jay Hunt.

THE POLITICIAN'S DREAM. November 27. 1,000 ft.
Frederick Thomson.

THE FRESHET. November 28. 1,000 ft. William Humphrey.

THE VOICELESS MESSAGE. November 29. 1,000 ft.
William V. Ranous.

HIS LAST CENT. December 1. 1,000 ft. Van Dyke Brooke.

THE HUSKING BEE. December 2. 1,000 ft.

SAVING THE SPECIAL. December 4. 1,000 ft. William
  V. Ranous.

HYPNOTIZING THE HYPNOTIST. December 5. 1,000 ft.
  (released on the same reel with A SLIGHT MISTAKE).
  Larry Trimble.

A SLIGHT MISTAKE. December 5. 1,000 ft. (released
  on the same reel with HYPNOTIZING THE HYPNO-
  TIST). William Humphrey.

THE BLACK CHASM. December 6. 1,000 ft. Rollin S.
  Sturgeon.

WAR. December 8. 1,000 ft.

HIS WIFE'S SECRET. December 9. 1,000 ft. Van Dyke
  Brooke and Maurice Costello.

ONE TOUCH OF NATURE. December 11. 1,000 ft. Larry
  Trimble.

THE MILITARY AIR SCOUT. December 12. 1,000 ft.
  William Humphrey.

THE VENTRILLOQUIST'S TRUNK. December 13. 1,000 ft.
  Frederick Thomson.

LOVE AT GLOUCESTER PORT. December 15. 1,000 ft.
  Van Dyke Brooke and Maurice Costello.

THE SICK MAN FROM THE EAST. December 16. 1,000 ft.

VANITY FAIR. December 19. 3,000 ft.

FIRES OF DRIFTWOOD. December 20. 1,000 ft.

A REFORMED SANTA CLAUS. December 22. 1,000 ft.

THE OLD DOLL. December 23. 1,000 ft.

SOME GOOD IN ALL. December 25. 1,000 ft.

THE YOUNGER BROTHER. December 26. 1,000 ft.

TESTING HIS COURAGE. December 27. 1,000 ft.

A DOUBLY DESIRED ORPHAN. December 29. 1,000 ft.

IN THE CLUTCHES OF A VAPOR BATH. December 30.
  1,000 ft.

1912

A ROMANCE OF WALL STREET. January 1. 1,000 ft.

A RED CROSS MARTYR. January 2. 1,000 ft.

THE HEART OF THE KING'S JESTER. January 3. 1,000 ft.

DESTINY IS CHANGELESS. January 5. 1,000 ft.

THE PATH OF TRUE LOVE. January 6. 1,000 ft.

CAPTAIN JENKS' DILEMMA. January 8. 1,000 ft.

HOW TOMMY SAVED HIS FATHER. January 9. 1,000 ft.

ALMA'S CHAMPION. January 10. 1,000 ft.

THE MEETING OF THE WAYS. January 12. 1,000 ft.

WILLIE'S SISTER. January 13. 1,000 ft.

FATHER AND SON. January 15. 1,000 ft.

CHUMPS. January 16. 1,000 ft.

CAUGHT IN THE RAIN. January 17. 1,000 ft.

TOM TILLING'S BABY. January 19. 1,000 ft.

A GIRL OF THE WEST. January 20. 1,000 ft.

THE BLIND MINER. January 22. 1,000 ft.

JEAN INTERVENES. January 23. 1,000 ft. Larry Trimble.*

CAPTAIN BARNACLE'S MESSMATE. January 24. 1,000 ft.

LOVE FINDS A WAY. January 26. 1,000 ft.

FOR THE HONOR OF THE FAMILY. January 27. 1,000 ft.

WHERE THE MONEY WENT. January 29. 1,000 ft.

INDIAN ROMEO AND JULIET. January 30. 1,000 ft.

A TIMELY RESCUE. January 31. 1,000 ft.

THE FIRST VIOLIN. February 2. 1,000 ft.

A PROBLEM IN REDUCTION. February 3. 1,000 ft.

THE LAW OR THE LADY. February 5. 1,000 ft.

UMBRELLAS TO MEND. February 6. 1,000 ft.

THE PICTURE WRITER. February 7. 1,000 ft.

HER BOY. February 9. 1,000 ft.

PLAYMATES. February 10. 1,000 ft.

THE HEART OF A MAN. February 12. 1,000 ft.

WINNING IS LOSING. February 13. 1,000 ft.

BUNNY AND THE TWINS. February 14. 1,000 ft.

THE CHOCOLATE REVOLVER. February 16. 1,000 ft.

THE HOBO'S REDEMPTION. February 17. 1,000 ft.

THE STRUGGLE. February 19. 1,000 ft.

THE LOVE OF JOHN RUSKIN. February 20. 1,000 ft.

HER LAST SHOT. February 21. 1,000 ft.

CURE FOR POKERITIS. February 23. 1,000 ft.

COWBOY DAMON AND PYTHIAS. February 24. 1,000 ft.

STENOGRAPHER WANTED. February 26. 1,000 ft.

JUSTICE OF THE DESERT. February 27. 1,000 ft.

THE PATCHWORK QUILT. February 28. 1,000 ft.

THE DIAMOND BROOCH. March 1. 1,000 ft.

THE TELEPHONE GIRL. March 2. 1,000 ft.

LULU'S ANARCHIST. March 4. 1,000 ft.

CARDINAL WOLSEY. March 5. 1,000 ft.

IRENE'S INFATUATION. March 6. 1,000 ft.

HOW STATES ARE MADE. March 8. 1,000 ft.

MRS. CARTER'S NECKLACE. March 9. 1,000 ft.

FIRST WOMAN JURY IN AMERICA. March 11. 1,000 ft.

THE FIVE SENSES. March 12. 300 ft.

A STORY OF THE CIRCUS. March 12. 700 ft.

MRS. 'ENRY 'AWKINS. March 13. 1,000 ft.

THE GREAT DIAMOND ROBBERY. March 15. 1,000 ft.

SUNSET, OR HER ONLY ROMANCE. March 16. 1,000 ft.

THE BLACK WALL. March 18. 1,000 ft.

THE OLD SILVER WATCH. March 19. 1,000 ft.

THE TWO PENITENTS. March 20. 1,000 ft.

MR. BOLTER'S INFATUATION. March 22. 1,000 ft.

HER FORGOTTEN DANCING SHOES. March 23. 500 ft.

TAFT AND HIS CABINET. March 23. 500 ft.

THE PRICE OF BIG BOB'S SILENCE. March 25. 1,000 ft.

HIS MOTHER'S SHROUD. March 26. 1,000 ft.

THE GOVERNOR WHO HAD A HEART. March 27. 1,000 ft.

THE HAUNTED ROCKER. March 29. 500 ft.

THE SUIT OF ARMOUR. March 29. 500 ft.

NEMESIS. March 30. 1,000 ft.

THE STAR REPORTER. April 1. 656 ft.

HIS MOTHER-IN-LAW. April 1. 346 ft.

SHE NEVER KNEW. April 2. 1,000 ft.

THE SEVENTH SON. April 3. 1,000 ft.

THE ILLUMINATION. April 5. 1,000 ft.

THE UNKNOWN VIOLINIST. April 6. 1,000 ft.

BURNT CORK. April 8. 800 ft.

PUSHMOBILE RACES. April 8. 200 ft.

AT SCOGGINSES' CORNER. April 9. 1,000 ft.

HIS FATHER'S SIN. April 10. 1,000 ft.

THE JOCULAR WINDS OF FATE. April 12. 1,000 ft.

CAPTAIN JINKS' DIPLOMACY. April 13. 1,000 ft.

THE PIPE. April 15. 1,000 ft.

THE CAVE MAN. April 16. 1,000 ft.

WORKING FOR HUBBY. April 17. 1,000 ft.

THE CRAVEN. April 19. 1,000 ft.

THE WAY OF A MAN WITH A MAID. April 20. 1,000 ft.

HOW HE PAPERED THE ROOM. April 22. 500 ft.

MARSHALL P. WILDER. April 22. 500 ft.

COUNSEL FOR THE DEFENSE. April 23. 1,000 ft.

THE WOMAN HATERS. April 24. 1,000 ft.

THE PINK PAJAMA GIRL. April 26. 1,000 ft.

THE VICTORIA CROSS. April 27. 1,000 ft.

FRANK COFFYN'S HYDRO-AEROPLANE FLIGHTS. April 29. 1,000 ft.

THE OLD KENT ROAD. April 30. 1,000 ft.

SHERIFF JIM'S LAST SHOT. May 1. 1,000 ft.

RED INK TRAGEDY. May 3. 500 ft.

OLD LOVE LETTERS. May 3. 500 ft.

THE HIEROGLYPHIC. May 4. 1,000 ft.

DR. LA FLEUR'S THEORY. May 6. 1,000 ft.

THOU SHALT NOT COVET. May 7. 1,000 ft.

THE SERPENTS. May 8. 1,000 ft.

WHEN DADDY WAS WISE. May 10. 1,000 ft.

THE GREATEST THING IN THE WORLD. May 11. 1,000 ft.

LOVE IN THE GHETTO. May 13. 1,000 ft.

THE SPIDER'S WEB. May 14. 1,000 ft.

LEAP YEAR PROPOSALS. May 15. 500 ft.

A PAGE IN CANADIAN HISTORY. May 15. 500 ft.

THE GREATER LOVE. May 17. 1,000 ft.

THE MAN UNDER THE BED. May 18. 1,000 ft.

PROFESSOR OPTIMO. May 20. 1,000 ft.

FORTUNES OF A COMPOSER. May 21. 1,000 ft.

THEIR GOLDEN ANNIVERSARY. May 22. 1,000 ft.

DIAMOND CUT DIAMOND. May 24. 1,000 ft.

THE REDEMPTION OF BEN FARLAND. May 25. 1,000 ft.

THE TRIUMPH OF RIGHT. May 27. 1,000 ft.

THE LADY OF THE LAKE. May 27. 3,000 ft.

AN INNOCENT THEFT. May 28. 1,000 ft.

ON HER WEDDING DAY. May 29. 1,000 ft.

THE PICTURE IDOL. May 31. 1,000 ft.

AN EVENTFUL ELOPEMENT. June 1. 1,000 ft.

WHO'S TO WIN. June 3. 1,000 ft.

THE PRAYERS OF MANUELO. June 4. 1,000 ft.

MOCKERY. June 5. 1,000 ft.

THE CYLINDER'S SECRET. June 7. 1,000 ft.

LULU'S DOCTOR. June 10. 1,000 ft.

PANDORA'S BOX. June 11. 1,000 ft.

YELLOW BIRD. June 12. 1,000 ft.

DAYS OF TERROR. June 14. 1,000 ft.

THE NIPPER'S LULLABY. June 17. 1,000 ft.

THE FRENCH SPY. June 17. 3,000 ft.

HER DIARY. June 18. 1,000 ft.

CHASED BY BLOODHOUNDS. June 19. 600 ft.

AUTOMOBILE RACE AT SANTA MONICA. June 19. 400 ft.

HER BROTHER. June 21. 1,000 ft.

THE GAMBLERS. June 22. 1,000 ft.

THE EXTENSION TABLE. June 24. 1,000 ft.

THE CARPATHIA. June 25. 1,000 ft. (released on the same reel with NEVER AGAIN).

NEVER AGAIN. June 25. 1,000 ft. (released on the same reel with THE CARPATHIA).

WHEN ROSES WITHER. June 26. 1,000 ft.

PSEUDO SULTAN. June 28. 1,000 ft.

AT THE END OF THE TRAIL. June 29. 1,000 ft.

AFTER MANY YEARS. July 1. 1,000 ft.

THE CHURCH ACROSS THE WAY. July 2. 1,000 ft.

LINCOLN'S GETTYSBURG ADDRESS. July 3. 1,000 ft.

ON THE PUPIL OF HIS EYE. July 5. 1,000 ft.

THE TROUBLESOME STEP-DAUGHTERS. July 6. 1,000 ft.

HER OLD SWEETHEART. July 8. 500 ft.

FATE'S AWFUL JEST. July 8. 500 ft.

THE CURSE OF THE LAKE. July 9. 1,000 ft.

A BUNCH OF VIOLETS. July 10. 1,000 ft.

THE FOSTER CHILD. July 12. 1,000 ft.

AUNTY'S ROMANCE. July 13. 1,000 ft.

THE MONEY KINGS. July 15. 3,000 ft.

CONSCIENCE. July 15. 1,000 ft.

A PERSISTENT LOVER. July 16. 400 ft.

A LIVELY AFFAIR.   July 16.   650 ft.

THE REDEMPTION OF RED RUBE.   July 17.   1,000 ft.

THE BLACK SHEEP.   July 19.   1,000 ft.

ROCK OF AGES.   July 20.   1,000 ft.

WANTED -- A SISTER.   July 22.   1,000 ft.

THE ADVENTURE OF THE THUMB PRINT.   July 23.
    1,000 ft.

MARTHA'S REBELLION.   July 24.   1,000 ft.

THE BARRIER THAT WAS BURNED.   July 26.   1,000 ft.

THE LIGHT OF ST. BERNARD.   July 27.   1,000 ft.

THE MIRACLE.   July 29.   1,000 ft.

A JUVENILE LOVE AFFAIR.   July 30.   1,000 ft.

THE ADVENTURE OF THE RETIRED ARMY COLONEL.
    July 31.   1,000 ft.

THE AWAKENING OF JONES.   August 2.   1,000 ft.

THE FATHERHOOD OF BUCK McGEE.   August 3.   1,000 ft.

AT THE ELEVENTH HOUR.   August 6.   1,000 ft.

THE CROSS ROADS.   August 7.   1,000 ft.

WANTED, A GRANDMOTHER.   August 9.   1,000 ft.

SUING SUSAN.   August 10.   1,000 ft.

BUNNY AND THE DOGS.   August 12.   300 ft.

INGENUITY.   August 12.   700 ft.

THE HEART OF ESMERALDA.   August 13.   1,000 ft.

VULTURES AND DOVES.   August 14.   1,000 ft.

THE BOGUS NAPOLEON.   August 16.   1,000 ft.

TWO BATTLES.   August 17.   1,000 ft.

RIP VAN WINKLE.   August 19.   2,000 ft.

HER GRANDCHILD.   August 19.   1,000 ft.

LOVESICK MAIDENS OF CUDDLETOWN.   August 20.
    1,000 ft.

THE ANCIENT BOW.   August 21.   1,000 ft.

SAVING AN AUDIENCE.   August 23.   1,000 ft.

THE PARTY DRESS.   August 24.   614 ft.

ON BOARD KAISER WILHELM THE SECOND.   August 24.
   388 ft.

A DOUBLE DANGER.   August 26.   1,000 ft.

FLIRT OR HEROINE.   August 27.   1,000 ft.

TWO CINDERS.   August 28.   555 ft.

BUMPS.   August 28.   447 ft.

WRITTEN IN THE SAND.   August 30.   1,000 ft.

BOND OF MUSIC.   August 31.   1,000 ft.

TOMMY'S SISTER.   September 2.   1,000 ft.

CORONETS AND HEARTS.   September 3.   1,000 ft.

CAPTAIN BARNACLE'S LEGACY.   September 4.   1,000 ft.

BUNNY'S SUICIDE.   September 6.   400 ft.

SHE WANTED A BOARDER.   September 6.   600 ft.

A WASTED SACRIFICE.   September 7.   1,000 ft.

THE ROAD TO YESTERDAY.   September 9.   1,000 ft.

THE HIGHER MERCY.   September 10.   1,000 ft.

THE HINDOO'S CURSE.   September 11.   1,000 ft.

THE LOYALTY OF SYLVIA.   September 13.   1,000 ft.

POPULAR BETTY.   September 14.   600 ft.

THE FORTUNE IN THE TEA-CUP.   September 14.   400 ft.

CAPTAIN BARNACLE'S WAIF.   September 16.   1,000 ft.

THE TROUBLED TRAIL.   September 17.   1,000 ft.

A VITAGRAPH ROMANCE.   September 18.   1,000 ft.
   James Young.*

THE INDIAN MUTINY.   September 20.   1,000 ft.   (released
   on the same reel with THE BURNING OF THE MATCH
   FACTORY).

THE BURNING OF THE MATCH FACTORY.   September 20.
   1,000 ft.   (released on the same reel with THE
   INDIAN MUTINY).

THE ADVENTURE OF THE ITALIAN MODEL.   September
   23.   1,000 ft.

HIS LORDSHIP, THE VALET.   September 24.   1,000 ft.

BILL WILSON'S GAL.   September 25.   1,000 ft.

THE SIGNAL FIRE. September 26. 1,000 ft.

THE COUNTS. September 27. 600 ft.

WEARY STARTS THINGS IN PUMPKINVILLE. September 27
    400 ft.

THE IRONY OF FATE. September 28. 1,000 ft.

HER CHOICE. September 30. 1,000 ft.

THE ADVENTURE OF THE SMELLING SALTS. October 1.
    1,000 ft.

BACHELOR BUTTONS. October 2. 1,000 ft. (released on
    the same reel with DIANA'S LEGACY).

DIANA'S LEGACY. October 2. 1,000 ft. (released on the
    same reel with BACHELOR BUTTONS).

SHE CRIED. October 3. 1,000 ft.

HER SPOILED BOY. October 4. 1,000 ft.

THE RED BARRIER. October 5. 1,000 ft.

NOTHING TO WEAR. October 7. 1,000 ft.

AS YOU LIKE IT. October 7. 3,000 ft.

THE GODMOTHER. October 8. 1,000 ft.

WHEN PERSISTENCY AND OBSTINACY MEET. October 9.
    1,000 ft.

AS FATE WOULD HAVE IT. October 10. 1,000 ft.

HER FATHER'S HAT. October 11. 700 ft.

MAMMOTH LIFE-SAVERS. October 11. 300 ft.

WHEN CALIFORNIA WAS YOUNG. October 12. 1,000 ft.

EVERY INCH A MAN. October 14. 1,000 ft. William
    Humphrey.

MRS. LIRRIPER'S LODGERS. October 15. 1,000 ft.

AN ELEPHANT ON THEIR HANDS. October 16. 1,000 ft.

FATHER'S HOT TODDY. October 17. 1,000 ft. (released
    on the same reel with EVENING PARADE AND GUN
    PRACTICE AT FORT HAMILTON).

EVENING PARADE AND GUN PRACTICE AT FORT
    HAMILTON. October 17. 1,000 ft. (released on
    the same reel with FATHER'S HOT TODDY).

BUNNY AT SEA. October 18. 1,000 ft. Larry Trimble.*

FOUR DAYS A WIDOW. October 19. 1,000 ft.

A MISTAKE IN SPELLING. October 21. 1,000 ft.

THE SPIRIT OF THE RANGE. October 22. 1,000 ft.

SCENES OF IRISH LIFE AT DUBLIN. October 23. 1,000 ft.
Larry Trimble.* (released on the same reel with AN
EXPENSIVE SHINE).

AN EXPENSIVE SHINE. October 23. 1,000 ft. (released
on the same reel with SCENES OF IRISH LIFE AT
DUBLIN).

THE TOYMAKER. October 24. 1,000 ft.

FAITHFUL UNTO DEATH. October 25. 1,000 ft.

IN THE FURNACE FIRE. October 26. 1,000 ft.

NONE BUT THE BRAVE DESERVE THE FAIR. October 28.
1,000 ft.

BUNNY AT THE DERBY. October 29. 1,000 ft. Larry
Trimble.* (released on the same reel with JUST
LUCK).

JUST LUCK. October 29. 1,000 ft. (released on the
same reel with BUNNY AT THE DERBY).

POET AND PEASANT. October 30. 1,000 ft.

ON THE LINE OF PERIL. October 31. 1,000 ft.

LESSONS IN COURTSHIP. November 1. 1,000 ft. (released on the same reel with BETTINA'S SUBSTITUTE).

BETTINA'S SUBSTITUTE. November 1. 1,000 ft. (released on the same reel with LESSONS IN COURTSHIP).

IN THE GARDEN FAIR. November 2. 1,000 ft.

THE MILLS OF THE GODS. November 4. 3,000 ft.

AN OFFICIAL APPOINTMENT. November 4. 1,000 ft.

THE FACE OR THE VOICE. November 5. 1,000 ft.

MICHAEL McSHANE, MATCHMAKER. November 6.
1,000 ft. Larry Trimble.*

OUT OF THE SHADOWS. November 7. 1,000 ft.

A MODERN ATLANTA. November 8. 1,000 ft.

THE HAND BAG. November 9. 1,000 ft. (released on
the same reel with ARABIAN SPORTS).

ARABIAN SPORTS. November 9. 1,000 ft. (released on the same reel with THE HAND BAG).

CAPTAIN BARNACLE, REFORMER. November 11. 1,000 ft.

THE PROFESSOR AND THE LADY. November 12. 1,000 ft. (released on the same reel with AQUATIC ELEPHANTS).

AQUATIC ELEPHANTS. November 12. 1,000 ft. (released on the same reel with THE PROFESSOR AND THE LADY).

LORD BROWNING AND CINDERELLA. November 13. 1,000 ft.

BILLY'S PIPE DREAM. November 14. 1,000 ft.

UNA OF THE SIERRAS. November 15. 1,000 ft.

THE MODEL FOR ST. JOHN. November 16. 1,000 ft.

THE UNUSUAL HONEYMOON. November 18. 1,000 ft.

ROMANCE OF A RICKSHAW. November 19. 1,000 ft.

TIMID MAY. November 20. 1,000 ft. (released on the same reel with DARKTOWN DUEL).

DARKTOWN DUEL. November 20. 1,000 ft. (released on the same reel with TIMID MAY).

SIX O'CLOCK. November 21. 1,000 ft.

THE SERVANT PROBLEM. November 22. 1,000 ft.

BILLY'S BURGLAR. November 22. 2,000 ft.

WILD PAT. November 23. 1,000 ft.

OMEN OF THE MESA. November 25. 1,000 ft.

IN THE FLAT ABOVE. November 26. 1,000 ft.

THE WOOD VIOLET. November 27. 1,000 ft.

THREE GIRLS AND A MAN. November 28. 1,000 ft. (released on the same reel with THE EAVESDROPPER).

THE EAVESDROPPER. November 28. 1,000 ft. (released on the same reel with THREE GIRLS AND A MAN).

SUSIE TO SUSANNE. November 29. 1,000 ft.

O'HARA, SQUATTER AND PHILOSOPHER. November 30. 1,000 ft.

THE ABSENT-MINDED VALET. December 2. 1,000 ft.

THE SCOOP. December 3. 1,000 ft.

THE CURIO HUNTERS. December 4. 1,000 ft.

MRS. LIRRIPER'S LEGACY. December 5. 1,000 ft.

TOO MANY CASEYS. December 6. 1,000 ft. (released on the same reel with CORK AND VICINITY).

CORK AND VICINITY. December 6. 1,000 ft. Larry Trimble. (released on the same reel with TOO MANY CASEYS).

THE DRAWING. December 6. 2,000 ft.

THE AWAKENING OF BIANCA. December 7. 1,000 ft.

THE SIGNAL OF DISTRESS. December 9. 1,000 ft.

DOCTOR BRIDGET. December 10. 1,000 ft.

NATOOSA. December 11. 1,000 ft.

ADAM AND EVE. December 12. 1,000 ft.

THE SONG OF THE SHELL. December 13. 1,000 ft.

ALL FOR A GIRL. December 14. 1,000 ft. (released on the same reel with THE DANDY, OR MR. DAWSON TURNS THE TABLES).

THE DANDY, OR MR. DAWSON TURNS THE TABLES. December 14. 1,000 ft. (released on the same reel with ALL FOR A GIRL).

A LEAP YEAR PROPOSAL. December 16. 1,000 ft.

THE NIGHT BEFORE CHRISTMAS. December 17. 1,000 ft.

WHO STOLE BUNNY'S UMBRELLA. December 18. 1,000 ft. (released on the same reel with AT THE DOG SHOW).

AT THE DOG SHOW. December 18. 1,000 ft. (released on the same reel with WHO STOLE BUNNY'S UMBRELLA).

THE HAT. December 19. 1,000 ft.

FOLLOWING THE STAR. December 20. 1,000 ft.

A MARRIAGE OF CONVENIENCE. December 21. 1,000 ft.

WHILE SHE POWDERED HER NOSE. December 23. 1,000 ft.

IT ALL CAME OUT IN THE WASH. December 24. 1,000 ft. (released on the same reel with IDA'S CHRISTMAS).

IDA'S CHRISTMAS. December 24. 1,000 ft. (released on
the same reel with IT ALL CAME OUT IN THE WASH).

TWO WOMEN AND TWO MEN. December 25. 1,000 ft.

FRECKLES. December 26. 1,000 ft.

THE BETTER MAN. December 27. 1,000 ft.

THE REINCARNATION OF KARMA. December 27. 2,000 ft.

SUE SIMPKINS' AMBITION. December 28. 1,000 ft.

PLANTING THE SPRING GARDEN. December 30. 1,000 ft.

A WOMAN. December 31. 1,000 ft.

1913

CASEY AT THE BAT. January 1. 1,000 ft. (released on
the same reel with LOVE HATH WROUGHT A MIRACLE).
James Young.

LOVE HATH WROUGHT A MIRACLE. January 1. 1,000 ft.
(released on the same reel with CASEY AT THE BAT).
James Young.

THE ADVENTURE OF THE COUNTERFEIT BILLS. January
2. 1,000 ft. Maurice Costello.

MR. BOLTER'S NIECE. January 3. 1,000 ft. Frederick
Thomson.

A BIT OF BLUE RIBBON. January 4. 1,000 ft. Rollin S.
Sturgeon.

THE ANGEL OF THE DESERT. January 6. 1,000 ft.
Rollin S. Sturgeon.

THE WINGS OF A MOTH. January 7. 1,000 ft. Larry
Trimble.

THE DELAYED LETTER. January 8. 1,000 ft. Ralph
Ince.

TWO OF A KIND. January 9. 1,000 ft. (released on the
same reel with BETTY'S BABY). Bert Angeles.

BETTY'S BABY. January 9. 1,000 ft. (released on the
same reel with TWO OF A KIND).

THE ADVENTURE OF THE AMBASSADOR'S DISAPPEARANCE.
January 10. 1,000 ft. Maurice Costello.

O'HARA HELPS CUPID.   January 11.   1,000 ft.   Van Dyke Brooke.

THE THREE BLACK BAGS.   January 13.   1,000 ft.   Frederick Thomson.

THE LITTLE MINISTER.   January 13.   3,000 ft.

OFF THE ROAD.   January 15.   1,000 ft.   Ralph Ince.

THE BRINGING OUT OF PAPA.   January 16.   1,000 ft.   Ralph Ince.

HIS WIFE'S RELATIVES.   January 17.   1,000 ft.   (released on the same reel with THE INTERRUPTED HONEY-MOON).   Ralph Ince.

THE INTERRUPTED HONEYMOON.   January 17.   1,000 ft. (released on the same reel with HIS WIFE'S RELA-TIVES).   James Young.

THOU SHALT NOT KILL.   January 18.   1,000 ft.   Hal Reid.

WHAT A CHANGE OF CLOTHES DID.   January 20.   1,000 ft.   Maurice Costello.

MA'S APRON STRINGS.   January 21.   1,000 ft.   Frederick Thomson.

THE JOKE ON HOWLING WOLF.   January 22.   1,000 ft.   Rollin S. Sturgeon.

THE VOLUNTEER STRIKE BREAKERS.   January 23. 1,000 ft.   Frederick Thomson.

THE WIDOW'S MIGHT.   January 24.   1,000 ft.   James Young.

THE VENGEANCE OF DURAND.   January 24.   2,000 ft.

EVERYBODY'S DOING IT.   January 25.   1,000 ft.   (re-leased on the same reel with WHEN BOBBY FORGOT). Larry Trimble.

WHEN BOBBY FORGOT.   January 25.   1,000 ft.   (released on the same reel with EVERYBODY'S DOING IT).

TWO SETS OF FURS.   January 27.   1,000 ft.   (released on the same reel with THE COKE INDUSTRY).   Maurice Costello.

THE COKE INDUSTRY.   January 27.   1,000 ft.   (released on the same reel with TWO SETS OF FURS).

WHEN MARY GREW UP.   January 28.   1,000 ft.   James Young.

AND HIS WIFE CAME BACK. January 29. 1,000 ft.
James Young.

THE SMOKE FROM LONE BILL'S CABIN. January 30.
1,000 ft. Rollin S. Sturgeon.

HOW FATTY MADE GOOD. January 31. 1,000 ft. Ralph
Ince.

IT MADE HIM MAD. February 1. 1,000 ft. James Young.

CUTEY AND THE TWINS. February 3. 1,000 ft. James
Young.

CLASSMATES' FROLIC. February 4. 1,000 ft. (released
on the same reel with ELEPHANT'S TOILET). Ralph
Ince.

ELEPHANT'S TOILET. February 4. 1,000 ft. (released
on the same reel with CLASSMATES' FROLIC).
Frederick Thomson.

THE SKULL. February 5. 1,000 ft. W. V. Ranous.

STENOGRAPHER TROUBLES. February 6. 1,000 ft.
Frederick Thomson.

THE WHISPERED WORD. February 7. 1,000 ft. Rollin
S. Sturgeon.

THE JOKE WASN'T ON BEN BOLT. February 8. 1,000 ft.
Charles Kent.

A TRIP TO CATCH A BURGLAR. February 10. 1,000 ft.
Van Dyke Brooke.

PAPA PUTS ONE OVER. February 11. 1,000 ft. Ralph
Ince.

BUTTERCUPS. February 12. 1,000 ft. (released on the
same reel with THE PANAMA CANAL). Frederick
Thomson.

THE PANAMA CANAL. February 12. 1,000 ft. (released
on the same reel with BUTTERCUPS).

THE WEAPON. February 13. 1,000 ft. Maurice Costello.

THE MAN HIGHER UP. February 14. 1,000 ft. Frederick
Thomson.

THE CHAINS OF AN OATH. February 14. 2,000 ft.

POLLY AT THE RANCH. February 15. 1,000 ft. Rollin
S. Sturgeon.

A CORNER IN CROOKS.   February 17.   1,000 ft.   Rollin
   S. Sturgeon.

JUST SHOW PEOPLE.   February 18.   1,000 ft.   Van Dyke
   Brooke.

BEAU BRUMMELL.   February 19.   1,000 ft.   James Young.

MR. FORD'S TEMPER.   February 20.   1,000 ft.   (released
   on the same reel with VIEWS OF IRELAND).   Frederick
   Thomson.

VIEWS OF IRELAND.   February 20.   1,000 ft.   (released
   on the same reel with MR. FORD'S TEMPER).   Larry
   Trimble.

CINDERELLA'S SLIPPER.   February 21.   1,000 ft.

THE LOCKET.   February 22.   1,000 ft.   Frederick Thomson.

FOUR DAYS.   February 24.

SUSPICIOUS HENRY.   February 24.   1,000 ft.   Frederick
   Thomson.

WHEN THE DESERT WAS KIND.   February 25.   1,000 ft.
   Rollin S. Sturgeon.

THE FINAL JUSTICE.   February 26.   1,000 ft.   Bert
   Angeles.

TIM GROGAN'S FOUNDLING.   February 27.   1,000 ft.   Van
   Dyke Brooke.

THE OLD GUARD.   February 28.   1,000 ft.   (released on
   the same reel with GOVERNOR WILSON).   James
   Young.

GOVERNOR WILSON.   February 28.   1,000 ft.   (released
   on the same reel with THE OLD GUARD).

PICKWICK PAPERS.   February 28.   2,000 ft.   Larry
   Trimble.

UNDER THE MAKE-UP.   March 1.   1,000 ft.   Larry
   Trimble.

O'HARA'S GODCHILD.   March 3.   1,000 ft.   Van Dyke
   Brooke.

HUBBY BUYS A BABY.   March 4.   1,000 ft.   Frederick
   Thomson.

A HEART OF THE FOREST.   March 5.   1,000 ft.   Ralph
   Ince.

THAT COLLEGE LIFE.   March 6.   1,000 ft.   William Humphrey.

THE ONE GOOD TURN.   March 7.   1 000 ft.   W. V. Ranous.

HE WAITED.   March 8.   1,000 ft.   (released on the same reel with BLACK DIAMONDS).   Frederick Thomson.

BLACK DIAMONDS.   March 8.   1,000 ft.   (released on the same reel with HE WAITED).

PUT YOURSELF IN THEIR PLACE.   March 10.   1,000 ft. (released on the same reel with NEW YORK FIRE DRILL).   James Young.

NEW YORK FIRE DRILL.   March 10.   1,000 ft.   (released on the same reel with PUT YOURSELF IN THEIR PLACE).

RED AND WHITE ROSES.   March 10.   2,000 ft.

THE WAY OUT.   March 11.   1,000 ft.   Maurice Costello and W. V. Ranous.

HIS HONOR, THE MAYOR.   March 12.   1,000 ft.   Frederick Thomson.

THE DECEIVERS.   March 13.   1,000 ft.   Rollin S. Sturgeon.

SISTERS ALL.   March 14.   1,000 ft.   Larry Trimble.

QUEBEC ZOUAVES.   March 15.

THE DOG HOUSE BUILDERS.   March 15.   1,000 ft.   James Young.

THE MOUSE AND THE LION.   March 17.   1,000 ft.   Van Dyke Brooke.

A BIRTHDAY GIFT.   March 18.   1,000 ft.   (released on the same reel with ACCORDING TO ADVICE).   Charles Kent.

ACCORDING TO ADVICE.   March 18.   1,000 ft.   (released on the same reel with A BIRTHDAY GIFT).   Rollin S. Sturgeon.

THE STRENGTH OF MEN.   March 19.   2,000 ft.

THE HOUSE IN SUBURBIA.   March 19.   1,000 ft.   Larry Trimble.

THE WONDERFUL STATUE.   March 20.   1,000 ft.   Frederick Thomson.

A MATTER OF MATRIMONY.   March 21.   1,000 ft.   Rollin S. Sturgeon and Major J. A. McGuire.

MINE RESCUE WORK OF THE AMERICAN RED CROSS.
 March 21.

BELINDA, THE SLAVEY, OR PLOT AND COUNTERPLOT.
 March 22. 1,000 ft. Bert Angeles.

BROTHER BILL. March 24. 1,000 ft. Ralph Ince.

DICK, THE DEAD SHOT. March 25. 1,000 ft. Van Dyke
 Brooke.

LOVE FINDS A WAY. March 26. 1,000 ft. (released on
 the same reel with IN OLD QUEBEC). Ralph Ince.

IN OLD QUEBEC. March 26. 1,000 ft. (released on the
 same reel with LOVE FINDS A WAY).

GETTING A PRACTICE. March 27. 1,000 ft. Maurice
 Costello and W. V. Ranous.

THE BLARNEY STONE. March 28. 1,000 ft. (released
 on the same reel with SCENES IN JAPAN).
 Larry Trimble.

SCENES IN JAPAN. March 28. 1,000 ft. (released on
 the same reel with THE BLARNEY STONE).

THE MODERN PRODIGAL. March 28. 2,000 ft.

TWO BROTHERS. March 29. 1,000 ft. Rollin S. Sturgeon.

TENYO MARU. March 29.

BEDELIA BECOMES A LADY. March 31. 1,000 ft. Rollin
 S. Sturgeon.

CHECKMATED. April 1. 1,000 ft. Larry Trimble.

ALIXE, OR THE TEST OF FRIENDSHIP. April 2. 1,000 ft.
 W. V. Ranous.

THE MIDGET'S ROMANCE. April 3. 1,000 ft. (released
 on the same reel with OUR COAST DEFENDERS).
 Bert Angeles.

OUR COAST DEFENDERS. April 3. 1,000 ft. (released
 on the same reel with THE MIDGET'S ROMANCE).

LET 'EM QUARREL. April 4. 1,000 ft. Larry Trimble.

THE GOLDEN HOARD, OR BURIED ALIVE. April 4.
 2,000 ft.

HE ANSWERED THE AD. April 5. 1,000 ft. Bert Angeles.

BUNNY'S HONEYMOON. April 7. 1,000 ft. Wilfred North.

THE TRANSITION. April 8. 1,000 ft. Rollin S. Sturgeon.

OUT OF THE STORM. April 9. 1,000 ft. Wilfred North.

CUTEY AND THE CHORUS GIRLS. April 10. 1,000 ft.
James Young.

THE WEB. April 11. 2,000 ft.

WANTED A STRONG HAND. April 11. 1,000 ft. (released on the same reel with LAYING A MARINE
CABLE). Van Dyke Brooke.

LAYING A MARINE CABLE. April 11. 1,000 ft. (released on the same reel with WANTED A STRONG
HAND).

MYSTERY OF THE STOLEN CHILD. April 12. 1,000 ft.
Maurice Costello and W. V. Ranous.

MR. MINTERN'S MISADVENTURES. April 14. 1,000 ft.
Maurice Costello and W. V. Ranous.

THE FORTUNE. April 15. 1,000 ft. Wilfred North.

AFTER THE HONEYMOON. April 16. 1,000 ft. Rollin
S. Sturgeon.

SLEUTHING. April 17. 1,000 ft. Bert Angeles.

PLAYING WITH FIRE. April 18. 1,000 ft. Bert Angeles.

SEEING DOUBLE. April 19. 1,000 ft. (released on the
same reel with JEAN AND HER FAMILY). Wilfred
North.

JEAN AND HER FAMILY. April 19. 1,000 ft. (released
on the same reel with SEEING DOUBLE). Larry
Trimble.*

MIXED IDENTITIES. April 21. 1,000 ft. (released on the
same reel with GALA DAY PARADE, YOKOHAMA,
JAPAN). William Humphrey.

GALA DAY PARADE, YOKOHAMA, JAPAN. April 21.
1,000 ft. (released on the same reel with MIXED
IDENTITIES).

THE ARTIST'S GREAT MADONNA. April 21. 2,000 ft.

THE MYSTERY OF THE STOLEN JEWELS. April 22.
1,000 ft. Maurice Costello and W. V. Ranous.

IN THE GOOD OLD SUMMER TIME. April 22.

THERE'S MUSIC IN THE HAIR. April 23. 1,000 ft.
Larry Trimble.

CROWDS ATTENDING GODS IN TEMPLE, TOKYO, JAPAN. April 23.

THE POWER THAT RULES. April 24. 1,000 ft. Rollin S. Sturgeon.

THE STRONGER SEX. April 25. 1,000 ft. Wilfred North.

A FIGHTING CHANCE. April 26. 1,000 ft. Ralph Ince.

O'HARA AND THE YOUTHFUL PRODIGAL. April 28. 1,000 ft. Van Dyke Brooke.

HEARTS OF THE FIRST EMPIRE. April 28. 2,000 ft.

TWO'S COMPANY, THREE'S A CROWD. April 29. 1,000 ft. (released on the same reel with STREET SCENES, YOKOHAMA, JAPAN). Ralph Ince.

STREET SCENES, YOKOHAMA, JAPAN. April 29. 1,000 ft. (released on the same reel with TWO'S COMPANY, THREE'S A CROWD).

A WINDOW ON WASHINGTON PARK. April 30. 1,000 ft. Larry Trimble.

BUNNY VERSUS CUTEY. May 1. 1,000 ft. (released on the same reel with USES OF DYNAMITE BY U.S. ENG. CORPS). Wilfred North.

USES OF DYNAMITE BY U.S. ENG. CORPS. May 1. 1,000 ft. (released on the same reel with BUNNY VERSUS CUPID).

CINDERS. May 2. 1,000 ft. Rollin S. Sturgeon.

CAPTAIN MARY BROWN. May 3. 1,000 ft. William Humphrey.

BINGLES MENDS THE CLOCK. May 5. 1,000 ft. Frederick Thomson.

OMENS AND ORACLES. May 6. 1,000 ft. Bert Angeles.

DISCIPLINING DAISY. May 7. 1,000 ft. (released on the same reel with INSPECTION OF THE QUEBEC POLICE). Wilfred North.

INSPECTION OF THE QUEBEC POLICE. May 7. 1,000 ft. (released on the same reel with DISCIPLINING DAISY).

THE DEERSLAYER. May 7. 2,000 ft.

THE WRATH OF OSAKA. May 8. 1,000 ft.

CUPID'S HIRED MAN. May 9. 1,000 ft. Wilfred North.

THE SEA MAIDEN. May 10. 1, 000 ft. Rollin S. Sturgeon.

THE WRONG PAIR. May 12. 1, 000 ft. (released on the same reel with THE GRAND CANYON). Rollin S. Sturgeon.

THE GRAND CANYON. May 12. 1, 000 ft. (released on the same reel with THE WRONG PAIR).

MR. HORATIO SPARKINS. May 13. 1, 000 ft. Van Dyke Brooke.

TWO SOULS WITH BUT A SINGLE THOUGHT. May 14. 1, 000 ft.

A SOUL IN BONDAGE. May 15. 1, 000 ft. Van Dyke Brooke.

THE VAMPIRE OF THE DESERT. May 16. 2, 000 ft.

HIS LIFE FOR HIS EMPEROR. May 16. 1, 000 ft. William Humphrey.

BUNNY AND THE BUNNY-HUG. May 17. 1, 000 ft. Wilfred North.

BUNNY'S BIRTHDAY SURPRISE. May 19. 1, 000 ft. (released on the same reel with VITAGRAPHERS AT KAMA KURA). Wilfred North.

VITAGRAPHERS AT KAMA KURA. May 19. 1, 000 ft. (released on the same reel with BUNNY'S BIRTHDAY SURPRISE).

THE AMATEUR LION TAMER. May 20. 1, 000 ft. Frederick Thomson.

COUNSELLOR BOBBY. May 21. 1, 000 ft. Larry Trimble.

A LADY AND HER MAID. May 22. 1, 000 ft. Bert Angeles.

THE MIDGET'S REVENGE. May 23. 1, 000 ft. (released on the same reel with GOING TO MEET PAPA). Bert Angeles.

GOING TO MEET PAPA. May 23. 1, 000 ft. (released on the same reel with THE MIDGET'S REVENGE).

THE STILL VOICE. May 24. 2, 000 ft.

CUPID THROUGH THE KEYHOLE. May 24. 1, 000 ft. Van Dyke Brooke.

UP AND DOWN THE LADDER. May 26. 1, 000 ft. Larry Trimble.

TRICKS OF THE TRADE.   May 27.   1,000 ft.   Frederick
Thomson.

CUTEY PLAYS DETECTIVE.   May 28.   1,000 ft.   Larry
Trimble.

THE ONLY VETERAN IN TOWN.   May 29.   1,000 ft.
Charles Kent.

A HUSBAND'S TRICK.   May 30.   1,000 ft.   William
Humphrey.

ONE CAN'T ALWAYS TELL.   May 31.   1,000 ft.   (released
on the same reel with WHO'D HAVE THUNK IT?).
Van Dyke Brooke.

WHO'D HAVE THUNK IT?   May 31.   1,000 ft.   (released
on the same reel with YOU CAN'T ALWAYS TELL).

THE WHITE SLAVE.   May 31.   2,000 ft.

WHAT GOD HATH JOINED TOGETHER.   June 2.   1,000 ft.
Rollin S. Sturgeon.

BUNNY AS A REPORTER.   June 3.   1,000 ft.   (released
on the same reel with THREE TO ONE).   Wilfred
North.

THREE TO ONE.   June 3.   1,000 ft.   (released on the
same reel with BUNNY AS A REPORTER).

A MODERN PSYCHE.   June 4.   1,000 ft.   Van Dyke Brooke.

THE HEART OF MRS. ROBINS.   June 5.   1,000 ft.   Van
Dyke Brooke.

THE BUTLER'S SECRET.   June 6.   1,000 ft.   William
Humphrey.

THE FORGOTTEN LATCHKEY.   June 7.   1,000 ft.   Ralph
Ince.

THE BACHELOR'S BABY.   June 9.   1,000 ft.   Van Dyke
Brooke.

CUTEY TRIES REPORTING.   June 10.   1,000 ft.   Bert
Angeles.

HIS HOUSE IN ORDER.   June 11.   1,000 ft.   Wilfred North.

THE REGIMENT OF TWO.   June 11.   2,000 ft.

HIS TIRED UNCLE.   June 12.   1,000 ft.   (released on the
same reel with CAPERS OF CUPID).   Wilfred North.

CAPERS OF CUPID.   June 12.   1,000 ft.   (released on the
same reel with HIS TIRED UNCLE).

AN INFERNAL TANGLE. June 13. 1,000 ft. William
Humphrey.

DOES ADVERTISING PAY? June 14. 1,000 ft. Larry
Trimble.

THE SILVER CIGARETTE CASE. June 16. 1,000 ft.
Van Dyke Brooke.

THE COMING OF GRETCHEN. June 17. 1,000 ft. Bert
Angeles.

THE DROP OF BLOOD. June 18. 1,000 ft. Frederick
Thomson.

BUNNY'S DILEMMA. June 19. 1,000 ft. Wilfred North.

DELAYED PROPOSALS. June 20. 1,000 ft. (released on
the same reel with YOKOHAMA FIRE DEPARTMENT).

YOKOHAMA FIRE DEPARTMENT. June 20. 1,000 ft.
(released on the same reel with DELAYED PROPOSALS).

'ARRIET'S BABY. June 21. 1,000 ft. Van Dyke Brooke.

THE LION'S BRIDE. June 23. 1,000 ft. Frederick
Thomson.

THE SNARE OF FATE. June 23. 3,000 ft. William
Humphrey.

NO SWEETS. June 24. 1,000 ft. Van Dyke Brooke.

JACK'S CHRYSANTHEMUM. June 25. 1,000 ft. Maurice
Costello and W. V. Ranous.

HER SWEETEST MEMORY. June 26. 1,000 ft. L. Rogers
Lytton.

ONE GOOD JOKE DESERVES ANOTHER. June 27. 1,000
ft. Wilfred North.

FIELD SPORTS, HONG KONG, CHINA. June 27.

ONE OVER ON CUTEY. June 28. 1,000 ft. (released on
the same reel with CLOISONNE WARE). Van Dyke
Brooke.

CLOISONNE WARE. June 28. 1,000 ft. (released on the
same reel with ONE OVER ON CUTEY).

ROUGHING THE CUB. June 30. 1,000 ft. Bert Angeles.

BINGLES AND THE CABARET. July 1. 1,000 ft. (released on the same reel with SIGHT-SEEING IN JAPAN).
Frederick Thomson.

SIGHT-SEEING IN JAPAN. July 1. 1,000 ft. (released
    on the same reel with BINGLES AND THE CABARET).

THE TIGER LILY. July 2. 3,000 ft.

THE SONG BIRD OF THE NORTH. July 2. 1,000 ft.
    Ralph Ince.

SWEET DECEPTION. July 3. 1,000 ft. Ralph Ince.

AN UNWRITTEN CHAPTER. July 4. 1,000 ft. William
    Humphrey.

LOVE'S QUARANTINE. July 5. 1,000 ft. Wilfred North.

THE GLOVE. July 7. 1,000 ft. William Humphrey.

COUNT BARBER. July 8. 1,000 ft. Bert Angeles.

SOLITAIRES. July 9. 1,000 ft. (released on the same
    reel with A MILLINERY BOMB). Van Dyke Brooke.

A MILLINERY BOMB. July 9. 1,000 ft. (released on
    the same reel with SOLITAIRES). Wilfred North.

THE CARPENTER. July 10. 1,000 ft. Wilfred North.

THE SPIRIT OF THE ORIENT. July 11. 1,000 ft. Maurice
    Costello.

THE MOULDING. July 12. 1,000 ft. Ralph Ince.

O'HARA AS A GUARDIAN ANGEL. July 14. 1,000 ft.
    Van Dyke Brooke.

THE DIAMOND MYSTERY. July 14. 2,000 ft.

MY LADY OF IDLENESS. July 15. 1,000 ft. William
    Humphrey.

THE MASTER PAINTER. July 16. 1,000 ft. L. Rogers
    Lytton.

HUBBY'S TOOTHACHE. July 17. 1,000 ft. (released on
    the same reel with SANDY AND SHORTY WORK TO-
    GETHER). Wilfred North.

SANDY AND SHORTY WORK TOGETHER. July 17. 1,000
    ft. (released on the same reel with HUBBY'S TOOTH-
    ACHE). Robert T. Thornby.

THE YELLOW STREAK. July 18. 1,000 ft. W. J. Bauman.

THE TAMING OF BETTY. July 19. 1,000 ft. M. Costello.

THE ONLY WAY. July 21. 1,000 ft. Wilfred North.

THE PICKPOCKET. July 22. 1,000 ft. George D. Baker.

AN ERROR IN KIDNAPPING.   July 23.   1,000 ft.
Frederick Thomson.

AN OLD MAN'S LOVE STORY.   July 24.   1,000 ft.   Van
Dyke Brooke.

THE TABLES TURNED.   July 25.   1,000 ft.   (released on
the same reel with SCENES IN HONOLULU).   Charles
Kent.

SCENES IN HONOLULU.   July 25.   1,000 ft.   (released on
the same reel with THE TABLES TURNED).

THE SPELL.   July 26.   1,000 ft.   Rollin S. Sturgeon.

A PRINCE OF EVIL.   July 26.   2,000 ft.

DR. CRATHERN'S EXPERIMENT.   July 28.   1,000 ft.   Van
Dyke Brooke.

THE TROUBLESOME DAUGHTERS.   July 29.   1,000 ft.
Frederick Thomson.

THE SIXTH COMMANDMENT.   July 30.   1,000 ft.

WHEN SOCIETY CALLS.   July 31.   1,000 ft.

COURAGE OF THE COMMONPLACE.   August 1.   1,000 ft.
Rollin S. Sturgeon.

THE INTRUDER.   August 2.   2,000 ft.   Maurice Costello
and Wilfred North.

THE FORTUNE HUNTER OF HICKSVILLE.   August 4.
1,000 ft.   (released on the same reel with THE
CELESTIAL REPUBLIC).   Robert Thornby.

THE CELESTIAL REPUBLIC.   August 4.   1,000 ft.   (released on the same reel with THE FORTUNE HUNTERS
OF HICKSVILLE).

A FAITHFUL SERVANT.   August 5.   1,000 ft.   Maurice
Costello.

THE LATE MR. JONES.   August 6.   1,000 ft.   James
Young.

THE PENALTIES OF REPUTATION.   August 7.   1,000 ft.
William Humphrey.

A GENTLEMAN OF FASHION.   August 8.   1,000 ft.   George
D. Baker.

THE LINE-UP.   August 9.   2,000 ft.   William Humphrey.

WHEN THE PRESS SPEAKS.   August 11.   1,000 ft.   George
D. Baker.

JOYS OF A JEALOUS WIFE. August 12. 1,000 ft. (re-
    leased on the same reel with BINGLES' NIGHTMARE).
    Maurice Costello.

BINGLES' NIGHTMARE. August 12. 1,000 ft. (released
    on the same reel with JOYS OF A JEALOUS WIFE).
    Ralph Ince.

THE FLIRT. August 13. 1,000 ft. William Humphrey.

KEEPING HUSBANDS HOME. August 14. 1,000 ft. Bert
    Angeles.

THE LADY AND THE GLOVE. August 15. 1,000 ft.
    Frederick Thomson.

THE LINE-UP. August 19. 2,000 ft.

SLIM DRISCOLL, SAMARITAN. August 18. 1,000 ft.
    W. J. Bauman.

THOSE TROUBLESOME TRESSES. August 19. 1,000 ft.
    George D. Baker.

BETTER DAYS. August 20. 1,000 ft. (released on the
    same reel with IN AND ABOUT CALCUTTA). Van
    Dyke Brooke.

IN AND ABOUT CALCUTTA. August 20. 1,000 ft. (re-
    leased on the same reel with BETTER DAYS).

A MAID OF MANDALAY. August 21. 1,000 ft. Maurice
    Costello.

PLAYING THE PIPERS. August 22. 1,000 ft. William
    Humphrey.

THE FEUDISTS. August 23. 1,600 ft. Wilfred North.

WHEN GLASSES ARE NOT GLASSES. August 25. 1,000 ft.
    Van Dyke Brooke.

A DOLL FOR THE BABY. August 26. 1,000 ft. W. J.
    Bauman.

WHICH WAY DID HE GO? August 27. 1,000 ft. George
    D. Baker.

HE FELL IN LOVE WITH HIS MOTHER-IN-LAW. August
    28. 1,000 ft. (released on the same reel with
    SIGHTS IN SINGAPORE). Bert Angeles.

SIGHTS IN SINGAPORE. August 28. 1,000 ft. (released
    on the same reel with HE FELL IN LOVE WITH HIS
    MOTHER-IN-LAW).

THE CLOWN AND THE PRIMA-DONNA. August 29. 1,000 ft. Maurice Costello and Wilfred North.

THE CALL. August 30. 2,000 ft. Ralph Ince.

THE PASSING OF JOE MARY. September 1. 1,000 ft. Robert T. Thornby.

HIS LORDSHIP, BILLY SMOKE. September 2. 1,000 ft. Robert T. Thornby.

THE KISS OF RETRIBUTION. September 3. 1,000 ft. Van Dyke Brooke.

THE LONELY PRINCESS. September 4. 1,000 ft. Maurice Costello.

PICKWICK PAPERS. September 5. 1,000 ft. (released on the same reel with THE BABY ELEPHANT). Larry Trimble.

THE BABY ELEPHANT. September 5. 1,000 ft. (released on the same reel with PICKWICK PAPERS).

WHEN WOMEN GO ON THE WARPATH. September 6. 2,000 ft. L. Rogers Lytton and James Young.

CUPID VERSUS WOMENS' RIGHTS. September 8. 1,000 ft. Maurice Costello.

OLD MODDINGTON'S DAUGHTERS. September 9. 1,000 ft. W. J. Bauman.

FORTUNE'S TURN. September 10. 1,000 ft. Wilfred North.

THE TIGER. September 11. 1,000 ft. Frederick Thomson.

SAUCE FOR THE GOOSE. September 12. 1,000 ft. L. Rogers Lytton and James Young.

THE LOST MILLIONAIRE. September 13. 2,000 ft. Ralph Ince.

PUMPS. September 15. 1,000 ft. (released on the same reel with SANDY GETS SHORTY A JOB). Larry Trimble.

SANDY GETS SHORTY A JOB. September 15. 1,000 ft. (released on the same reel with PUMPS). Robert T. Thornby.

THEIR MUTUAL FRIEND. September 16. 1,000 ft. Frederick Thomson.

THE HINDOO CHARM. September 17. 1,000 ft. Maurice Costello.

SUNNY, OR THE CATTLE THIEF. September 18. 1,000 ft.
W. J. Bauman.

JOHN TOBIN'S SWEETHEART. September 19. 1,000 ft.
George D. Baker.

OUR WIVES. September 20. 2,000 ft. James Lackaye.

DADDY'S SOLDIER BOY. September 22. 1,000 ft. Robert
T. Thornby.

EXTREMITIES. September 23. 1,000 ft. (released on the
same reel with SCENES IN SINGAPORE). Maurice
Costello.

SCENES IN SINGAPORE. September 23. 1,000 ft. (released on the same reel with EXTREMITIES).

THE OTHER WOMAN. September 24. 1,000 ft. Van Dyke
Brooke.

THE RACE. September 25. 1,000 ft. Robert T. Thornby.

BUNNY FOR THE CAUSE. September 26. 1,000 ft.
Wilfred North.

UNDER THE DAISIES. September 27. 2,000 ft. Van Dyke
Brooke.

WHEN THE WEST WAS YOUNG. September 29. 1,000 ft.
W. J. Bauman.

WHICH? September 30. 1,000 ft. James Lackaye.

SALVATION SAL. October 1. 1,000 ft. Robert T. Thornby.

THE AUTOCRAT OF FLAPJACK JUNCTION. October 2.
1,000 ft. George D. Baker.

THE TREASURE OF DESERT ISLE. October 3. 1,000 ft.
Ralph Ince.

THE MYSTERY OF THE SILVER SKULL. October 4.
2,000 ft. Wilfred North and Maurice Costello.

ANN OF THE TRAILS. October 6. 1,000 ft. W. J.
Bauman.

A HOMESPUN TRAGEDY. October 7. 1,000 ft. James W.
Castle and Ned Finley.

WHEN FRIENDSHIP CEASES. October 8. 1,000 ft. Robert
T. Thornby.

HEARTBROKEN SHEP. October 9. 1,000 ft. L. Rogers
Lytton and James Young.

CUTEY'S WATERLOO. October 10. 1,000 ft. James
Lackaye.

THE TEST. October 11. 2,000 ft. Captain Harry Lambert.

MRS. UPTON'S DEVICE. October 13. 1,000 ft. James W.
Castle.

THE BALLYHOO'S STORY. October 14. 1,000 ft. Rollin
S. Sturgeon.

MASTER FIXIT. October 15. 1,000 ft. (released on the
same reel with BUDDHIST TEMPLES AND WORSHIP-
PERS). Ralph Ince.

BUDDHIST TEMPLES AND WORSHIPPERS. October 15.
1,000 ft. (released on the same reel with MASTER
FIXIT).

THE OUTLAW. October 16. 1,000 ft. Robert T. Thornby.

MATRIMONIAL MANOEUVRES. October 17. 1,000 ft.
Maurice Costello and Wilfred North.

THE PIRATES. October 18. 2,000 ft. George D. Baker.

THE WHITE FEATHER. October 20. 1,000 ft. W. J.
Bauman.

LUELLA'S LOVE STORY. October 21. 1,000 ft. L. Rogers
Lytton and James Young.

SLEUTHS UNAWARES. October 22. 1,000 ft. (released on
the same reel with LOW CASTE BURMESE). Robert
T. Thornby.

LOW CASTE BURMESE. October 22. 1,000 ft. (released
on the same reel with SLEUTHS UNAWARES).

THE DOCTOR'S SECRET. October 23. 1,000 ft. Van Dyke
Brooke.

ON THEIR WEDDING NIGHT   October 24. 1,000 ft.
Maurice Costello.

THE NEXT GENERATION. October 25. 2,000 ft. L.
Rogers Lytton.

AT THE SIGN OF THE LOST ANGEL. October 27. 1,000
ft. Rollin S. Sturgeon.

IN THE SHADOW. October 28. 1,000 ft. James Lackaye.

FATHER'S HATBAND. October 29. 1,000 ft. Van Dyke
Brooke.

BIANCA. October 30. 1,000 ft. Robert T. Thornby.

FATTY'S AFFAIR OF HONOR. October 31. 1,000 ft. (released on the same reel with PEGGY'S BURGLAR). Ralph Ince.

PEGGY'S BURGLAR. October 31. 1,000 ft. (released on the same reel with FATTY'S AFFAIR OF HONOR).

THE WAR-MAKERS. November 1. 2,000 ft. Maurice Costello and Robert Gaillord.

THE KING'S MAN. November 3. 1,000 ft. W. J. Bauman.

HIS SILVER BACHELORHOOD. November 4. 1,000 ft. Van Dyke Brooke.

THE HOODOO UMBRELLA. November 5. 1,000 ft. (released on the same reel with ANCIENT TEMPLES OF KARNAK). Bert Angeles.

ANCIENT TEMPLES OF KARNAK. November 5. 1,000 ft. (released on the same reel with THE HOODOO UMBRELLA).

A BROKEN MELODY. November 6. 1,000 ft. Robert T. Thornby.

FLAMING HEARTS. November 7. 1,000 ft. George D. Baker.

THE DIVER. November 8. 2,000 ft. Captain Harry Lambart.

THIEVES. November 10. 1,000 ft. W. J. Bauman.

THE PRICE OF THOUGHTLESSNESS. November 11. 1,000 ft. (released on the same reel with THE CANALS AT VENICE). Ned Finley.

THE CANALS AT VENICE. November 11. 1,000 ft. (released on the same reel with THE PRICE OF THOUGHTLESSNESS).

AN ELOPEMENT AT HOME. November 12. 1,000 ft. Van Dyke Brooke.

THE RIGHT MAN. November 13. 1,000 ft. Frederick Thomson.

FANNY'S CONSPIRACY. November 14. 1,000 ft. Van Dyke Brooke.

JERRY'S MOTHER-IN-LAW. November 15. 2,000 ft. L. Rogers Lytton and James Young.

TANGLED THREADS. November 17. 1,000 ft. Robert T. Thornby.

HIS LAST FIGHT. November 18. 1,000 ft. Ralph Ince.

WHY I AM HERE. November 19. 1,000 ft. (released on the same reel with FARMING IN ANCIENT THEBES). Ralph Ince.

FARMING IN ANCIENT THEBES. November 19. 1,000 ft. (released on the same reel with WHY I AM HERE).

THE SALE OF A HEART. November 20. 1,000 ft. Maurice Costello and Robert Gaillord.

THE SCHEMERS. November 21. 1,000 ft. George D. Baker.

THE WHIMSICAL THREADS OF DESTINY. November 22. 2,000 ft. Frederick Thomson.

THE LEADING LADY. November 24. 1,000 ft. Ned Finley.

LITTLE KAINTUCK. November 25. 1,000 ft. Robert T. Thornby.

FELLOW VOYAGERS. November 26. 1,000 ft. (released on the same reel with TEMPLES AND STATUES OF ROME). Maurice Costello.

TEMPLES AND STATUES OF ROME. November 26. 1,000 ft. (released on the same reel with FELLOW VOYA-GERS).

THE CURE. November 27. 1,000 ft. Ned Finley and James W. Castle.

BETTY IN THE LION'S DEN. November 28. 1,000 ft. George D. Baker.

THE GOLDEN PATHWAY. November 29. 2,000 ft. Maurice Costello and Robert Gaillord.

A GAME OF CARDS. December 1. 1,000 ft. Ned Finley.

THE WRECK. December 2. 3,000 ft. Ralph Ince.

A PAIR OF PRODIGALS. December 3. 850 ft. Robert T. Thornby.

THE COLISEUM OF ROME. December 3. 150 ft.

THE SWAN GIRL. December 4. 1,000 ft. Ralph Ince.

A LESSON IN JEALOUSY. December 5. 1,000 ft. Captain Harry Lambart.

BEAUTY UNADORNED. December 6. 2,000 ft. L. Rogers Lytton and James Young.

MID KENTUCKY HILLS. December 8. 1,000 ft. Ned Finley.

DECEPTION. December 9. 1,000 ft. W. J. Bauman.

THAT SUIT AT TEN. December 10. 700 ft. Bert Angeles.

PERFORMING LIONS. December 10. 300 ft.

SACRIFICE. December 11. 1,000 ft. Hardee Kirkland.

THE LIFE-SAVER. December 12. 1,000 ft. Wilfred North.

LOVE'S SUNSET. December 13. 2,000 ft. Frederick Thomson.

THE UPRISING OF ANN. December 15. 1,000 ft. Hardee Kirkland.

UP IN A BALLOON. December 16. 700 ft. James Young.

ELEPHANTS AT WORK. December 16. 300 ft.

ANY PORT IN A STORM. December 17. 1,000 ft. W. J. Bauman.

THE FACE OF FEAR. December 18. 1,000 ft. W. J. Bauman.

THE GIRL AT THE LUNCH COUNTER. December 19. 1,000 ft. George D. Baker.

THE ANCIENT ORDER OF GOODFELLOWS. December 20. 2,000 ft. Captain Harry Lambart.

A CHRISTMAS STORY. December 22. 1,000 ft. James W. Castle and Tefft Johnson.

HER FAITH IN THE FLAG. December 23. 1,000 ft. Robert T. Thornby.

THE HONORABLE ALGERNON. December 24. 1,000 ft. Van Dyke Brooke.

THE SPIRIT OF CHRISTMAS. December 25. 1,000 ft. William Humphrey and Tefft Johnson.

THE GOLF GAME AND THE BONNET. December 26. 1,000 ft. George D. Baker.

HEARTSEASE. December 27. 1,000 ft. L. Rogers Lytton and James Young.

HER HUSBAND'S FRIEND. December 29. 1,000 ft. Hardee Kirkland.

HIS SECOND WIFE. December 30. 800 ft. Ralph Ince.

THE BABY SHOW. December 30. 200 ft.

THE EDUCATION OF AUNT GEORGIANNA. December 31. 1,000 ft. Maurice Costello and Robert Gaillord.

1914

THE SECRET OF THE BULB. January 1. 1,000 ft. W. J. Bauman.

THE MISADVENTURES OF A MIGHTY MONARCH. January 2. 1,000 ft. George D. Baker.

THE STREET SINGERS. January 3. 2,000 ft. Wilfred North and Wally Van.

FRANCINE. January 5. 1,000 ft. Ulysses Davis.

JERRY'S UNCLE'S NAMESAKE. January 6. 2,000 ft. L. Rogers Lytton and James Young.

DIANA'S DRESS REFORM. January 7. 1,000 ft. Ralph Ince.

THEIR INTEREST IN COMMON. January 8. 600 ft. Rollin S. Sturgeon.

MONTANA STATE FAIR. January 8. 400 ft.

BUNNY'S MISTAKE   January 9. 1,000 ft. George D. Baker.

OFFICER JOHN DONOVAN. January 10. 2,000 ft. Van Dyke Brooke.

THE RIGHT AND THE WRONG OF IT. January 12. 1,000 ft. Ralph Ince.

THE MASKED DANCER. January 13. 2,000 ft. Burton King.

TIMING CUPID. January 14. 1,000 ft. Captain Harry Lambart.

THE BRUTE. January 15. 800 ft. Hardee Kirkland.

BASEBALL STARS. January 15. 200 ft.

CUTEY'S VACATION. January 16. 1,000 ft. Captain Harry Lambart.

LOCAL COLOR. January 17. 2,000 ft. Ned Finley.

QUANTRELL'S SON. January 19. 1,000 ft. Robert T. Thornby.

THE VAVASOUR BALL. January 20. 2,000 ft. Van Dyke Brooke.

LOVE'S OLD DREAM. January 21. 1,000 ft. George D. Baker.

ANNE OF THE GOLDEN HEART. January 22. 1,000 ft.
Ulysses Davis.

THE PERPLEXED BRIDEGROOM. January 23. 650 ft.
Maurice Costello.

DECORATION DAY AT OLD SOLDIERS' HOME. January 23.
350 ft.

HEARTS OF WOMEN. January 24. 2,000 ft. William
Humphrey and Tefft Johnson.

THE RETURN OF JACK BELLEW. January 26. 1,000 ft.
Robert T. Thornby.

PICKLES, ART AND SAUERKRAUT. January 27. 2,000 ft.
James Young.

SCOTLAND FOREVER. January 28. 1,000 ft. Captain
Harry Lambart.

THE LITTLE BUGLER. January 29. 1,000 ft. Robert T.
Thornby.

THE LUCKY ELOPEMENT. January 30. 1,000 ft. Ralph
Ince.

THE LOVE OF TOKIWA. January 31. 2,000 ft. Ulysses
Davis.

HOW GOD CAME TO SONNY BOY. February 2. 1,000 ft.
Burton King.

CAUGHT WITH THE GOODS. February 3. 2,000 ft. Ned
Finley.

HOW BURKE AND BURKE MADE GOOD. February 4.
1,000 ft. Captain Harry Lambart.

LINCOLN, THE LOVER. February 5. 1,000 ft. Ralph
Ince.

MARRYING SUE. February 6. 1,000 ft. Tefft Johnson.

TAINTED MONEY. February 7. 2,000 ft. Burton King.

THE WINNER WINS. February 9. 1,000 ft. W. J. Bauman.

THE MASTER OF THE MINE. February 10. 2,000 ft.
W. J. Bauman.

SONNY JIM IN SEARCH OF A MOTHER. February 11.
1,000 ft. Tefft Johnson.

SOME STEAMER SCOOPING. February 12. 700 ft.
Maurice Costello.

NIAGARA FALLS. February 12. 300 ft.

BUNNY'S BIRTHDAY.   February 13.   1,000 ft.   George D. Baker.

CHILDREN OF THE FEUD.   February 14.   2,000 ft.   Ned Finley.

SAWDUST AND SALOME.   February 16.   1,000 ft.   Van Dyke Brooke.

BACK TO BROADWAY.   February 17.   2,000 ft.   Ralph Ince.

FATTY ON THE JOB.   February 18.   600 ft.   Ralph Ince.

LUMBERING IN SWEDEN.   February 18.   400 ft.

THE FIRST ENDORSEMENT.   February 19.   1,000 ft. Captain Harry Lambart.

HIS LITTLE PAGE.   February 20.   1,000 ft.   Van Dyke Brooke.

IRON AND STEEL.   February 21.   2,000 ft.   Maurice Costello and Robert Gaillord.

IN THE OLD ATTIC.   February 23.   1,000 ft.   Frederick Thomson.

DOCTOR POLLY.   February 24.   2,000 ft.   Wilfred North and Wally Van.

THE HERO.   February 25.   750 ft.   Frederick Thomson.

CRAWFISHING.   February 25.   250 ft.

THE OLD OAK'S SECRET.   February 26.   1,000 ft.   Robert T. Thornby.

A CHANGE IN BAGGAGE CHECKS.   February 27.   1,000 ft. George D. Baker.

THE DRUDGE.   February 28.   2,000 ft.   Tefft Johnson.

BUFFALO JIM.   March 2.   1,000 ft.   Ulysses Davis.

THE SACRIFICE OF KATHLEEN.   March 3.   2,000 ft. Van Dyke Brooke.

A PAIR OF FRAUDS.   March 4.   1,000 ft.   Theodore Marston.

SILENT TRAILS.   March 5.   750 ft.   Rollin S. Sturgeon.

SCENES IN NORDLAND.   March 5.   250 ft.

THE SPEEDERS' REVENGE.   March 6.   1,000 ft.   Wilfred North and Wally Van.

THE MISCHIEF-MAKER.   March 7.   2,000 ft.   Frederick Thomson.

GINGER'S REIGN. March 9. 1,000 ft. Burton King.

THE PORTRAIT. March 10. 2,000 ft. James Young.

ART FOR A HEART. March 11. 1,000 ft. Wilfred North and Wally Van.

THE WAY TO HEAVEN. March 12. 1,000 ft. Ulysses Davis.

MRS. MALONEY'S FORTUNE. March 13. 1,000 ft. Theodore Marston.

AN OFFICER AND A GENTLEMAN. March 14. 2,000 ft. Captain Harry Lambart.

AUNTIE. March 16. 1,000 ft. Burton King.

THE PRICE OF VANITY. March 17. 2,000 ft. Captain Harry Lambart.

THE GHOSTS. March 18. 1,000 ft. W. J. Bauman.

THE IDLER. March 19. 1,000 ft. Tefft Johnson.

A MODEL YOUNG MAN. March 20. 1,000 ft. James Young.

OLD RELIABLE. March 21. 2,000 ft. Van Dyke Brooke.

THE WOMAN IN BLACK. March 23. 1,000 ft. Maurice Costello and Robert Gaillord.

HER HUSBAND. March 24. 2,000 ft. Theodore Marston.

THE HALL ROOM RIVALS. March 25. 1,000 ft. Tefft Johnson.

CHANLER RAO, CRIMINAL EXPERT. March 26. 1,000 ft. Ned Finley.

MILLIONS FOR DEFENSE. March 27. 1,000 ft. Ulysses Davis.

NEVER AGAIN. March 28. 2,000 ft. Sidney Drew.

THE SILVER SNUFF BOX. March 30. 1,000 ft. Theodore Marston.

A HELPFUL SISTERHOOD. March 31. 2,000 ft. Van Dyke Brooke.

STAGE-STRUCK. April 1. 1,000 ft. Ned Finley.

TOMMY'S TRAMP. April 2. 1,000 ft. Robert T. Thornby.

BUNNY'S SCHEME. April 3. 1,000 ft. George D. Baker.

THE CRUCIBLE OF FATE.   April 4.   2,000 ft.   Captain Harry Lambart.

CHERRY.   April 6.   650 ft.   James Young.

PUPS ON A RAMPAGE.   April 6.   350 ft.

THE MEMORIES THAT HAUNT.   April 7.   2,000 ft. Captain Harry Lambart.

'FRAID CAT.   April 8.   1,000 ft.   Tefft Johnson.

THE LITTLE SHERIFF.   April 9.   1,000 ft.   George C. Stanley.

AN EASTER LILY.   April 10.   1,000 ft.   Tefft Johnson.

THE GIRL FROM PROSPERITY.   April 11.   2,000 ft.

THE BATTLE OF THE WEAK.   April 13.   1,000 ft. Theodore Marston.

HE NEVER KNEW.   April 14.   2,000 ft.   Ralph Ince.

THE CHICKEN INSPECTOR.   April 15.   1,000 ft.   Wally Van and Wilfred North.

THE KISS.   April 16.   1,000 ft.   Ulysses Davis.

INNOCENT BUT AWKWARD.   April 17.   1,000 ft.   Sidney Drew.

THE VANITY CASE.   April 18.   2,000 ft.   Theodore Marston.

SONNY JIM AT THE NORTH POLE.   April 20.   1,000 ft. Tefft Johnson.

THE SPIRIT AND THE CLAY.   April 21.   2,000 ft. Captain Harry Lambart.

FANNY'S MELODRAMA.   April 22.   1,000 ft.   Wilfred North and Wally Van.

A LITTLE MADONNA.   April 23.   1,000 ft.   Ulysses Davis.

TANGLED TANGOISTS.   April 24.   1,000 ft.   George D. Baker.

HER BIG SCOOP.   April 25.   2,000 ft.   Maurice Costello and Robert Gaillord.

THE AWAKENING OF BARBARA DARE.   April 27.   1,000 ft.   Wilfred North.

THE TATTOO MARK.   April 28.   2,000 ft.

SETTING THE STYLE.   April 29.   1,000 ft.   George D. Baker.

TONY, THE GREASER. April 30. 1,000 ft. Rollin S. Sturgeon.

BUNCO BILL'S VISIT. May 1. 1,000 ft. George D. Baker.

MAREEA, THE HALF-BREED. May 2. 2,000 ft. Ulysses Davis.

CUPID VERSUS MONEY. May 4. 1,000 ft. Van Dyke Brooke.

THE OLD FIRE HORSE AND THE NEW FIRE CHIEF. May 5. 2,000 ft. George D. Baker.

SANDY AND SHORTY START SOMETHING. May 6. 1,000 ft. Robert T. Thornby.

HIS LAST CALL. May 7. 1,000 ft. Tefft Johnson.

BUNNY IN DISGUISE. May 8. 1,000 ft. George D. Baker.

THE ANTIQUE ENGAGEMENT RING. May 9. 2,000 ft. Theodore Marston.

MISTER MURRAY'S WEDDING PRESENT. May 11. 1,000 ft. Van Dyke Brooke.

THE ACID TEST. May 12. 2,000 ft. Maurice Costello and Robert Gaillord.

BUDDY'S FIRST CALL. May 13. 1,000 ft. Tefft Johnson.

THE SEA GULL. May 14. 1,000 ft. Rollin S. Sturgeon.

BUNNY BUYS A HAREM. May 15. 1,000 ft. George D. Baker.

THE COUNTESS VESCHI'S JEWELS. May 16. 2,000 ft. Ned Finley.

DOROTHY DANEBRIDGE, MILITANT. May 18. 1,000 ft. Theodore Marston.

JOHANNA, THE BARBARIAN. May 19. 2,000 ft. Ulysses Davis.

THE RIVAL UNDERTAKERS. May 20. 1,000 ft. Lee Beggs.

OUT IN HAPPY HOLLOW. May 21. 1,000 ft. Ulysses Davis.

BUNNY'S SWELL AFFAIR. May 22. 1,000 ft. Lee Beggs.

ETTA OF THE FOOTLIGHTS. May 23. 2,000 ft. Maurice Costello and Robert Gaillord.

A SENTIMENTAL BURGLAR. May 25. 1,000 ft. Maurice
Costello and Robert Gaillord.

CUTEY'S WIFE. May 26. 2,000 ft. Wilfred North and
Wally Van.

HUNGER KNOWS NO LAW. May 28. 1,000 ft. Ulysses
Davis.

MR. BUNNYHUG BUYS A HAT FOR HIS BRIDE. May 29.
1,000 ft. George D. Baker.

THE MYSTERY OF THE HIDDEN HOUSE. May 30. 2,000
ft. Ulysses Davis.

MISS RAFFLES. June 1. 1,000 ft. Theodore Marston.

THE LAST WILL. June 2. 2,000 ft. Ulysses Davis.

WANTED, A HOUSE. June 3. 1,000 ft. Lee Beggs.

A FALSE MOVE. June 4. 1,000 ft. Robert T. Thornby.

THE MAID FROM SWEDEN. June 5. 1,000 ft. Lee Beggs.

TOO MANY HUSBANDS. June 6. 2,000 ft. Sidney Drew.

EVE'S DAUGHTER. June 8. 1,000 ft. Wilfred North.

THE RIGHT OF WAY. June 9. 2,000 ft. Van Dyke Brooke.

THE WIDOW OF RED ROCK. June 10. 1,000 ft. Wally
Van.

THE POWER TO FORGIVE. June 11. 1,000 ft. George
C. Stanley.

THE ACCOMPLISHED MRS. THOMPSON. June 12. 1,000
ft. Wilfred North.

OUR FAIRY PLAY. June 13. 2,000 ft. Lee Beggs.

THE CRIME OF CAIN. June 15. 1,000 ft. Theodore
Marston.

A WAYWARD DAUGHTER. June 16. 2,000 ft. Van Dyke
Brooke.

THE LADIES' WAR. June 17. 1,000 ft. Wilfred North.

ONLY A SISTER. June 18. 1,000 ft. Ulysses Davis.

THE PERSISTENT MR. PRINCE. June 19. 1,000 ft.
Wilfred North.

FATHER'S FLIRTATION. June 20. 2,000 ft. George D.
Baker.

MARIA'S SACRIFICE. June 22. 1,000 ft. William Humphrey.

THE PASSING OF DIANA. June 23. 2,000 ft. Theodore Marston.

THE 'BEAR' FACTS. June 24. 1,000 ft. Tefft Johnson.

HAPPY-GO-LUCKY. June 25. 1,000 ft. James Young.

THE OLD MAID'S BABY. June 26. 1,000 ft. George D. Baker.

HIS WIFE AND HIS WORK. June 27. 2,000 ft.

THE GANG. June 29. 1,000 ft. Ned Finley.

THE POOR FOLKS' BOY. June 30. 2,000 ft. Ulysses Davis.

THE CIRCUS AND THE BOY. July 1. 1,000 ft. Tefft Johnson.

TWO STEPCHILDREN. July 2. 1,000 ft. Theodore Marston.

A TRAIN OF INCIDENTS. July 3. 1,000 ft. George D. Baker.

THE TOLL. July 4. 2,000 ft. Theodore Marston.

THE FALSE AND THE TRUE. July 6. 1,000 ft. Theodore Marston.

THE MOONSTONE OF FEZ. July 7. 2,000 ft. Maurice Costello and Robert Gaillord.

DOCTOR SMITH'S BABY. July 8. 1,000 ft. Maurice Costello and Robert Gaillord.

PROSECUTION. July 9. 1,000 ft. Ulysses Davis.

THE VASES OF HYMAN. July 10. 1,000 ft. George D. Baker.

LILLIAN'S DILEMMA. July 11. 2,000 ft. Wilfred North.

THE SOUL OF LUIGI. July 13. 1,000 ft. Theodore Marston.

FOGG'S MILLIONS. July 14. 2,000 ft. Van Dyke Brooke.

THE ARRIVAL OF JOSIE. July 15. 1,000 ft. Lee Beggs.

THE LITTLE CAPTAIN. July 16. 1,000 ft. Tefft Johnson.

PIGS IS PIGS. July 17. 1,000 ft. George D. Baker.

THE SONG OF THE GHETTO. July 18. 2,000 ft. William Humphrey.

LOVE, THE CLAIRVOYANT. July 20. 1,000 ft. Maurice Costello and Robert Gaillord.

BREAD UPON THE WATERS. July 21. 2,000 ft. Wilfred North.

BUDDY'S DOWNFALL. July 22. 1,000 ft. Tefft Johnson.

THE APPLE. July 23. 1,000 ft. Theodore Marston.

THE WINNING TRICK. July 24. 1,000 ft. Wilfred North.

ROMANTIC JOSIE. July 25. 2,000 ft. Lee Beggs.

HIS KID SISTER. July 27. 2,000 ft. Ulysses Davis.

JOHN RANCE, GENTLEMAN. July 28. 2,000 ft. Van Dyke Brooke.

OFFICER KATE. July 29. 1,000 ft. Ned Finley.

THE GREATER MOTIVE. July 30. 1,000 ft. Theodore Marston.

PRIVATE BUNNY. July 31. 1,000 ft. George D. Baker.

THE VIOLIN OF M'SIEUR. August 1. 2,000 ft. James Young.

DETECTIVE AND MATCHMAKER. August 3. 1,000 ft. Ulysses Davis.

WARFARE IN THE SKIES. August 4. 2,000 ft. Frederick Thomson.

SECOND SIGHT. August 5. 1,000 ft. Ned Finley.

MEMORIES IN MEN'S SOULS. August 6. 1,000 ft. Van Dyke Brooke.

THE LOCKED HOUSE. August 7. 1,000 ft. George D. Baker.

THE HOUSE ON THE HILL. August 8. 2,000 ft. Tefft Johnson.

THROUGH LIFE'S WINDOW. August 10. 1,000 ft. Maurice Costello and Robert Gaillord.

DAVID GARRICK. August 11. 2,000 ft. James Young.

THE NEW STENOGRAPHER. August 12. 1,000 ft. Wilfred North.

THE HORSE THIEF. August 13. 1,000 ft. Ulysses Davis.

POLISHING UP. August 14. 1,000 ft. George D. Baker.

THE WHEAT AND THE TARES. August 15. 2,000 ft.
Theodore Marston.

PRIVATE DENNIS HOGAN. August 17. 1,000 ft. Captain
Harry Lambart.

AN INNOCENT DELILAH. August 18. 2,000 ft. Ulysses
Davis.

TAKEN BY STORM. August 19. 1,000 ft. James Young.

THE WOES OF A WAITRESS. August 20. 1,000 ft.
Maurice Costello and Robert Gaillord.

THE HONEYMOONERS. August 21. 1,000 ft. George D.
Baker.

LILY OF THE VALLEY. August 22. 2,000 ft. Wilfred
North.

WARD'S CLAIM. August 24. 1,000 ft. Ulysses Davis.

RAINEY, THE LION KILLER. August 25. 2,000 ft.
Sidney Drew.

JOSIE'S DECLARATION OF INDEPENDENCE. August 26.
1,000 ft. Lee Beggs.

THE MYSTERIOUS LODGER. August 27. 1,000 ft.
Maurice Costello and Robert Gaillord.

SUCH A HUNTER. August 28. 1,000 ft. George D. Baker.

JOSIE'S CONEY ISLAND NIGHTMARE. August 29. 2,000 ft.
Lee Beggs.

THE WRONG FLAT. August 31. 1,000 ft. Captain Harry
Lambart.

THE HIDDEN LETTERS. September 1. 2,000 ft. Van
Dyke Brooke.

THE LOST CORD. September 2. 1,000 ft. Wilfred North.

THE UPPER HAND. September 3. 1,000 ft. William
Humphrey.

THE BARREL ORGAN. September 4. 1,000 ft. Edmond F.
Stratton.

TOO MUCH UNCLE. September 5. 2,000 ft. Ralph Ince.

THE UNWRITTEN PLAY. September 7. 1,000 ft. Theodore
Marston.

BRANDON'S LAST RIDE. September 8. 2,000 ft. Ulysses
Davis.

THE BAND LEADER. September 9. 1,000 ft. Edmond F. Stratton.

BELLA'S ELOPEMENT. September 10. 1,000 ft. Maurice Costello and Robert Gaillord.

A STUDY IN FEET. September 11. 1,000 ft. Captain Harry Lambart.

HE DANCED HIMSELF TO DEATH. September 12. 2,000 ft. Ralph Ince.

THE MAN WHO KNEW. September 14. 1,000 ft. William Humphrey.

STEVE O'GRADY'S CHANCE. September 15. 2,000 ft. Ned Finley.

THE AGELESS SEX. September 16. 1,000 ft. Captain Harry Lambart.

POLITICS AND THE PRESS. September 17. 1,000 ft. Van Dyke Brooke.

FATHER'S TIMEPIECE. September 18. 1,000 ft. Lee Beggs.

THE REWARD OF THRIFT. September 19. 2,300 ft. Ned Finley and Tefft Johnson.

FINE FEATHERS MAKE FINE BIRDS. September 21. 1,000 ft. William Humphrey.

THE BLOOD RUBY. September 22. 2,000 ft. Maurice Costello and Robert Gaillord.

A DOUBLE ERROR. September 23. 1,000 ft. Theodore Marston.

A CLOSE CALL. September 24. 1,000 ft. Wilfred North.

A HORSESHOE-- FOR LUCK. September 25. 1,000 ft. Sidney Drew.

HEARTS AND DIAMONDS. September 26. 2,000 ft. George D. Baker.

WHEN THE GODS FORGIVE. September 28. 1,000 ft. Ulysses Davis.

REGAN'S DAUGHTER. September 29. 2,000 ft. Theodore Marston.

THE HEART OF SONNY JIM. September 30. 1,000 ft. Tefft Johnson.

THE LOVE OF PIERRE LAROSSE. October 1. 1,000 ft.
Theodore Marston.

EATS. October 2. 1,000 ft. Lee Beggs.

THE ROYAL WILD WEST. October 3. 2,000 ft. Sidney
Drew.

FISHERMAN KATE. October 5. 1,000 ft. Captain Harry
Lambart.

HIS UNKNOWN GIRL. October 6. 2,000 ft. Captain Harry
Lambart.

KILL OR CURE. October 7. 1,000 ft. Captain Harry
Lambart.

THE LOAN SHARK KING. October 8. 1,000 ft. Van Dyke
Brooke.

JOSIE'S LEGACY. October 9. 1,000 ft. Lee Beggs.

THE ROSE AND THE THORN. October 10. 2,000 ft.
Captain Harry Lambart.

MIDST WOODLAND SHADOWS. October 12. 1,000 ft.
Ralph Ince.

MAREEA, THE FOSTER-MOTHER. October 13. 2,000 ft.
Ulysses Davis.

THE PEACEMAKER. October 14. 1,000 ft. Van Dyke
Brooke.

HIS DOMINANT PASSION. October 15. 1,000 ft. William
Humphrey.

FATTY'S SWEETHEART. October 16. 1,000 ft. Ralph Ince.

THE GIRL IN THE CASE. October 17. 2,000 ft. Maurice
Costello and Robert Gaillord.

HIS WEDDED WIFE. October 19. 2,000 ft. William
Humphrey.

ANNE OF THE MINES. October 20. 2,000 ft. Ulysses
Davis.

UNDER FALSE COLORS. October 21. 1,000 ft. Van Dyke
Brooke.

THE MILL OF LIFE. October 22. 1,000 ft. Maurice
Costello and Robert Gaillord.

A COSTUME PIECE. October 23. 1,000 ft. Wilfred North.

GOODBYE SUMMER. October 24. 1,000 ft. Van Dyke
Brooke.

THE CAVE DWELLERS. October 26. 1,000 ft. Tefft
    Johnson.

THE BUTTERFLY. October 27. 2,000 ft.

WILLIAM HENRY JONES' COURTSHIP. October 28. 1,000
    ft. Sidney Drew.

KIDDING THE BOSS. October 29. 1,000 ft. Ulysses Davis.

BUNNY BACKSLIDES. October 30. 1,000 ft. George D.
    Baker.

WITHIN AN ACE. October 31. 2,000 ft. Theodore Marston.

THE MYSTERY OF BRAYTON COURT. November 2. 1,000
    ft. Maurice Costello and Robert Gaillord.

ON THE STROKE OF FIVE. November 3. 2,000 ft.
    Captain Harry Lambart.

THE EVOLUTION OF PERCIVAL. November 4. 1,000 ft.
    Lee Beggs.

THE CHOICE. November 5. 1,000 ft. Ulysses Davis.

THANKS FOR THE LOBSTER. November 6. 750 ft.
    Wally Van.

IN THE LAND OF ARCADIA. November 7. 2,000 ft.
    Wilfred North.

MISS TOMBOY AND FRECKLES. November 9. 1,000 ft.
    Wilfred North.

THE SENATOR'S BROTHER. November 10. 2,000 ft.
    William Humphrey.

IN BRIDAL ATTIRE. November 11. 1,000 ft. Lee Beggs.

LOLA, THE RAT. November 12. 1,000 ft. Maurice
    Costello and Robert Gaillord.

THE ROCKY ROAD OF LOVE. November 13. 1,000 ft.
    George D. Baker.

ANN, THE BLACKSMITH. November 14. 1,362 ft.
    Ulysses Davis.

MAKING OF A NEWSPAPER. November 14. 638 ft.

SISTERS. November 16. 1,000 ft. Ulysses Davis.

HOPE FOSTER'S MOTHER. November 17. 2,000 ft.
    Lionel Belmore.

FIXING THEIR DADS. November 18. 1,000 ft. George D.
    Baker.

TOO MUCH BURGLAR. November 19. 1,000 ft. Maurice Costello and Robert Gaillord.

THE PROFESSIONAL SCAPEGOAT. November 20. 1,000 ft. Sidney Drew.

MARY JANE ENTERTAINS. November 21. 2,000 ft. George D. Baker.

THE LEVEL. November 23. 1,000 ft. Ulysses Davis.

THE OLD FLUTE-PLAYER. November 24. 1,000 ft. Lionel Belmore.

NETTY OR LETTY. November 25. 1,000 ft. Theodore Marston.

CAUSE FOR THANKSGIVING. November 26. 1,000 ft. Tefft Johnson.

THE CURING OF MYRA MAY. November 27. 1,000 ft. Van Dyke Brooke.

CONVICT, COSTUMES AND CONFUSION. November 28. 2,000 ft. Lee Beggs.

EVERYTHING AGAINST HIM. November 30. 1,000 ft. Ulysses Davis.

SAVED FROM A LIFE OF CRIME. December 1. 2,000 ft. Theodore Marston.

THE MYSTERIOUS MR. DAVEY. December 2. 1,000 ft. Sidney Drew.

THE MAN THAT MIGHT HAVE BEEN. December 3. 1,000 ft. William Humphrey.

THE METHODS OF MARGARET. December 4. 1,000 ft. Wilfred North.

BUNNY'S LITTLE BROTHER. December 5. 1,500 ft. George D. Baker.

PICTURESQUE CALIFORNIA. December 5. 500 ft.

THE MOONSHINE MAID AND THE MAN. December 7. 1,000 ft. Charles L. Gaskill.

SUNSHINE AND SHADOWS. December 8. 2,000 ft. Van Dyke Brooke.

THE ATHLETIC FAMILY. December 9. 1,000 ft. Edmond F. Stratton.

PURE GOLD. December 10. 1,000 ft. Ulysses Davis.

A STRAND OF BLOND HAIR.   December 11.   1,000 ft.
George D. Baker.

HOW TO DO IT AND WHY, OR CUTEY AT COLLEGE.
December 12.   2,000 ft.   Wally Van.

THE GREATER LOVE.   December 14.   1,000 ft.   Theodore
Marston.

OUT OF THE PAST.   December 15.   2,000 ft.   Lionel
Belmore.

THE EGYPTIAN MUMMY.   December 16.   1,000 ft.   Lee
Beggs.

A QUESTION OF CLOTHES.   December 17.   1,000 ft.   Van
Dyke Brooke.

WHO WAS WHO IN HOGG'S HOLLOW.   December 18.
1,000 ft.   Sidney Drew.

MR. SANTA CLAUS.   December 19.   2,000 ft.   George
Ridgewell.

ARTHUR TRUMAN'S WARD.   December 21.   1,000 ft.
Wilfred North.

BY THE GOVERNOR'S ORDER.   December 22.   2,000 ft.
Maurice Costello and Robert Gaillord.

THE PROFESSOR'S ROMANCE.   December 23.   1,000 ft.
Sidney Drew.

THE KNIGHT BEFORE CHRISTMAS.   December 24.   1,000 ft.
Tefft Johnson.

SWEENEY'S CHRISTMAS BIRD.   December 25.   1,000 ft.
George D. Baker.

AN AFFAIR FOR THE POLICE.   December 26.   2,000 ft.
William Humphrey.

THE PRODUCT.   December 28.   1,000 ft.   Maurice
Costello and Robert Gaillord.

THE PLOT.   December 29.   2,000 ft.   Maurice Costello
and Robert Gaillord.

FORCING DAD'S CONSENT.   December 30.   1,000 ft.   Lee
Beggs.

LOVE WILL OUT.   December 31.   1,000 ft.   Ulysses Davis.

1915

AUNTIE'S PORTRAIT. January 1. 820 ft. Sidney Drew.

RATTLESNAKES. January 1. 180 ft.

IN THE LATIN QUARTER. January 2. 2,000 ft. Lionel Belmore.

TREACHERY IN THE CLOUDS (Part One of THE FATES AND FLORA FOURFLUSH). January 4. 1,000 ft. Wally Van.

TWO WOMEN. January 5. 3,000 ft. Ralph Ince.

BILLY'S WAGER. January 6. 1,000 ft. Lee Beggs.

THE MAN, THE MISSION AND THE MAID. January 7. 1,000 ft. Theodore Marston.

THE SMOKING OUT OF BELLA BUTTS. January 8. 1,000 ft. George D. Baker.

A DAUGHTER OF ISRAEL. January 9. 2,000 ft. Van Dyke Brooke.

THE TREASURE TEMPLE OF BHOSH (Part Two of THE FATES AND FLORA FOURFLUSH). January 11. 1,000 ft. Wally Van.

A MIX-UP IN DRESS SUIT CASES. January 12. 2,000 ft. Lee Beggs.

THE HAIR OF HER HEAD. January 13. 1,000 ft. Sidney Drew.

THE LEGEND OF THE LONE TREE. January 14. 1,000 ft. Ulysses Davis.

CHIEFLY CONCERNING MALES. January 15. 1,000 ft. Tefft Johnson.

THE SAGE-BRUSH GAL. January 16. 3,000 ft. Rollin S. Sturgeon.

A RACE FOR LIFE (Part Three of THE FATES AND FLORA FOURFLUSH). January 18. 1,000 ft. Wally Van.

THE EVIL MEN DO. January 19. 3,000 ft. Maurice Costello and Robert Gaillord.

THE RIGHT GIRL? January 20. 1,000 ft. Ralph Ince.

THE NAVAJO RING. January 21. 1,000 ft. Ulysses Davis.

WANTED, A NURSE. January 22. 1,000 ft. Sidney Drew.

WAR. January 23. 2,000 ft.

THE SLIGHTLY WORN GOWN. January 25. 1,000 ft.
William Humphrey.

THE GAME OF LIFE. January 26. 2,000 ft. Ulysses
Davis.

THE HOMECOMING OF HENRY. January 27. 1,000 ft.
Sidney Drew.

THE BARRIER OF FAITH. January 28. 1,000 ft. Van
Dyke Brooke.

THE CHIEF'S GOAT. January 29. 1,000 ft. Wally Van.

UNDERNEATH THE PAINT. January 30. 3,000 ft. Charles
L. Gaskill.

CABMAN KATE. February 1. 1,000 ft. C. Jay Williams.

HOW CISSY MADE GOOD. February 2. 3,000 ft. George
D. Baker.

THE COMBINATION. February 3. 1,000 ft. Sidney Drew.

THE UNDERSTUDY, OR BEHIND THE SCENES. February 4.
1,000 ft. Maurice Costello and Robert Gaillord.

THE GREEN CAT. February 5. 1,000 ft. Lee Beggs.

FOR ANOTHER'S CRIME. February 6. 2,000 ft. William
Humphrey.

HEARTS TO LET. February 8. 1,000 ft. William
Humphrey.

THE WRONG GIRL. February 9. 2,000 ft. Wally Van.

BREAKING IN. February 10. 1,000 ft. Wilfred North.

ON THE ALTAR OF LOVE February 11. 1,000 ft.
Maurice Costello and Robert Gaillord.

WHEN GREEK MEETS GREEK. February 12. 1,000 ft.
Sidney Drew.

MOTHER'S ROSES. February 13. 3,000 ft. Theodore
Marston.

THE PROFESSOR'S NIGHTMARE. February 15. 800 ft.
C. Jay Williams.

SCENES IN SWEDISH NORRLAND. February 15. 200 ft.

O'GARRY OF THE ROYAL MOUNTED. February 16.
3,000 ft. Ned Finley.

SOME WHITE HOPE? February 17. 1,000 ft. Ralph Ince.

THE QUALITY OF MERCY. February 18. 1,000 ft.
Lionel Belmore.

A MADCAP ADVENTURE. February 19. 1,000 ft. Theodore Marston.

TWICE RESCUED. February 20. 2,000 ft. Theodore
Marston.

WHEN SAMUEL SKIDDED. February 22. 1,000 ft. Edmond
F. Stratton.

THE STILL, SMALL VOICE. February 23. 2,000 ft.
Charles L. Gaskill and Helen Gardner.

THE YOUNG MAN WHO FIGGERED. February 24. 600 ft.
Lee Beggs.

SPORTS IN BALTIC ARCHIPELAGO. February 24. 400 ft.

THE WORTHIER MAN. February 25. 1,000 ft. Ulysses
Davis.

A MAN OF PARTS. February 26. 1,000 ft. Wally Van.

A DAUGHTER'S STRANGE INHERITANCE. February 27.
3,000 ft. Van Dyke Brooke.

BURGLARIOUS BILLY. March 1. 1,000 ft. Lee Beggs.

THE SILENT PLEA. March 2. 3,000 ft. Lionel Belmore.

THE GIRL AT NOLAN'S. March 3. 1,000 ft. Ulysses
Davis.

PEGGY OF FIFTH AVENUE. March 4. 1,000 ft. Wilfred
North.

TWO AND TWO. March 5. 1,000 ft. C. Jay Williams.

ROSELYN. March 6. 2,000 ft. Captain Harry Lambart.

THE JARR FAMILY DISCOVERS HARLEM. March 8.
1,000 ft. Harry Davenport.

SNATCHED FROM A BURNING DEATH. March 9. 2,000 ft.
Charles L. Gaskill.

A STUDY IN TRAMPS. March 10. 750 ft. Lee Beggs.

A VERY RARE COMPANIONSHIP. March 10. 250 ft.

THE BLACK WALLET. March 11. 1,000 ft. Ulysses Davis.

CUPID'S COLUMN. March 12. 1,000 ft. Sidney Drew.

THE RADIUM THIEVES. March 13. 3,000 ft. William Humphrey.

MR. JARR BRINGS HOME A TURKEY. March 15. 1,000 ft. Harry Davenport.

FROM HEADQUARTERS. March 16. 3,000 ft.

POSTPONED. March 17. 1,000 ft. Wally Van.

THE BATTLE OF FRENCHMAN'S RUN. March 18. 1,000 ft. Theodore Marston.

THE CAPITULATION OF THE MAJOR. March 19. 1,000 ft. Wilfred North.

THE MILLIONAIRE'S HUNDRED DOLLAR BILL. March 20. 2,000 ft. William Humphrey.

MR. JARR AND THE LADY REFORMER. March 22. 1,000 ft. Harry Davenport.

A WIRELESS RESCUE. March 23. 2,000 ft. Theodore Marston.

THE MASTER OF HIS HOUSE. March 24. 1,000 ft. Lee Beggs.

THE OTHER MAN'S WIFE. March 25. 1,000 ft. Ulysses Davis.

THE LADY OF SHALOTT. March 26. 1,000 ft. C. Jay Williams.

LIFTING THE BAN OF COVENTRY. March 27. 2,000 ft.

CUTEY BECOMES A LANDLORD. March 29. 1,000 ft. Wally Van.

THE ENEMIES. March 30. 3,000 ft. Harry Davenport.

A FORTUNE HUNTER. March 31. 1,000 ft. Theodore Marston.

THE HEART OF JIM BRICE. April 1. 1,000 ft. Maurice Costello and Robert Gaillord.

WHEN DUMBLEIGH SAW THE JOKE. April 2. 1,000 ft. Sidney Drew.

JANET OF THE CHORUS. April 3. 2,000 ft. Van Dyke Brooke.

MR. JARR TAKES A NIGHT OFF. April 5. 1,000 ft. Harry Davenport.

THE TIMID MR. TOOTLES. April 6. 2,000 ft. Sidney Drew.

EASY MONEY. April 7. 1,000 ft. Theodore Marston.

HER GETHSEMANE. April 8. 1,000 ft. David Smith.

THEY LOVED HIM SO. April 9. 1,000 ft. C. Jay Williams.

THE RETURN OF MAURICE DONNELLY. April 10. 3,000 ft. William Humphrey.

MR. JARR'S MAGNATE FRIEND. April 12. 1,000 ft. Harry Davenport.

BETWEEN THE TWO OF THEM. April 13. 3,000 ft. Sidney Drew.

HIS PHANTOM SWEETHEART. April 14. 1,000 ft. Ralph Ince.

STRENGTH. April 15. 1,000 ft. Ulysses Davis.

THE LOVE WHIP. April 16. 1,000 ft. Wilfred North.

ELSA'S BROTHER. April 17. 2,000 ft. Van Dyke Brooke.

THE TAMING OF RITA. April 19. 1,000 ft. Ulysses Davis.

THE JUGGERNAUT. April 19. 5,000 ft. Ralph Ince.

THE CLOSING OF THE CIRCUIT. April 20. 2,000 ft. Harry Davenport.

THE GUTTERSNIPE. April 21. 1,000 ft. Wilfred North.

SONNY JIM AND THE VALENTINE. April 22. 1,000 ft. Tefft Johnson.

WHOSE HUSBAND? April 23. 1,000 ft. C. Jay Williams.

PAWNS OF MARS. April 24. 3,000 ft. Theodore Marston.

BOOBLEY'S BABY. April 26. 1,000 ft. Sidney Drew.

THE LADY OF THE LIGHTHOUSE. April 27. 3,000 ft. Captain Harry Lambart and George Ridgewell.

THE BOARDING HOUSE FEUD. April 28. 1,000 ft. Lee Beggs.

STRICTLY NEUTRAL. April 29. 1,000 ft. C. Jay Williams.

THE-SORT-OF-A-GIRL-WHO-CAME-FROM-HEAVEN. April 30. 1,000 ft. Ralph Ince.

A PILLAR OF FLAME. May 1. 2,000 ft. Van Dyke Brooke.

CUTEY'S SISTER. May 3. 1,000 ft. Wally Van.

A CHILD OF THE NORTH. May 4. 2,000 ft. Rollin S. Sturegon.

A LILY IN BOHEMIA. May 5. 1,000 ft. Wilfred North.

THE PARK HONEYMOONERS. May 6. 1,000 ft. Tefft Johnson.

THE VANISHING VAULT. May 7. 1,000 ft. Lee Beggs.

THE BREATH OF ARABY. May 8. 3,000 ft. Charles L. Gaskill.

THE JARRS VISIT ARCADIA. May 10. 1,000 ft. Harry Davenport.

THE GIRL WHO MIGHT HAVE BEEN. May 11. 3,000 ft. Lionel Belmore.

WHEN A FELLER'S NOSE IS OUT OF JOINT. May 12. 1,000 ft. Tefft Johnson.

TO SAVE HIM FOR HIS WIFE. May 13. 1,000 ft. Wilfred North.

THE PROFESSOR'S PAINLESS CURE. May 14. 1,000 ft. Sidney Drew.

THE VALLEY OF HUMILIATION. May 15. 2,000 ft. Ulysses Davis.

MR. JARR AND THE DACHSHUND. May 17. 1,000 ft. Harry Davenport.

THE ISLAND OF REGENERATION. May 17. 6,000 ft. Harry Davenport.

THE AWAKENING. May 18. 2,000 ft. Ralph Ince.

ALMOST A HERO. May 19. 1,000 ft. Ulysses Davis.

DIMPLES, THE AUTO SALESGIRL. May 20. 1,000 ft. Wilfred North.

CUPID PUTS ONE OVER ON THE SHATCHEN. May 21. 1,000 ft. Wally Van.

IN THE DAYS OF FAMINE. May 22. 3,000 ft. Theodore Marston.

MR. JARR VISITS HIS HOME TOWN. May 24. 1,000 ft. Harry Davenport.

THE ESTERBROOK CASE. May 25. 3,000 ft. Lorimer Johnston.

THE STORY OF A GLOVE. May 26. 1,000 ft. Sidney Drew.

HILDA OF THE SLUMS. May 27. 1,000 ft. Ulysses Davis.

THE STARRING OF FLORA FINCHURCH. May 28. 1,000 ft. Lee Beggs.

JANE WAS WORTH IT. May 29. 2,000 ft. George D. Baker.

MRS. JARR'S AUCTION BRIDGE. May 31. 1,000 ft. Harry Davenport.

PLAYING THE GAME. June 1. 2,000 ft. Wilfred North.

BUNNY IN BUNNYLAND. June 2. 1,000 ft. Carl Lederer (animator).

SONNY JIM AT THE MARDI GRAS. June 3. 1,000 ft. Tefft Johnson.

JONES' HYPNOTIC EYE. June 4. 1,000 ft. David Smith.

THE WAY OF THE TRANSGRESSOR. June 5. 3,000 ft. William Humphrey.

MRS. JARR AND THE BEAUTY TREATMENT. June 7. 1,000 ft. Harry Davenport.

LOVE, SNOW AND ICE. June 8. 3,000 ft. Wally Van.

SPADES ARE TRUMPS. June 9. 1,000 ft. Lee Beggs.

MR. BLINK OF BOHEMIA. June 10. 1,000 ft. Sidney Drew.

FAIR, FAT AND SAUCY. June 11. 1,000 ft. C. Jay Williams.

FOUR GRAINS OF RICE. June 12. 2,000 ft. Theodore Marston.

MR. JARR AND THE LADIES' CUP. June 14. 1,000 ft. Harry Davenport.

SINS OF THE MOTHERS. June 14. 5,000 ft. Ralph Ince.

THE LITTLE DOLL'S DRESSMAKER. June 15. 2,000 ft. Wilfred North.

PHILANTHROPIC TOMMY. June 16. 1,000 ft. Harry Davenport.

TO THE DEATH. June 17. 1,000 ft. Ulysses Davis.

A MISTAKE IN TYPESETTING.   June 18.   1,000 ft.   Lee
  Beggs.

MISS JEKYLL AND MADAME HYDE.   June 19.   3,000 ft.
  Charles L. Gaskill.

MR. JARR AND LOVE'S YOUNG DREAM.   June 21.
  1,000 ft.   Harry Davenport.

VICTOR'S AT SEVEN.   June 22.   3,000 ft.   C. Jay Williams.

AN INTERCEPTED VENGEANCE.   June 23.   1,000 ft.
  Ulysses Davis.

WHAT'S OURS.   June 24.   1,000 ft.   S. Rankin Drew.

THEIR FIRST QUARREL.   June 25.   1,000 ft.   Sidney Drew.

THE SILENT W.   June 26.   1,500 ft.   Wilfred North.

WHEN WE WERE TWENTY-ONE.   June 26.   450 ft.

MR. JARR AND THE CAPTIVE MAIDEN.   June 28.
  1,000 ft.   Harry Davenport.

THE HAND OF GOD.   June 29.   1,550 ft.   Captain Harry
  Lambart.

A CUTE LITTLE BEAR.   June 29.

THE EVOLUTION OF CUTEY.   June 30.   1,000 ft.   Wally
  Van.

THE HONEYMOON PACT.   July 1.   1,000 ft.   Wilfred North.

HUNTING A HUSBAND.   July 2.   1,000 ft.   Ulysses Davis.

THE CRIMINAL.   July 3.   3,000 ft.   Van Dyke Brooke.

THE REVOLT OF MR. WIGGS.   July 5.   1,000 ft.   Edmond
  F. Stratton.

THE MAN FROM THE DESERT.   July 6.   3,000 ft.   Ulysses
  Davis.

THE WHITE AND BLACK SNOWBALL.   July 7.   1,000 ft.
  Tefft Johnson.

BERTIE'S STRATAGEM.   July 8.   1,000 ft.   Lee Beggs.

LOVE'S WAY.   July 9.   1,000 ft.   S. Rankin Drew.

INSURING CUTEY.   July 10.   2,000 ft.   Wally Van.

MR. JARR AND GERTRUDE'S BEAUX.   July 12.   1,000 ft.
  Harry Davenport.

A NATURAL MAN.   July 13.   2,000 ft.   Ulysses Davis.

THE HONEYMOON BABY. July 14. 1,000 ft. Sidney Drew.

BILLY, THE BEAR TAMER. July 15. 1,000 ft. Lee Beggs.

WELCOME TO BOHEMIA. July 16. 1,000 ft. Wally Van.

THE CONFESSION OF MADAME BARASTOFF. July 17. 3,000 ft. Charles L. Gaskill.

CROOKY. July 19. 5,000 ft. C. Jay Williams.

THE HIGHWAYMAN. July 19. 1,000 ft. Wally Van.

THE LORELEI MADONNA. July 20. 3,000 ft. Rollin S. Sturgeon.

FOLLOWING THE SCENT. July 21. 1,000 ft. Sidney Drew.

ALL ON ACCOUNT OF TOWSER. July 22. 1,000 ft. Ulysses Davis.

MR. BIXBIE'S DILEMMA. July 23. 1,000 ft. Edmond F. Stratton.

A PAIR OF QUEENS. July 24. 2,000 ft. George D. Baker.

MR. JARR'S BIG VACATION. July 26. 1,000 ft. Harry Davenport.

THE RED STEPHANO. July 27. 2,000 ft. Ulysses Davis.

THE MISSING CLUE. July 28. 1,000 ft. Lee Beggs.

CUTEY, FORTUNE HUNTING. July 29. 1,000 ft. Wally Van.

SOME DUEL. July 30. 1,000 ft. George D. Baker.

THE MYSTERY OF MARY. July 31. 3,000 ft. Captain Harry Lambart.

THE SERPENT'S TOOTH. August 2. 1,000 ft. Wally Van.

THE SCAR. August 3. 3,000 ft. William Humphrey.

THE REPENTANCE OF DR. BLINN. August 4. 1,000 ft. David Smith.

A DISCIPLE OF PLATO. August 5. 1,000 ft. Lee Beggs.

DIMPLES AND THE RING. August 6. 1,000 ft. Wilfred North.

PAT HOGAN, DECEASED. August 7. 1,000 ft. George D. Baker.

WHAT DID HE WHISPER? August 9. 1,000 ft. Ulysses Davis.

THE CHALICE OF COURAGE. August 9. 6,000 ft. Rollin S. Sturgeon.

LIFE'S YESTERDAYS. August 10. 2,000 ft. Lorrimer Johnston.

HIS FAIRY GODMOTHER. August 11. 1,000 ft. Wally Van.

HIS BUNKIE. August 12. 1,000 ft. Lionel Belmore.

A KEYBOARD STRATEGY. August 13. 1,000 ft. Courtlandt Van Deusen.

HEAVY VILLAINS. August 14. 3,000 ft. George D. Baker.

MR. JARR AND CIRCUMSTANTIAL EVIDENCE. August 16 1,000 ft. Harry Davenport.

MY LOST ONE. August 17. 3,000 ft. Harry Handsworth.

SHE TOOK A CHANCE. August 18. 1,000 ft. C. Jay Williams.

THE QUEST OF THE WIDOW. August 19. 1,000 ft. Ulysses Davis.

CUTEY'S AWAKENING. August 20. 804 ft. Wally Van.

SWEDISH ARMY AND NAVY. August 20. 196 ft.

THE DAWN OF UNDERSTANDING. August 21. 2,000 ft. Van Dyke Brooke.

THE WHEELS OF JUSTICE. August 23. 4,000 ft. Theodore Marston.

THE CUB AND THE DAISY CHAIN. August 23. 1,000 ft. Sidney Drew.

FROM THE DREGS. August 24. 2,000 ft. Lionel Belmore.

A CITY RUBE. August 25. 740 ft. Ulysses Davis.

PEARLS OF THE BALTIC. August 25. 260 ft.

THE GOOD IN THE WORST OF US. August 26. 1,000 ft. William Humphrey.

THE WARDROBE WOMAN. August 27. 1,000 ft. Theodore Marston.

THE TIGRESS. August 28. 3,000 ft. Lorrimer Johnston.

JARR AND THE VISITING FIREMEN. August 30. 1,000 ft. Harry Davenport.

HEARTS ABLAZE. August 31. 3,000 ft. Lorrimer Johnston.

THE QUARREL. September 1. 1,000 ft. Ulysses Davis.

THE FIRE ESCAPE. September 2. 1,000 ft. Courtlandt Van Deusen.

THEIR AGREEMENT. September 3. 1,000 ft. Sidney Drew.

THE OFFENDING KISS. September 4. 2,000 ft. Ulysses Davis.

MRS. JARR AND THE SOCIETY CIRCUS. September 6. 1,000 ft. Harry Davenport.

MORTMAIN. September 6. 5,000 ft. Theodore Marston.

THE KIDNAPPED STOCKBROKER. September 7. 2,000 ft. Harry Handsworth.

THE SIREN. September 8. 1,000 ft. Ulysses Davis.

THE ROMANCE OF A HANDKERCHIEF. September 9. 1,000 ft. Van Dyke Brooke.

UNLUCKY LOUEY. September 10. 1,000 ft. Sidney Drew.

ONE PERFORMANCE ONLY. September 11. 3,000 ft. Eugene Mullin.

SONNY JIM AND THE AMUSEMENT COMPANY LTD. September 13. 1,000 ft. Tefft Johnson.

WEST WIND. September 14. 3,000 ft. Lionel Belmore.

SAVE THE COUPONS. September 15. 1,000 ft. Courtlandt Van Deusen.

THE SHADOW OF FEAR. September 16. 1,000 ft. William Humphrey.

THE PROFESSIONAL DINER. September 17. 1,000 ft. Sidney Drew.

HIS GOLDEN GRAIN. September 18. 2,000 ft. Ulysses Davis.

PLAYING DEAD. September 20. 5,000 ft. Sidney Drew.

WILLIE STAYED SINGLE. September 20. 1,000 ft. Ulysses Davis.

DOROTHY. September 21. 2,000 ft. Van Dyke Brooke.

GETTING RID OF AUNT KATE. September 22. 1,000 ft. C. Jay Williams.

THE LESSON OF NARROW STREET. September 23. 1,000 ft. S. Rankin Drew.

BACK TO THE PRIMITIVE. September 24. 1,000 ft.
Sidney Drew.

FROM OUT OF THE BIG SNOWS. September 25. 3,000 ft.
Theodore Marston.

THE BUTTERFLY LESSON. September 27. 1,000 ft.
William Humphrey.

THROUGH TROUBLED WATERS. September 28. 3,000 ft.
Ulysses Davis.

RAGS AND THE GIRL. September 29. 1,000 ft. Van Dyke
Brooke.

THE PLAGUE SPOT. September 30. 1,000 ft. Theodore
Marston.

THE FOX-TROT FINESSE. October 1. 1,000 ft. Sidney
Drew.

A QUEEN FOR AN HOUR. October 2. 2,000 ft. George
D. Baker.

THE REWARD. October 4. 1,000 ft. S. Rankin Drew.

THE DUST OF EGYPT. October 4. 6,000 ft. George D.
Baker.

BARRIERS OF PREJUDICE. October 5. 2,000 ft. Ulysses
Davis.

FITS AND CHILLS. October 6. 1,000 ft. C. Jay Williams.

OLD GOOD FOR NUTHIN'. October 7. 1,000 ft. George
Ridgewell.

MISS STICKY-MOUFIE-KISS. October 8. 1,000 ft. Sidney
Drew.

YOUTH. October 9. 3,000 ft. Harry Handsworth.

THE LURE OF A WIDOW. October 11. 1,000 ft. Wally
Van.

LILLIAN'S HUSBANDS. October 12. 3,000 ft. Wilfred
North.

ON WITH THE DANCE. October 13. 1,000 ft. C. Jay
Williams.

THE THIRD PARTY. October 14. 1,000 ft. Theodore
Marston.

HOW JOHN CAME HOME. October 15. 1,000 ft. Sidney
Drew.

THE WOMAN IN THE BOX. October 16. 2,000 ft. Harry Davenport.

QUITS. October 18. 1,000 ft. Wally Van.

THE MAN WHO COULDN'T BEAT GOD. October 18. 5,000 ft. Maurice Costello and Robert Gaillord.

THE GODS REDEEM. October 19. 2,000 ft. Van Dyke Brooke.

BROWN'S SUMMER BOARDERS. October 20. 1,000 ft. George Ridgewell.

ON THE TURN OF A CARD. October 21. 1,000 ft. William Humphrey.

A SAFE INVESTMENT. October 22. 1,000 ft. Sidney Drew.

THE RULING POWER. October 23. 3,000 ft. Lionel Belmore.

THE PRINCE IN DISGUISE. October 25. 1,000 ft. Tefft Johnson.

TO CHERISH AND PROTECT. October 26. 3,000 ft. William Humphrey.

ITSKY, THE INVENTOR. October 27. 1,000 ft. C. Jay Williams.

THE UNFORGIVEN. October 28. 1,000 ft. Lorrimer Johnston.

A CASE OF EUGENICS. October 29. 1,000 ft. Sidney Drew.

THE SHABBIES. October 30. 2,000 ft. Wilfred North.

BETWEEN TWO FIRES. November 1. 1,000 ft. Courtlandt Van Deusen.

THE TURN OF THE ROAD. November 1. 5,000 ft. Tefft Johnson.

THE SULTAN OF ZULON. November 2. 2,000 ft. Wally Van.

A FAMILY PICNIC. November 3. 1,000 ft. Edmond F. Stratton.

THE EBONY CASKET. November 4. 1,000 ft. Ulysses Davis.

BEAUTIFUL THOUGHTS. November 5. 1,000 ft. Sidney Drew.

ANSELO LEE. November 6. 3,000 ft. Harry Handsworth.

NO TICKEE-- NO WASHEE. November 8. 550 ft. Edmond
F. Stratton.

CALIFORNIA SCRAP BOOK. November 8. 450 ft.

FOR THE HONOR OF THE CREW. November 9. 3,000 ft.
William P. S. Earle.

HATS IS HATS. November 10. 1,000 ft. Wally Van.

SIS. November 11. 1,000 ft. George Ridgewell.

ROMANTIC REGGIE. November 12. 1,000 ft. Sidney Drew.

THE WOMAN'S SHARE. November 13. 2,000 ft. Rollin S.
Sturgeon.

SONNY JIM AND THE GREAT AMERICAN GAME. November 15. 1,000 ft. Tefft Johnson.

THE HEIGHTS OF HAZARD. November 15. 5,000 ft.
Harry Lambart.

GONE TO THE DOGS. November 16. 2,000 ft. Harry
Handsworth.

THE COUNTS. November 17. 1,000 ft. Ralph Ince.

A MOTORCYCLE ELOPEMENT. November 18. 1,000 ft.
C. Jay Williams.

DIPLOMATIC HENRY. November 19. 1,000 ft. Sidney
Drew.

HEREDITY. November 20. 3,000 ft. William Humphrey.

LOVE AND LAW. November 22. 1,000 ft. Rollin S.
Sturgeon.

SAINTS AND SINNERS. November 23. 3,000 ft. Van Dyke
Brooke.

SONNY JIM AND THE FAMILY PARTY. November 24.
1,000 ft. Tefft Johnson.

GHOSTS AND FLYPAPER. November 25. 1,000 ft.
Ulysses Davis.

ALL FOR THE LOVE OF A GIRL. November 26. 1,000 ft.
Sidney Drew.

A 'MODEL' WIFE. November 27. 2,000 ft. Wilfred North.

ONE PLUS ONE EQUALS ONE. November 29. 1,000 ft.
Tefft Johnson.

THE CAVEMAN. November 29. 5,000 ft. Theodore
Marston.

THE MYSTERY OF THE EMPTY ROOM. November 30.
2,000 ft. Courtlandt Van Deusen.

A SCANDAL IN HICKVILLE. December 1. 1,000 ft.
Ulysses Davis.

THE CONQUEST OF CONSTANTIA. December 2. 1,000 ft.
Courtlandt Van Deusen.

THE HOME CURE. December 3. 1,000 ft. Sidney Drew.

CAL MARVIN'S WIFE. December 4. 3,000 ft. Ulysses
Davis.

HER LAST FLIRTATION. December 6. 1,000 ft. Ulysses
Davis.

WASTED WIVES. December 7. 3,000 ft. Theodore Marston.

SONNY JIM'S FIRST LOVE AFFAIR. December 8. 1,000 ft.
Tefft Johnson.

SAM'S SWEETHEART. December 9. 1,000 ft. William
Humphrey.

ROONEY'S SAD CASE. December 10. 1,000 ft. Sidney
Drew.

HUGHEY OF THE CIRCUS. December 11. 2,000 ft. Wally
Van.

BENJAMIN BUNTER, BOOK AGENT. December 13. 1,000
ft. Courtlandt Van Deusen.

A PRICE FOR FOLLY. December 13. 5,000 ft. George
D. Baker.

A QUESTION OF RIGHT OR WRONG. December 14. 2,000
ft. Van Dyke Brooke.

THE FAITH OF SONNY JIM. December 15. 1,000 ft.
Tefft Johnson.

A FLOWER OF THE HILLS. December 16. 1,000 ft.
William Humphrey.

THE DECEIVERS. December 17. 1,000 ft. Sidney Drew.

A MAN'S SACRIFICE. December 18. 3,000 ft. George
D. Baker.

LEVY'S SEVEN DAUGHTERS. December 20. 1,000 ft.
Wally Van.

ON HER WEDDING NIGHT.   December 20.   4,000 ft.
William Humphrey.

THE PATENT FOOD CONVEYOR.   December 20.   1,000 ft.
C. Jay Williams.

IS CHRISTMAS A BORE?   December 24.   1,000 ft.   Sidney
Drew.

THE THIRTEENTH GIRL.   December 25.   3,000 ft.   Theodore Marston.

HE GOT HIMSELF A WIFE.   December 27.   1,000 ft.
George Stanley.

WHAT HAPPENED TO FATHER.   December 27.   5,000 ft.
C. Jay Williams.

THE MAKING OVER OF GEOFFREY MANNING.   December
27.   4,000 ft.   Harry Davenport.

THE PEST VAMOOSER.   December 27.   1,000 ft.   C. Jay
Williams.

BY MIGHT OF HIS RIGHT.   December 31.   1,000 ft.
Sidney Drew.

INDEX

This index refers to the text only, and does not include films and personalities included in "A Vitagraph Who's Who" or "The Films of the Vitagraph Company, 1910-1915." All major references are underscored. As the names J. Stuart Blackton and Albert E. Smith appear on almost every page, references thereto have not been included.

Abbott, Rev. Lyman 74 75
Academy of Motion Picture
   Arts and Sciences,
   The 32
Adventure Shop, The 66
Adventures of Kathlyn, The
   94
Adventures of Raffles, the
    Amateur Cracksman,
   The 13, 17
Alberti Madame 49
Alexander, Frank 92
 Lefty 23
All in the Family 84
Allen, Viola 64
American Academy of Dramatic
   Arts 49
American Home, An 78
American Tobacco Company
   67, 68
American Vitagraph Company
   7
Anderson, Broncho Billy see
   Anderson, G. M.
 G. M. 12, 38
 Mary 32
Angeles, Bert 61
Anne of the Golden Heart 52
Arbuckle, Maclyn 102
Armat, Thomas 32
Arthur, Julia 22
 Walker 59, 64
Aubrey, James 83, 91
Aunty's Romance 53

Babcock, "Dad" 54
Babes and Boobs 91
Bainbridge, Sherman J. 27
Baird, Leah 57
Baker George D. 46, 57
Barrie, J. M. 112
Barrymore, Ethel 85
 John 85
 Lionel 85
Battle Cry of Peace, The 20,
   64, 72-79, 82, 115
Battle Cry of War, The see
   Womanhood, the Glory
   of a Nation
Battle of Manilla Bay, The 9,
   26
Beach, Rex 78
Beaudet, Louise 49, 74
Beckett 58
Behold This Woman 109
Belasco, David 108
Bellew, Kyrle 13
Belmore, Lionel 61
Beloved Brute, The 24, 109,
   111
Bergman, Ingmar 105
Bernhardt, Sarah 38
Bertram, William 97
Betty Becomes a Maid 53
Between Friends 109
Big Boobs and Bathing Beau-
   ties 91
Biograph Company, The 1,
   18, 52, 115